Spike Milligan was one of the greatest and most influential comedians of the twentieth century. Born in India in 1918, he was educated in India and England before joining the Royal Artillery at the start of the Second World War and serving in North Africa and Italy. At the end of the war, he forged a career as a jazz musician, sketch-show writer and performer, touring Europe with the Bill Hall Trio and the Ann Lenner Trio, before joining forces with, among others, Peter Sellers and Harry Secombe, to create the legendary *Goon Show*. Broadcast on BBC Radio, the ten series of the *Goon Show* ran from 1951 until 1960 and brought Spike to international fame, as well as to the edge of sanity and the break-up of his first marriage. He had subsequent success as a stage and film actor, as the author of over eighty books of fiction, memoir, poetry, plays, cartoons and children's stories, and with his long-running one-man show. In 1992 he was made a CBE and in 2001 an honorary KBE, and in 2000 and 2001 he received two Lifetime Achievement Awards for writing and for comedy. He died in 2002.

Spike Milligan

GOODBYE SOLDIER

PENGUIN BOOKS

PENGUIN BOOKS

Published by the Penguin Group
Penguin Books Ltd, 80 Strand, London WC2R ORL, England
Penguin Group (USA) Inc., 375 Hudson Street, New York, New York 10014, USA
Penguin Group (Canada), 90 Eglinton Avenue East, Suite 700, Toronto, Ontario, Canada M4P 2Y3
(a division of Pearson Penguin Canada Inc.)
Penguin Ireland, 25 St Stephen's Green, Dublin 2, Ireland (a division of Penguin Books Ltd)
Penguin Group (Australia), 250 Camberwell Road, Camberwell, Victoria 3124, Australia
(a division of Pearson Australia Group Pty Ltd)
Penguin Books India Pvt Ltd, 11 Community Centre, Panchsheel Park, New Delhi – 110 017, India
Penguin Group (NZ), 67 Apollo Drive, Rosedale, Auckland 0632, New Zealand
(a division of Pearson New Zealand Ltd)
Penguin Books (South Africa) (Pty) Ltd, Block D, Rosebank Office Park,
181 Jan Smuts Avenue, Parktown North, Gauteng 2193, South Africa

Penguin Books Ltd, Registered Offices: 80 Strand, London WC2R ORL, England

www.penguin.com

First published in Great Britain by Michael Joseph 1986
Published in Penguin Books 1987
Reissued in this edition 2012

013

Copyright © Spike Milligan Productions Ltd, 1986
All rights reserved

Printed in England by Clays Ltd, Elcograf S.p.A.

ISBN: 978-0-241-95814-8

www.greenpenguin.co.uk

Penguin Books is committed to a sustainable
future for our business, our readers and our planet.
This book is made from Forest Stewardship
Council™ certified paper.

MIX
Paper from
responsible sources
FSC
www.fsc.org   FSC™ C018179

To Jennie Davies, for her help

FOREWORD

Find a Place – Stop the Clock

Sitting here at the typewriter, stop the clock. When I think of the kind of human being I was then, I can't believe that it was me. I was twenty-eight, with the best years of my life spent in the Army. I had found the transformation from civilian life painless: it allowed freedoms I hadn't had before. No longer did I have my mother's dictatorship about going to mass – we had unending rows over it, in fact I left home for a time. No longer did I have that voice on the landing when I came home at night, 'Is that you, Terry? What time do you call this?' type rows. I had always given my mother my entire wage packet, £5.00. In return, I got half-a-crown pocket money at the age of twenty-one. Now I kept *all* my pay, came in late and didn't have to go to mass. It was freedom! I was living for the moment. If there was any future, it was the next band job. I loved being there, playing the trumpet, me the music maker, me being asked by officers, 'I say, Milligan, can you play such and such a tune?', me singing, flirting with the girls. Now here I was in Italy on £10.00 a week with officer status, playing with a trio that I thought would bring us fame and fortune, and all this and a pretty ballerina. This was Italy, the sun shone, free of all responsibilities except the show, free all day. Oh, life was good! One day that would all end.

Spike Milligan

Monkenhurst
1 May 1986

The view we left behind! From my bedroom window, showing the now dormant Mount Vesuvius

ROME

Maria Antoinetta Fontana

ROMANCE

June 1946

The charabanc, with its precious cargo of bisexual soldier artistes, see-saws through the narrow Neapolitan streets. It is a day of high summer. We pull up at our destination, the Albergo Rabacino. The sunlight plays on its golden baroque chiselled façade. Lieutenant Ronnie Priest hurries into its mahogany portals, only to return downcast of visage. 'The bloody girls will be a while; they've just got back from mass.' He lights up a cigarette. 'Bloody females,' he adds. We all debouch to stretch our legs and other parts. Immediately, we are set on by street vendors. I was taken up with a tray of chrome and gilt watches – I needed a watch badly, a good heavy one that would stop me being blown away. As we barter, the Italian Corps de Ballet usher forth with their luggage. Our balding driver, Luigi, is rupturing himself stowing the bulging cases into the rear locker – all this while I have just clinched a deal for a watch that looks like a burnished gold Aztec altar, a huge lump of a thing. On me, it made my wrist look like an Oxfam appeal for food. I had bargained the price down from ten million lire to seven thousand and the vendor was running away at full speed while counting the money. I was winding it when a female voice diverted me: ''Ow much you payer for that?' I turned to see a petite, mousy-haired, blue-eyed, doll-like girl.

The first clash of eyes was enough. It was, no, not *love* at first sight – that came later – but it most certainly was *something* at first sight. (Darling, I feel in something at first sight.)

'I paid seven thousand lire.'

She 'tsu-tsu-tsued' and shook her head. 'You know all watch stolen.' No, I didn't know that. 'Let me see,' she said, in a semi-commanding voice. She examined the watch. 'Maybe, yes,' she said, returning it.

3

I said it was a very good watch, it told the time in Italian as well as English. What was her name?

'My namer is Maria Antoinetta Fontana, but everyone call me Toni.'

'I'm Spike,' sometimes known as stop thief or hey you!

'Yeser, I know.' She had found my name on the programme and had obviously set her sights on me. I would make good target practice. Maria Antoinetta Fontana was understudy for the première ballerina at the Royal Opera House in Rome. From now on, it was goodbye Bing Crosby, lead soldiers and Mars bars. She was so petite! Five feet four inches! We are 'all aboarding' the Charabong, I notice that Toni has lovely legs and the right amount, two. I tried to sit next to her, but in the mêlée I ended up in the seat behind her as Riccy Trowler, our crooner, had fancied her and beat me to it. If he looked at her, I would kill. Do you hear me? K I L L! Didn't he know with me around he hadn't a chance! Me, the Brockley Adonis? Poor blind little fool. Me, the Harry James of St Cyprian's Hall, S E 26! 'Hold very tight and fares please,' says Lieutenant Priest in mock cockney bus conductor tones as we set off for the Holy City.

The journey passes with Toni turning to cast me eye-crippling glances. She dangles her hand in the lee of her seat for me to hold. Arghhhhhhhhhh! It's small, sensuous, soft and perfumed. It's giddy-making. Oh, but how lovely!!! I'm falling, falling, falling! and no safety net!

Mulgrew's keen Scottish eye has noticed my new watch. He assesses it and says, 'That's the sort of present a mean millionaire would buy for a blind son.' He asks how much. I tell him. He bursts out laughing. Laugh he may, in a year's time that selfsame watch would save him and the Bill Hall Trio from ruin. Of that, more in my next book! Bill Hall is killing the boredom by playing his fiddle. I join in on the guitar. We play some jazz and a few Neapolitan melodies, 'Cuore Napolitano', 'Non Me Scorde', 'Ah Zaz Zaz Za'.

Ceprano is a halfway halt. We are taken to a large N A A F I where we are given lunch. Ahhhhhhhgghhhh, Cold

4

Clowning at a wayside break. Toni (left) feeds Jimmy Molloy (centre) and Riccy Trowler (right)

5

Collation!!! The most dreaded meal in the English Culinary calendar: the dead chicken, the dead lettuce, the watery mayonnaise, the lone tomato ring! It's the sort of meal you

The Bill Trio in a now derelict prisoner-of-war cage, trying desperately to be funny en route to Rome, where the Pope lives

leave in your will to your mother-in-law.

'You no lak,' says Toni who is sitting opposite.

'No, I no lak,' I said.

'Can I have you chicken?' she says, her head inclined to one side. I watch as the dead fowl disappears through her delectable lips. I sip the red tannic-acid-ridden tea that must have been put on to boil the day after we all landed at Salerno.

Toni and I saunter out to the Charabong, the journey continues. The swine Trowler assumes his seat next to *my* Toni, the blind fool. Hasn't he noticed her adoring glances?? My matchless profile from Brockley S E 26?

Bill Hall is laughing, I've told him the price of the watch. So far Bornheim has passed the journey immersed in the *Union Jack* newspaper. He walks down the Charabong, swaying and bumping. He makes reference to my new amour.

'Is there something going on?' he said, nodding towards my Toni.

I told him most certainly there was a lot going on. I had met her, according to my new watch, at ten-thirty precisely. Yes, there was a lot going on but as conditions improved I'd hoped for a lot coming off. He grins like a fiend.

'The poor girl,' he said. 'You'd better not show it to her all at once.'

He slunk away chuckling, the swine! This was not *that* kind of affair, this was *true* romance. No tawdry thoughts entered my head, but they were entering other areas. South of Rome we lumber through hot dusty villages, the grapes are heavy on the vine and on sale are large luscious red bunches for a few lire. But I don't have eyes for the delights of the Campagna, only Toni's glances and the squeeze of her little hand.

Late evening and the dusty chugging Charabong enters Rome through the Porta Maggiore. It's a Sunday evening and the sunlight is turning to rose-petal pink. The streets are full of the populace taking their evening strolls – elegant

Romans are *really* elegant, they wear clothes well. But! None of them are wearing sensible brown English shoes like me. More of them later. The Charabong comes to rest ouside the Albergo Universo. *I'll* help Toni with her luggage to her bedroom. Her mother wants her to go home, but, because she wants to be near me, lies, and tells Momma the company rules insist she stays at the hotel. Ha! Ha! Love finds a way.

I take me to my chamber – a very nice no-nonsense double bedroom. Thank God, this time there's no screaming, chattering, farting Secombe. No, he's in his hammock and a thousand miles away. Instead, I have Wino of the Year, Trooper Mulgrew, J., who by just throwing his kit down can make the room look like the Wandsworth Municipal Rubbish Tip. I hang up my civvies.

'This is the life, Johnny,' I say.

'Oh, you've noticed,' he says.

To activate his Scottish mind, I say, 'I wonder what your folks in Glasgow are doing?'

And he says, 'A bank.' He's looking at the ceiling, there's nothing there to tax his tartan mind. 'What's the time?' he says.

And I say, 'It's time you bought a watch that I can laugh at.'

From our floor we take the lift.

'*Che piano?*' says the ageing lift attendant.

'*La terra piano,*' says Mulgrew which translated means 'the earth floor'.

The dining-room is full. Another E N S A party has booked in, among them Tony Fayne who in post-war years would become well known for his partnership with David Evans. As Fayne and Evans, they did funny sporting commentaries and were used by the B B C till it had sucked them dry and discarded them. I noticed that this new intake all wore their shirts outside their trousers. This struck me as amusing because, dear reader, during my boyhood days in India we, the Raj, laughed at the 'wogs' for that selfsame reason. What I didn't know is that this was the 'latest fashion' from Ameri-

8

ca! Suddenly, tucking shirts in was old-fashioned. I remember whenever Tony Fayne passed me there was the faint aroma of marijuana, for which he was later 'busted'! I remember one dinner-time, when the smell of pot emanated from their table as I passed it on my way to bed, a pale ENSA female of some forty summers grabbed the seat of my trousers and whooped 'Wot ho, Monty' and fell face-down into the soup.

Our lesbian javelin-thrower manageress remembers me.

'Come sta, Terri?' she says.

We chatted over coffee. Had I any spare tickets for the show? Of course. How many? She'd like to bring the family, thirty-two. She 'buys' us a bottle of wine and we discuss post-war Italy – the political scene was very woolly with the Christian Democrats holding the wolf of Communism at bay. She doesn't want Communism, she loves democracy and have we anything for sale on the black market? We repair to her private suite where we continue drinking and she shows me a photo album. There she is in all her athletic glory, throwing the javelin at the All Italia Games. Gad! In her running shorts and vest, she's a fine figure of a man. She shows me photos of Mussolini's execution – ghastly – then, a turn-up for the book, a picture of Clara Petacci looking very sexy in a net dress (see picture).

A knock at the door. It's the late Bill Hall and fiddle, can he come in? His eyes fall on the Petacci photo.

'Cor, 'oo's the bird? Clara Petacci? Wot, the one that Musso was givin' it to? Cor, 'ow could they shoot her, all that lovely stuff!'

He was right, she would have made a lovely stuff.

Bill has been out visiting 'a friend'. This is usually some old boiler with a turkey trot neck, one foot in the grave and very grateful for any that's going. He wants to know if it's too late for dinner. The manageress says no, what's he want? Spaghetti. We watch Bill eating it. He cuts it all up with a knife, then shovels it in on a spoon.

I retire to bed, first taking a luxurious bath. Mulgrew is already abed, smoking and sipping red wine from a glass by his bedside. 'How did you get on with the Italian bird?'

Italian *bird*? If he meant Miss Toni Fontana, I was indeed much favoured by her and would see her on the morrow and

Clara Petacci turning on the Fascist party

be immediately hypnotized by her 'petite beauty'. Mulgrew is given to silent evil laughter with heavy shoulders.

'Wait till she gets a look at your petite beauty.'

He was a dirty little devil and would never go to heaven.

BARBARY COAST

Barbary Coast opened at the Argentina Theatre on Monday, 24 June. It was an immediate success and the Bill Hall Trio again the hit of the show. Wait till England heard about us, rich, rich, rich!!!

It's a busy show for me: I have to appear in sketches, in the Bowery Quartette singing 'Close the Shutters, Willy's Dead', play trumpet in the orchestra and the guitar in the Bill Hall Trio – all at no extra charge. Bornheim has a dastardly trick. During my solo in 'Close the Shutters', he drops a lone ping-pong ball that bounces slowly and re-

The Bill Hall Trio on stage in Rome, where the Pope lives

BARBARY COAST

The Boss, "Honest" Sam Shane – – – JIMMY MOLLOY
"Gaga" Gallagher – – – – – Chalky White
The Chuckers-Out – – – – – Max Beermann
– – – – – – Terry Pelici
– – – – – – Keith Knapp
The Soft Shoe Shuffler – – – – Teddy Grant
The Man About Town – – – – Spike Milligan
The Master-Mind Detective – – – Chalky White
The Doer of the Foul Deed – – – Terry Pelici
The Corpse – – – – – John Angove
Willie, the Other Corpse –

Frisco Lil – – – – – TIOLA SILENZI
The Sentimental Tenor – – – Fulvio Pazzaglia
The Three Russians – – – – Bill Woodhouse,
Norman Lee and
Frank Prescott
The Permanent Drunk – – – John Angove
The Dude – – – – – Keith Knapp
The Bathing Beauty – – – – Alda Elliston
The Betrayed Woman – – – Bill Woodhouse
The Knuckle-Fighter – – – Terry Pelici

The Singing Waiters

Spike Milligan, Jack Escott, Johnny Bornheim,
and Eric Trowler

The Salvation Navy

THE BILL HALL TRIO

THE BARBARY COAST BELLES
ALDA ELLISTON – GRETA WEINGARTNER
MARIANI LOUISA – PONTIANI ANTONIETTA
ANDREATTA GERMANA

THE BARBARY BAND
DICKIE WRIGHT – EDDIE GARVEY
TOMMY HUGHES – FREDDIE PARKER
PETER ROSOKHA – STAN COLE
RAY LOXLEY – FRANK PRESCOTT
DENNIS SAXTON

THE BOOK

Cardsharpers, Customers, Wide Boys, Smart Guys,
Not-so-Smart Guys, Odds and Clods

Johnny Midgrew, "Zen" Dargue, Dennis Evans,
Jim Whitlock, and ALL OF YOU in the audience

Devised and Written by
ELIZABETH AGOULT, RAYMOND AGOULT
JIMMY MOLLOY AND PADRAIG MANNING
O'BRNE
Stage Direction
NORMAN LEE AND JOHN ANGOVE
Production by
PADRAIG MANNING O'BRNE

Musical Director
& Associate Producer
RAYMOND AGOULT

Dance Ensemble
GIOVANNI BRIMATI

Lighting and Sound Effects
JIM WHITLOCK

SETTING and COSTUMES
Created by CSE Staff under
supervision of
JOHN CROKER &
ELIZABETH AGOULT

Wardrobe Mistress
ADA WHITLOCK

The programme of the Barbary Coast *opening night, Rome, where the Pope
lives*

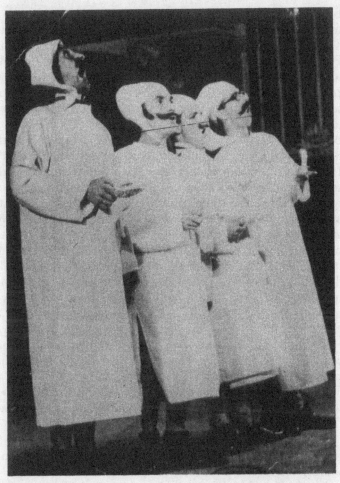

The Barbary Coast Quartet – left to right, Milligan, Bornheim, Trowler, Escott

peatedly and faster into the orchestra pit, where he has arranged for a man to drop a brick into a bucket of water. It was a simple but funny idea.

Of others in the show, the lead comic was Jimmy Molloy, about forty, overweight, a cockney, very left wing, his comedy all aggressive. After the war not a word was heard of him in the profession, so . . . There's one born every minute and we had one who was, Sergeant Chalky White, ex-Marine Para Commando. What he was doing in the entertainment world was as baffling as finding Adolf Eichmann in the Israeli government. His only claim to fame was he once leapt off Bari Bridge into the harbour with an umbrella – all very clever, but there's a limit to how many times. He was a bouncing all-noise cockney boy: if you were in a pub with him, you all *had* to sing and do 'Knees Up Mother Brown'. He had a brain that would have fitted into a thimble with room to spare. He was i/c transport and scenery, both of which strained his mental capacities to the limit. Yes, he was a nice bouncing thirty-year-old cockney lad who should have stayed on his barrow. However, he was turned on by the bright lights and birds of show biz, so he wheedled his way into the show. He couldn't act, he couldn't sing, he couldn't dance, but he could fight . . . So, for no reason at all, in the middle of the show a mock fight breaks out and we all have to pretend to be floored by Sergeant White.

'Don't worry, I won't 'urt yer, I'll miss you by a whisker.'

This didn't work out. Every night he would mistime and render one of the cast unconscious. As I had boxed in the past, I rode his punches. Even then, to this day I have a chipped front tooth and a scarred inner lip. Finally, after we'd all been hit, Lieutenant Priest had to put a stop to the 'Fight'. White sulked off.

'It's professional jealousy,' he said.

White truly believed that after the war he would 'become someone'. He did, a dustman.

Maxie – just Maxie – was a short, squat mid-European. A huge head dwarfed his body and his neck didn't exist, so much so that he couldn't turn his head but had to revolve his whole body. He spoke very little English. His 'act' consisted of bending iron bars on his head and shoulders, concluding with his bending an iron bar on his forearm.

'Maxie has developed this special muscle that "no living human has developed". In this attempt, if he misses the muscle he could break his arm,' announced Molloy.

There followed great grunts and thwacks as the sweating strong man beat the shit out of himself, finally holding up the now bent bar and collapsing into the wings.

ROMANCE AND TEA

27 June 1946

On the day she visited her mother, Toni arranged to meet me in the gardens of the Villa Borghese. There, we would have tea. I was walking on air! Our budding romance was the talk of the company.

'We will meeta under theee statue of Goethe,' she had said smilingly.

Of course, Frederick von Goethe the well-known German singer dancer! I wore my dark blue trousers, white silk shirt, satin blue tie, navy blue velvet jacket and my sensible strong brown outsized convulsed English shoes. I took one of Rome's dying Fiat taxis. He had never heard of the statue of Frederick von Goethe, singer and dancer, but we kept driving till we found it.

I arrived early as I wished to choose a suitable pose to strike for when Toni arrived. I chose a Spanish oak against which I leaned like Gary Cooper and smoked a cigarette like Humphrey Bogart. By the time she arrived, I'd run out. Toni drew up in a taxi, I posed heavily as Robert Taylor. As she approached, all the juices in my metabolism started to revolve. I think I was actually vibrating: as she drew near I would appear to her as a blue blur. She was dressed in a blue polka-dot dress, her clean brown limbs glowed in the Roman sun and I was speechless in the face of her smile.

'Buon giorno, Toni,' I said going light-headed, only the weight of my sensible English shoes keeping me earthbound.

'Hello Terr-ee,' *she said and held out her hand.

---

* She had discovered I was also Terence and Terry. She liked the latter.

*My first
photograph of
Maria Antoinetta
Fontana – the
Villa Borghese
gardens, Rome,
where the Pope
lives*

I took it and she led me away.

'Come,' she said.

Through leafy glades she led me to a teahouse. We sat at a table, all the others were deserted, how perfect! A crisp white-coated waiter still smelling of shaving soap attended us. Would I like tea, asks Toni. Yes, I say. What kind, she says. What's she mean what kind? Tea, there's only one kind. Toni orders in Italian and the waiter speeds to her bidding.

'Isn't it a lovely day?'

Yes, Toni, and I love you.

'The trees are at their best this time of the year.'

Yes, Toni, and I love you.

The tea arrives – ah! and Italian pastries. Good old Char. Toni watches as I mix mine with half milk, five spoons of sugar and stir it into a treacly goo. What's that she's drinking in a tall glass enclosed in a silver holder? There's a lemon floating in it. Careless waiter! Shall I get it out for her? What? It's meant to be there? Russian tea? Oh, I'm sorry I can't speak Russian, so how should I know?

16

Temple of Aesculapius. 'You have temple like that in England?' No, I say. We have only Nat Temple and his diseased Band.

The Italian pastries are all small multicoloured fiddly things. Haven't they any jam doughnuts or currant buns? She pours tea like a duchess, eats like a bird, picks up pastries like an angel and sits upright ballerina-style. I had met a lady.

I pay the bill. I must have tipped too heavily as the waiter clutches his heart and runs crying to the kitchen.

'I show you nice things,' says Toni arising. 'Having you ever seen Temple of Aesculapius?'

No I have never seen his temple; the only Temple I've seen is Shirley. We walk through boulevards of roses, many a small fountain laughing in the sun. We talked, I know we talked but it was all coming to me through a long tube. I was spellbound by this girl by my side. We saw the temple and I took an amateur snapshot to enshrine the moment.

So we walk, walk, walk, talk, talk, talk. The walking involves my sensible brown English brogues. Let me describe them. At first glance they look like semi-deflated rugby balls. I have a small foot, size seven, but the shoe is size ten. The leather is convulsed, the soles are an inch thick with a rubber heel. I had bought them off a stall in Deptford. Basically, they made me look like a cripple. I wondered why people stood up for me in buses. Now Toni, elegant Toni, has noticed them. I suppose to her Italian mind they would appear to look like two giant stale salamis with shoelaces inserted. She tries to be tactful.

'Terr-ee, why you wear you Army boots with nice clothes?'

Army boots???? What was wrong with the girl? I told her these were my best shoes and the height of fashion in England in the 7s. 6d. range. I was the talk of Deptford! She stifled a laugh with her handkerchief. She is wearing delightful feather-light Ferragamo shoes.

'You only 'ave one pair of shoes?'

Of course, that's all one needs – one sensible pair weighing ten pounds each.

'You must buy one more best pair,' she said and we left it at that. That magic afternoon wandered on and still does . . . We stop at a stall and have a lemonade each. We sit sipping them through straws.

Toni points to the range of cakes and confectionary, 'You have like this in England?'

Oh, yes, I tell her, we have very good sweets in England and I reel them off: spotted dick, rice and jam, plum duff, suet and treacle pud. Oh, yes, we have sweet things. I offer her a cigarette from my Erinmore Mixture tin. No, she 'no lak smoke', she thinks that smoking is dangerous to one's health. Is she mad? Smoking is lovely: all the film stars do it, smoking never hurt anyone, I said. I smoke sixty a day and am as fit as a fiddle, I said, coughing and bringing up a ton of it.

We have arrived at the Spanish Steps. The flower sellers fade into drabness among the urgently growing flowers. Red roses! of course! I buy Toni a small bouquet – I had never bought flowers for a girl before. I passed them to her, they glowed red in the afternoon sun. She took them, looking intently at me as she did. Still looking at me, she withdrew one lone rose and gave it to me. It's a moment in time frozen in my memory. I take the rose and try to put it into my buttonhole. But there isn't one, is there, so I stick it in my pocket. Toni giggles, it sounds like water splashing in a pond.

'My love is like a red, red rose that blooms in early spring.'

She smiled with her eyes, 'You write that?'

'Yes,' I said.

If you're going to tell a lie, tell a big one. She holds her hand out and we are off up the steps to visit the apartment of Keats's overlooking the Piazza di Spagna. A bored sixty-year-old guide points out items of interest – Keats's bed, his writing table, his chair, his po, etc. etc. – then holds out his hands for the Keats fund. I tip him fifty lire. He is well pleased and I am not. I want change. He tells us that Keats's grave can be seen in the Protestant cemetery. I say, thanks, we only visit Catholic stiffs. Time for us to part, she to home to see Mother and I to the Albergo. We will meet again at the theatre that evening.

The *Barbary Coast* show was a sell-out again. Some brass hats and their females were introduced to the cast, among them General Tuker from the 4th Indian Div. He was delighted when I spoke to him in Hindi – even more stunning, he knew my grandfather, Trumpet Sergeant Major H. Kettleband and his wife!! That night I went straight to bed and dreamed the whole day through again, nude.

FAREWELL OLD SHOES

28 June 1946

Toni and I meet at the Café Minosko on the Via Veneto. Toni wants to get me to a shoe shop to buy a pair of decent shoes. I arrive first and order.

'Tea,' I say. 'Tea à la russe con lemone.'

I am quick to learn. Suddenly, as I'm sipping the new-found concoction, she draws up beside me. She, too, has Russian Tea. Tea over, she holds out her hand; I take it and follow. We walk and talk. We could have run and talked, I suppose; or, rather, Toni could have run and talked while I stood and listened. God she had lovely legs. Those lovely legs stop outside a shoe shop. In she hikes me. A totally bald fat Italian salesman with a fixed grin attends us. Tony rattles off something in Italian, during which the salesman glances in horror at my sensible English shoes. He is gone and returns with a pair of black moccasins.

'Terr-ee,' she smiles. 'You try theseeeee.'

I sit while the salesman unlaces my shoes. He braces himself like a man about to neutralize an unexploded bomb. With a low moan, he eases them off and drops them to the floor with a loud Thud!

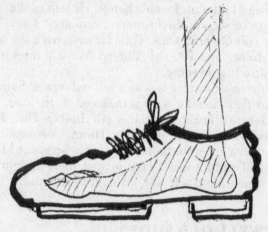

My shoes lie on their sides looking like an accident. He slips on one moccasin, then the other. I feel light-headed. I feel naked. I look in the mirror – gone are the two Frankenstein lumps at the bottom of my legs. Now, all is trim and elegant. Toni has made her first move in civilizing me.

The salesman wants to know if I want the old shoes. Yes, I say, I want to take them to Lourdes to see if there's a cure.

The change in shoes is unbelievable. I'm a stone lighter, I can cross my legs without having to lift my leg manually, dogs have stopped barking at or trying to mate with them. A small step for Spike Milligan, a giant step for mankind.

Toni wants me to meet her family. Why not? I've already met mine and it took to me. We sit in a café on the Via Veneto with Rome passing by. She tells me her father died at the beginning of the war, that he had owned various enterprises in Abyssinia but they had all collapsed and been impounded by the British whom he hated. The main one was a soap factory; when they closed that, he had a heart attack and died. I had been out with a girl whose father was a mechanic in Norwood, one who was a bookmaker in Crofton Park and one who was a thief in Brockley, but never a soap factory owner. Still, everything comes to he who waits. But before I meet her family, she must break the news to her 'boyfriend' Arturo who is an officer in the Alpine Brigade. She has already written to him saying it was *finito*.

'I only know him a leetle,' she said.

29 JUNE 1946

Saturday morning and I take a taxi to 53 Via Appennini. Toni meets me, smiling, at the door. Why she smiled at doors, I don't know.

''Ello Terr-ee.'

I had dressed in my battledress with all my medal ribbons on. I wanted her to present a heroic liberator-of-her-country image to her mother. So to Mother in the lounge, a homely chintzy loose covers affair. This was the first time I'd had a loose covers affair.

Her mother is tall, fair-haired and blue-eyed and I was soon to know she was French by descent, like parachuting from the Eiffel Tower. She is very pleased to meet me as is her younger sister, Lily, who is the living image of Ingrid Bergman! The maid, Gioia, is introduced and she is a giggle of shyness. She curtsies to me.

21

I am to have a lunch of soup, then pasta and a fish course with a white wine – the latter must have been made from stewed guardsmen's socks, mixed with vinegar. Apart from that, it was a delightful lunch with me acting up to Toni's mother. I think as I was the first Allied soldier they'd met, they were all excited, including Gioia who giggled every time she served me. I tried to avoid an amorous glance to Toni so her mother didn't worry about what was going to be a real love affair.

That night I stood in the wings and watched Toni pirouetting to Ponchielli's 'Dance of the Hours'. It was all so romantic. It had echoes of Hemingway's *Farewell to Arms*, though I doubt if anyone would have judged the man with the clip-on moustache, long white nightshirt, holding a candle and singing 'Close the Shutters, Willy's Dead', was the boyfriend of the stunning petite ballerina on the stage. Toni liked Johnny Mulgrew and Bill Hall but a) didn't like Bill's scruffy appearance and b) Mulgrew's drinking habits. It was her fear that I, too, would become like them.

Bill Hall is still disappearing for twenty-three out of the twenty-four hours, only appearing – shagged out – minutes before the act is due on stage. Where does he go? Bornheim knows.

'He has to hop it sharp after the show. If daylight touches him, he turns into a werewolf and raids NAAFI dustbins.'

Mulgrew shakes with silent laughter.

'I tell yew if he did turn into a werewolf no one would notice the difference.'

Mulgrew has an evil sense of humour i.e. Hall rolls his cigarettes, so Mulgrew manages to mix magnesium powder with hall's baccy. With blackened face and singed eyebrows, Hall walks the hotel corridors with a stick shouting 'Orrite 'oo fuckin' dun it.' Worse to come, Mulgrew, who by damping brown paper had made a realistic 'Richard' * places it in Gunner Hall's bed with the note 'The Phantom strikes again'.

* Richard. Richard the Third = turd.

Oh, dear! Maxie has overdone it, he thinks he has fractured his arm! I watched from the wings as it happened. Maxie, for a start, looked like Neanderthal man, his forehead was every bit of two inches and his arms reached below his knees. I think in his paybook it said 'Place of birth: tree'.

He is telling the audience, 'Laddies and Gintzleman, hai makada act zo, I tak dees hiron barrr and I mak bend bye hitting special muscle hin mie arm.'

Then he used to start this terrible Thwack Thwack Thwack on his forearm, mixed with grunts and occasional screams. This night, he staggers off clutching his arm and moaning Oh Fuck in Hungarian. He was off the show for weeks; I think he convalesced in a zoo.

After the show, I take Toni for a glass of wine at the trattoria next to the theatre. We sit at a table on the pavement and talk, what about? *Anything*, it's just lovely being with her, looking into those eyes, at that waspish smile and listening to her small childlike voice. I am falling head over heels.

PADUA

SUNDAY, 30 JUNE 1946

All packed up and on to the Charabong. This time, I sit next to Toni. Our destination, the ancient town of Padua. We are travelling on a Sunday morning and families are coming or going to church. The sound of church bells hangs on the morning air; we pass several religious processions.

'One fing about Caflicks,' says Gunner Hall. 'They always play ter full 'ouses.'

Bornheim agrees. 'It's all that communion wine they swig free, that gets 'em in' – he who hasn't been inside a church since his christening day.

I, too, had lost touch with my religion. I had stopped going to church the moment I joined the Regiment. No more could my mother nag me into God's presence. However, Toni was a practising Catholic. Why are they always practising? When do they become good enough not to?

When I put that to Toni, she said, 'I don't understand you, what are you talking about.'

I said about twenty words a minute.

She didn't understand, but laughed and said, 'I love you beautiful eyes.'

How strange! All those years in the Army and my sergeant never said I had beautiful eyes. 'Beautifulll eyeeesss front!' No, it doesn't sound right.

We are driving across Italy from west to east. We can't make Padua in a day; it's some six hundred kilometres away. We stay that night in a hotel on the sea at Riccione. It's a large rambling hotel built in the thirties, a square building built by squares for squares. The rooms are comfortable – strange I've *never* found an uncomfortable Italian bed.

We all hike ourselves off the Charabong carrying our chattels. We're here for three nights – we do two shows

27

starting tomorrow night. It's only seven o'clock, a velvet starlit night is slipping overhead. I tap at Toni's door: would she like to go for a swim? Oh, yes, it's a warm night. Dinner is at eight, so we have time. The beach is deserted and the water soft and warm. We frolic around for a bit – all that idiot ducking and diving between her legs, etc. We run back to the lee of a fishing boat and dry off.

'Before the war, these beach very many people,' she says, and it wouldn't be long before there were twice as many people as there were then.

I went back in 1965 on a nostalgia trip: you couldn't see the sea for people and when you did see it, there was no room in it. Signs should have read 'Sorry, Adriatic Full Up Today'.

We hold hands and lean against the boat and I kiss her for the first time . . . There were love whispers in the all-embracing night. We return to dinner in a nice airy room opening on to a verandah. Toni asks about the family.

'Wot you fadder do?'

'As little as possible. He's a soldier, a captain.'

'He fight in theese war?'

'No, no, not this one. He's too old – "vecchio". He fight in last war, this one is an encore.'

'And you mother? You look like her or you fadder?'

'I think I like my father.'

'Oh, he must be veree 'ansome,' she laughed.

'Yes, he was. Not so much now.'

'You have sisters, brothers?'

'One brother.'

'Is he old or young?'

'He's younger than me, eight years.'

'Wot he do?'

'He's in the Army in Germany.'

'Before war?'

'Before he was studying to be an artist.'

'You family all artist . . . how you say *artistico*?'

'Yes, my mother was a trained singer and she played the piano. My father sing and dance.'

28

'What kind dance?'

'Tap dance.'

'Oh, like American, Fred Astairs?'

'Yes, Fred Astairs – a little more Bill Robinson.'

'Who Bill Robinson?'

'Oh dear.'

It was the sort of conversation that millions of people make when they first meet. Looking at it these forty years later, it looks boring. So, what made it worthwhile at the time? The sound of her voice? The movement of her lips? The look in her eyes and that peculiar tilt of her head when she spoke? Her hand gesturing to make a point? Yes, I suppose all those things and the unexplainable biological call of matching chemistry that takes charge of the entire you and dedicates it to another person. It's all pretty miraculous stuff. It does wear off, but it will always haunt you – a sudden tune, a perfume, a flower, a word, and the ghost of all those yesterdays returns for a fleeting moment, like a wind's caress. Ahhh, youth . . .

From the windows in the passage off our bedrooms, we can see the outdoor cinema which is showing Nelson Eddy and Jeanette MacDonald in something like 'give me some men who are stout-hearted men', etc. etc. etc. Toni and I stand at the window for the freebie. I have my arm round her waist; it's like an electric shock. We watch as Jeanette and Nelson shriek at each other, face to face. 'I am thineeeeeeee, for everrrrrrr.' It ends with them kissing on a balcony. So to bed. I kiss Toni goodnight only to be caught by Johnny Bornheim.

'Here, here, here,' he cautions. 'No kissing ballerinas between six and midnight.' He pretends to produce a notebook and pencil. 'Now then, how many kisses and what time?'

Toni giggles and disappears into her bedroom. 'Goodnight Terr-ee.'

Bornheim tells me he has found a grand piano in a room. Would I like to hear it? I troop down with him and he plays Puccini, Ellington and more Ellington. By then it is midnight. I hie me to my bed, my head full of flowers and Toni.

29

Oh, those kisses, there must be a word somewhere that explains the feeling. Spazonkled! That's it, it was like being Spazonkled, Spazonklified!! I lay in bed smoking a cigarette and steaming with love. Where will it all end?

RICCIONE DAY 2

I slept late, missed breakfast, couldn't find Toni anywhere. She'd gone with the girls for a swim. I find an Italian café and order *caffelatte* and a brioche which I wolf down. Bornheim appears at the door:

'Missed breakfast,' he said.

'Oh, you little Sherlock Holmes,' I said.

'Not with Toni?' he went on.

'No, not with Toni. Very good, very observant.'

He settles down to a coffee. 'Seen the theatre?'

No, I hadn't.

'Very nice, small but very nice. Called La Galleria. Been for a swim yet?'

'Yes, last night with Toni.'

'Ohhhhhh, you dirty devil! Midnight swims, eh???'

Bornheim doesn't understand the purity of this romance.

'When you going to give it to her,' he says, and I shudder. I'm above all this. I'm no longer lecherous Gunner Milligan but nice Terri Milligan.

Bill Hall thinks we need to practise and think of some new ideas. So we retire to my room for two hours, play those jazz standards I still love, 'Georgia Brown', 'Poor Butterfly', 'What's New', 'Sophisticated Lady'. We get carried away and the practice becomes a swing session, lovely.

The show that night as per usual, with glances between Toni and me whenever we passed as we rushed to change for the next scene. It's a very warm night and the smell of frangipani is wafting through the window of our dressing-room – all very nice. Taiola Silenzi, a name to conjure with: she is our monumental Italian soprano. She and her smaller

30

husband Fulvio Pazzaglia sing excerpts from opera and popular ballads – 'Violetta', etc. Taiola is in her early forties and must have been very pretty in her day. Alas, I wasn't in town that day. She is overweight but insists on wearing skin-tight clothes. Layers of fat poke all over the place as though she is wearing a series of bicycle inner tubes. She is not far off looking like a Michelin man. She's billed as Frisco Lil and with that name launches into 'One Fine Day'. Tonight, as she and Fulvio are going for one of those last high screaming notes, her dress rips across her abdomen with resultant raw soldier laughter from the audience. She is furious and storms off into her dressing-room where we can hear her yelling at her innocent little husband. She was so loud in her protestations that during the Bill Hall Trio act we could hear her ranting on, to which Bill Hall yells *'Silencio!'* Which got more laughter.

Show over, we all clean up and pile in the Charabong. Toni is already in and pats the place next to her. Every time I sit next to her, there's a sort of howl from the males in the coach. Through twenty minutes of streets to our hotel, it's a moonlit night. From the hotel, we can see the waves breaking on the beach. A swim? A crowd of us ran up and don our costumes, then a race to the beach and splash bang into the warm waters of the Adriatic. Lots of whooping and high jinks. I swim out about a thousand yards and look back at the shore, the winking lights, the shouts of the swimmers – I swim back.

'Where you been, Terr-ee?' says a little wet thing. 'It ees dangerous to swim long way.'

Ah, she's mothering me! We dry off. I smoke a cigarette holding up a towel for Toni to change behind, seeing as much of her as I can. Contrary to the legend Bornheim has spread, I now know that Italian girls have pubic hairs like all the others.

It's minestrone soup and scampi for dinner and a carafe of white wine. How different from my mother's boiled hake, boiled potatoes, boiled meat and two boiled veg, and spotted dick. I was living in another world. That night, I wrote home to my parents telling them about Toni. I concluded, 'How would you like an Italian as a daughter-in-law?' My mother writes, 'Be careful, son. I've heard these Italian girls are diseased.' Never mind, she'll be all right when she's boiled. But then my mother would have only been satisfied if I had married a nun or the Virgin Mary. She is now ninety, I am sixty-seven and she's still warning me: 'They only want your money or your body.' If she only knew how run down both were.

Our two days at Riccione over, we lump it all on the Charabong and with groans of 'Oh not again' and *'Che stufa'* we set off for ancient Padua. Bill Hall is missing.

'We can't wait for the bugger,' says despairing Lieutenant Priest and away we go.

Another bright, sunny but hot day. We open the windows for air, but that lets in the dust of passing cars. So it's the alternative – shouting 'Look out, here comes a bloody lorry,' slamming the windows then opening them again. Such interesting work. What if Hall *doesn't* show up, inquires Mulgrew. I say he always does. But Mulgrew says,

'You see, one time he *won't* show. Then what?'

Then I say we become the Bill Hall Duo.

Padua is some 120 miles up the coast; the coach averages forty miles an hour; inside the coach, we seem to manage sixty miles an hour. The journey passes with some singing, smoking and me mooning over Toni. We stop every hour for leg stretches and easing of springs, etc. We drive through wonderful Rimini but don't stop, and so much to see! A town crawling with history and us shooting right through it.

We stop at Ferrara for lunch at a large NAAFI canteen. It's full of soldiers and when the girls enter, they get the treatment. Aggggggghhhhhhhh COLD COLLATION!!!! It's following me around Italy. In desperation I wolf it down.

'You don't like thesse dinner,' says Toni.

'No, I don't like it.'

'Why you no like?'

'Because it is without imagination and it's cold – *senza immaginazione anche freddo*. Another thing, it's not boiled.'

She smiles because I'm so serious. Why, why, why do females always laugh at males in distress????? Whenever my father struck his head on a beam in the cellar my mother, her sister and my grandmother burst into hysterical laughter and locked themselves in the sewing-room so my father wouldn't hear. Is it the ultimate triumph of woman over man? Did Eve laugh when she first saw Adam's willy?

No, I loathed Cold Collation mainly because it's the English's answer to shutting the kitchen early so the chef can get to the boozer before eleven. The number of nights I had been trapped in boarding houses with just me alone with Cold Collation in an empty seaside dining-room. The horror still lingers. How could Toni ever understand? There was only one thing worse than Cold Collation and that was the 'Warsaw Concerto'. When the meal was over, several of the cast came and congratulated me on eating it. On, then, to Padua and away from the reek of Cold Collations!!!!

> Ohhh never go to Ferrara
> The curse of the nation
> It's known to weary travellers
> For serving Cold Collation
> Do not then you wonder
> At travellers' faces stricken
> A lettuce leaf, tomato half
> A lump of long-dead chicken.

Toni is telling me about how she always wanted to be a ballerina. She had started at eleven when she must have been two inches high. She was trained by Madame Cold Collation. No, no, no, I'm sorry, dear reader. It's that terrible meal twisting my mind. No, not Madame Collation but Madame Esteve. Under her strict supervision, it was considered impolite to smile without placing a kerchief over your mouth; laughing out loud was forbidden. It was all the discipline of the ballet with Victorianism. And this training showed – Toni never raucous, always polite and, wonders

33

for an Italian, never angry. Her gestures were always controlled. At first, she had difficulty in understanding me. I talked lunatic things all day so much that even people who spoke English didn't understand.

MILLIGAN: Bornheim, it's the spludles again.
BORNHEIM: The what?
MILLIGAN: The spludles, they're activating again.
BORNHEIM: (*warming to it*) Ah, yes, and where are they this day?
MILLIGAN: They are aggropilating just below the swonnicles.
BORNHEIM: The usual place.
MILLIGAN: The danger is they might swarm.
BORNHEIM: Yes.
MILLIGAN: Read all about it – man found dead in matchbox.

It's very hot inside the coach.

'Ask the driver if he knows a cooler route,' says Hall.

'Like Iceland,' I call out. 'Anyone for iced swonnicles?'

We are crossing numerous Bailey bridges built on those destroyed in the fighting. The odd sign still says 'You are crossing this river by courtesy of 202 Royal Engineers'. I reflect on how much blood was spilt in building them. Toni is fanning herself with a piece of card.

'*Che stufa,*' she says.

Indeed, it is very *stufa*. Through the village of Polecella, the towns of Rovigo and Stranghella – the names roll by on city limits signs – past old Mussolini slogans fading on the walls, murals of the deceased dictator with his jutting jaw, now vandalized, flashes of red which are tomatoes ripening on walls.

'Not long now,' says Lieutenant Priest in a cheery voice.

Lots of things aren't long. Mulgrew wasn't very long, Maxie at five feet five was even less long. There was indeed a great shortage of longs.

34

PADUA

Let's see, what do I know about Padua? There was St Anthony's, and 'Fred' Giotto had some murals in the Palazzo della Regione. So I didn't know much about Padua. If only the coach stopped in Catford. I knew a lot about Catford. There was the Fifty Shilling Tailors, where I had ordered a dreadful suit that made me look deformed. It was like something you get on prescription from a doctor.

It's evening when the dusty Charabong with its passengers singing 'Hey, Girra, Girra, Girrica' shudders to a steaming halt outside the Leone Bianco Hotel.

'Ah, Leone Bianco,' says Bornheim, 'The Blancoed Lion.'

'Che stufa,' says Toni.

It's her twentieth *che stufa* of the journey. We sort out our luggage. Mulgrew says, 'Oh fuck,' the handle of his suitcase has come off.

'Ah, now you can join the knotted string brigade,' I say.

We lollop into the hotel which is soon echoing to the sound of lollops. Blast! I am sharing a room with Mulgrew and his second-hand clothes store. Toni's bedroom is the next floor up, blast again.

'It'll never stretch that far,' says Mulgrew.

'Will you stop making suggestive remarks about me and Toni,' I said. 'Our love is pure,' I said with hand over heart and the other raised heavenwards.

A tap on the door and enter a pretty girl with tea trolley.

'Signori tak tea, yes?'

Yes, please! We sipped our tea and smoked.

'Sooo,' says Mulgrew. 'This is New York.'

I unpack.

'You know, Johnny, you look taller in bed.'

'What are you suggesting? I only meet people lying down?'

'Well, yes. You can get up for shaking hands and then lie down again.'

35

There was a silence and Mulgrew blew smoke ceiling-wards.

'I wonder where that silly bugger Hall is.'

It was a worry. Hall had this horror film visage – he was lucky no one had tried to drive a stake through his heart. We were to open in Venice tomorrow. Would Hall make it?

'I mean, the streets are made of water. No good trying to run,' says Mulgrew, scratching his groins.

'Is it the old trouble?' I say.

'That was a wee smasher who brought in the tea,' he said.

More groin scratching. Aloud, he starts to read the notice on the door – anything to save buying a book.

'Dinner between eight and ten-thirty, unless a late meal is requested.'

There it is at the bottom . . . Arghhhhhhh Cold Collation! It's followed me, there are special Cold Collation units that are following me.

'Sir, he's heading for Padua.'

'Quick, send a despatch rider with several Cold Collations, and hurry.'

I run a bath; I undress in front of the mirror. The more clothes I remove, the more I look like a Belsen victim. I immerse what is called a body in the bath. I sing merrily, adjusting the taps with my toes.

I spruce up and take the lift down to see Toni, who is walking down the stairs to meet me. I go down to meet her, she comes up to meet me, and so on until we make it. A lovers' stroll through the town: being a university town, there are numerous book shops and the cafés are full of students talking excitedly. Toni stops at a sweet shop and buys coloured sugared almonds.

'Thee blues ones are for your eyes.'

Gad, I must have been lovely then. One thing for sure, she must never see me naked. I had a body that invited burial, that and my ragged underwear.

We walked and talked. Sometimes, we stood still and talked – that's like walking with your legs together (eh?).

Back to the Blancoed Lion and dinner. *Gnocchi?* What's a Gnocki? Who's that Gnocking at my door? It was the first time I'd had it.

'Eeet is a Roman speciality,' says Toni.

She asks me if I've ever been to Venice. I say no, but I've seen it in a book. 'All the city built on – how you say?'

'Piles,' I said.

Yes, the whole of Venice suffered from damp piles. She doesn't understand.

Lieutenant Priest approaches, 'Is everything all right?'

Yes, *molto buono*.

He tells us that Chalky White has gone forward with the scenery, which will be transported to the theatre by barge. Priest laughs at the thought.

'My God, he had difficulty unloading on dry land.'

We repair to the lounge bar where most of the cast are drinking.

'What will you have?' says Bornheim.

'I will have a Cognac and Toni will have a lemonade.'

'Well, I'm sure the barman will serve you,' he laughed – the swine! 'Sorry, Spike, I'm broke. You'll have to lash out.'

'You sure Bornheim isn't a Jewish name?' I said. 'So, what'll *you* have?'

Of course, it's double whisky, isn't it. Wait, what's this? Through the door, covered in dust, unshaven, his fiddle case under his arm, is the late Gunner Bill Hall.

''Ere, they didn't bleedin' wait for me,' he says. 'I bin cadging lifts all day. My bloody thumb's nearly coming off.'

He wants to know if dinner is still on. I gaze at my Aztec gold watch and, holding it in a position for the whole room to see, I tell him he is just on the right side of ten-thirty. He departs, him and his reeking battledress – the jacket is open from top to waist, over a crumpled shirt (off-white shirt). Because of his thin legs he wears two pairs of trousers – they billow out like elephants' legs. God, what a strange man, but a genius of a musician. When he died a few years ago, I realized that a genius could die unsung.

So, as the surgeon said, we're opening tonight. All excitement – we're on our way to the Theatre Fenice in Venice. Toni gave my arm a squeeze but nothing came out.

'Now,' she says. 'Theese is for you.'

It's a small tissue-wrapped package.

'Oh, how lovely! It's what I've always wanted, a tissue-wrapped package!'

I remove the tissue. It's a silver cigarette case. I look for the price tag.

'Now you throw away dirty tin, eh?'

'No, no I can't throw it away. That tin has been under mortar and shell fire with me, danced with girls with me, even had an attack of piles with me!' From now on, I'll have to keep it out of sight.

A FAG SHOP IN CATFORD SE6

CUSTOMER: A packet of out-of-sight cigarettes, please.

SHOPKEEPER: There, sir.

CUSTOMER: This packet is empty.

SHOPKEEPER: Yes, sir. That's because they're out of sight.

VOICE: Yes, get the new out-of-sight cigarette!

Maria Antoinetta Fontana swimming from the knees down in Riccione

VENICE

VENICE

The Charabong is taking us through medieval Mestre and on to the causeway. The sun bounces off the yellow waters of the Lagoon. On the right, the blue-grey of the Adriatic, neither of which looked clean. We de-bus in the Piazza Roma where a CSE* barge is waiting – oh, the fun!

Barbary Coast Co. on the Grand Canal. Bornheim reading the Union Jack

* Combined Services Entertainment.

'Hello sailor,' I say to a deckhand.

I lift my guitar case carefully on board, then turn to help Toni – blast! A deckhand is helping her. I'll kill him, he *touched* her, my Brockley SE 26 blood boiled. He's lucky to be alive.

We glide down the Grand Canal: on our right, the magnificent Palace Vendramin Calergi, its mottled stone catching the sun, pigeons roosting along its perimeters. We slide under the Ponte Rialto and look up people's noses – the sheer *leisure* of water travel. Toni and I are in the back of the barge by the rudder; I look into the brown waters to see romantic discharge from a sewer. Slowly, we come to the landing stage for the theatre.

Our dressing-rooms are wonderful: red plush with gilt mirrors, buttoned furniture.

Our pier – at 86 Area HQ, Venice

42

'Och, now! Och, this is more like it,' says Mulgrew.

What it is och more like, he doesn't say. That bugger Bill Hall is missing again! Will he turn up? Mulgrew shrugs his shoulders. Suddenly, he notices my new cigarette case.

'It's from Toni,' I tell him.

An evil grin on his face, Mulgrew says, 'Is that for services rendered.'

How dare he! Now he wants to borrow a fag.

'God, Mulgrew, you're always on the ear'ole. What do you do with your fags?'

'Didn't you know I smoke them!' A pause, then, 'Are you thinking of marrying her?'

'Hardly, I mean my worldly savings are eighty pounds.'

Mulgrew claws the air like a beggar.

'Rich – R I C H,' he says.

'I can't take Toni from all this to a steaming sink in Deptford.'

'Why not? It's good enough for your mother.'

'My mother's used to it, but this girl is upper middle class. They've got a maid.'

'Then,' he laughs, 'marry the maid. She's used to it.'

As he speaks, he is undressing – he's down to his vest when there's a knock at the door.

'Just a minute,' he says, and pulls the front of his vest between his legs. 'Come in.'

Lieutenant Priest sticks his head round the door.

'Any signs of your vagrant?' he says.

'We need notice of that question,' says Mulgrew. He releases his vest and lets his wedding tackle swing freely in the night air.

'He is a bugger,' says Priest, and departs.

Another knock on the door.

'Just a minute,' says Mulgrew, again tucking his vest between his legs. 'Come in.'

It's buxom dancer Greta Weingarten. She wants to know would we swop our chocolate ration for her cigarettes. Alas, we have eaten it all. She departs and again Mulgrew lets it all swing free.

'Ohhh, Rita,' groaned Mulgrew, making a well-known sign.

'I must change,' I say.

'What's it this time, Dr Jekyll?' says Mulgrew.

It's an hour to curtain up. I'm on first, playing trumpet in the band, then a nightshirted singer in 'Close the Shutters, Willy's Dead', then on guitar in the Bill Hall Trio – or the Mulgrew-Milligan Duo. The show starts with no sign of Hall: the entire cast are on-stage singing 'San Francisco'. This is followed by our M C, Jimmy Molloy, with a dreadful American accent.

'Howdee folks,' he says, 'welcome to *Barbary Coast*. For the next two hours we will be' etc. etc., as the girls go into the can-can.

Interval and Hall appears. 'Wots orl the fuss I'm in time for the act aren't I?' We are again the hit of the evening. The applause was longer than normal; we do an extra encore and busk 'Undecided'.

The Barbary Coast Belles heavily posed with Keith Grant

PADUA AGAIN

'Ah Ter-ee, today we go see Basilica St Anthony of Padua.'
She is a little bossy boots.
'OK. Mulgrew wants to tag along.'
'OK.'
Ah! That basilica! Built in the eleventh century!! And looking fresh and magnificent. Seven weathered bronze cupolas are its roof; it looks like a multiple Santa Sophia. As you approach the entrance, there is a Donatello, a magnificent bronze equestrian statue of Erasmo di Narni (Rasmus the Nana). Inside is a treasure house of marble statues and paintings. Suddenly, the outside noise is subdued, voices become sibilant. Toni has covered her head with a black lace shawl; mine is covered in Brylcreem. Catholics all, we cross ourselves with Holy Water that looks like a breeding ground for typhoid. I recalled how a priest at St Saviour's, Brockley Rise, a hygiene fanatic, used to add Dettol to the Holy Water. When we returned from mass, my father asked 'Have you been to church or had an operation?'

Here, mass is about to be said. Holding candlesticks, a chanting string of choirboys with faces like cherubim precede a grim-faced priest and retinue. He is mouthing the words, but not singing. He's heard it all before.

'You want stay for mass?' whispers Toni.
'OK, just a little.'
We slide our knees into an empty pew. The chanting echoes round the vaulted ceiling like trapped birds trying to escape. The gloom of the interior is punctured by a pointillism of candles flickering before statues with sightless eyes and marbled brains. The waft of stale incense is being topped up with fresh ignitions. Old ladies in black eschew older prayers. They pass the Stations of the Cross, each one jostling

47

Mirror, mirror! Toni fixes her hair with the aid of Mulgrew

with her neighbour for a better place in heaven. Why are the poor so rich in religion? Do the godless rich rely on St Peter taking bribes? '*Sanctus, sanctus, sanctus,*' intones the priest. The communicants, heads hanging like condemned murderers, scuffle to the Communion rail, their heads jerk back to receive the Host. It's rather like a petrol station, each one being refilled for their spiritual journey.

It was nice to hear the tongue of the Romans still in use. There's the final blessing – *Dominus vobiscum;* we reply, *Et cum spirito tuo*, and Ta raaaa . . . that's the end. We walk out into the bright sunshine. Mulgrew is gasping for a fag, especially one of mine. I open my silver case, he takes one, I snap the case shut like Bogart. I tap my cigarette on the lid. With a flick, I send the cigarette up my nose.

'That's the first time I've been in a Catholic church,' said Mulgrew (a lapsed Scottish Presbyterian).

'I promise I won't tell anyone,' I said. Toni wants to tidy up her hair, 'That lace shawl catch my hair.' She got Mulgrew to hold her mirror.

I drop these photos in from time to time so you don't think I'm making this all up.

The occasion is marred by rain. We run for the covered walkways by the shops and finally make a dash for the Blancoed Lion. Ah! There's some more mail. My folks have sent me a parcel of books and magazines, so I settle down for a good afternoon's read. I read we now have a Labour government with Clem Attlee as Prime Minister. After having that wonderful man Churchill, we now have someone who looks like an insurance clerk on his way to a colonic irrigation appointment. I ask Mulgrew what he thinks of Attlee.

'I never think of Attlee.'

'Do you think of any politicians?'

'I sometimes think of what Bessie Braddock looks like with her clothes off. It's therapeutic! Something else, politicians should only be allowed to make speeches with their trousers down. It would be a test of their sincerity.'

Is Mulgrew mad? Could Churchill have made his 'Blood, Sweat and Tears' speech with his trousers down?

SPEAKER: Will the honourable gentleman lower his trousers and answer the question.

CHURCHILL: I'm sorry, Mr Speaker, but I've forgotten my underpants . . .

VENICE AGAIN

VENICE AGAIN

The rain continues, thunder added to the downpour. I read Mulgrew bits of spicy headlines:

Nude trombone player in bath mystery

FILM STAR SWALLOWS OIL SLICK

... etc. etc. The *Daily Mirror* wins the prize with its headline about a vicar molesting choir boys:

REVEREND SMITH GO UNFROCK YOURSELF

It was in deluge conditions that we set out for the theatre, the windows steamed up, the roar of the rain incessant.

'Christ,' says Bornheim. 'We'll end up on Mount Ararat with two of each animal.' He peers through the window. Bornheim enjoyed a good peer.

Lieutenant Priest is poking the driver, pointing up and saying, 'Sunny Italy, *si*?' Luigi grins and shrugs his shoulders. Luigi liked a good shrug.

MY MOTHER: Where have you been to this time of night?
ME: I've been out shrugging, Mum.

Thank God, the barge has put up canvas awnings. We push
out into the Lagoon show, the spray washing over us all
crouched in the back. Some people like a good crouch.

MY MOTHER: Have you been out shrugging again?
ME: No, I've been out crouching.

We arrive at the theatre damp. Bill Hall is missing again. I
discover him asleep in the dressing-room, covered in an army
overcoat. Stretched out, his feet protruding, he looked like
an effigy of a very down-market crusader tomb. He tells me
he missed the transport home last night. What kept him?

'I met this girl from the box office.'

Girl?? She's this side of fifty, wears pebble-dash glasses . . .

'Be grateful for bad eyesight, Bill,' says Mulgrew.

What a mess! This dressing-room that once housed Caruso,
Pavlova, Tibaldi, now has Hall's laundry strung across it.

The show is a bit of a fiasco (which bit I'm not sure). The
thunder drowns out most of the dialogue. This was the night
when during the mock fight Chalky White split my lip. In a
rage, I shouted above the thunder, 'You cunt!' The soldier
audience dissolved into laughter. It didn't end there. When
White made his next entrance, a drunken voice from the
gallery shouted, 'Look, it's that cunt again.'

The show finishes but the rain doesn't. 'It's a serial,' says
Bornheim. We sat huddled in our motor barge.

'*Che pioggia*,' says the helmsman.

'Wots 'ee say?' says Hall.

'He says what rain,' I said.

'Tell him King George the Sixth.'

The thunder rackets overhead, the sky is gashed by light-
ning. The Lagoon lights up like a silver tray, the surface is a
fleece of raindrops. We make the causeway soaked to the
skin. I help Toni from the barge and give them a quick
squeeze. 'Pleaseeeee, Tereeee,' she exclaimed. 'You are
naughty, *cattivo* boy.' Why do men want to squeeze women's

54

boobs? It only puts them out of shape. It's something to do with being weaned.

By eleven o'clock we are back at the Blancoed Lion. We rush upstairs to dry off and rush down for dinner. I'm staring into Toni's eyes. Waiter, waiter, a double bed please! Would *signor* like anything on it? Yes, Miss Fontana with as little dressing as possible! Arggghhhhhh! The rain has stopped and after dinner the Trio play for dancing. We invite the waitresses to join in. May I have the next Spaghetti Neapolitan with you? The dance leads to trouble, some of the local yobs have started to gather outside at the large glass window and now start shouting threats at the Italian girls for dancing with Allied soldiers. They make that nasty sign of cutting women's hair. We stop the dance as they are trying to break in, so we phone the Military Police. We block the doorway, standing shoulder to shoulder. Terry Pellici, a cockney Italian, was remonstrating with them. There's a lot of barging, chest to chest. Maxie, our strong man, bodily picks up one of the mob and hurls him back into the crowd. It stems the tide long enough for the Redcaps' arrival in a jeep, and disperses what could have been a nasty situation. And so to bed – first, a tap on Toni's door to say goodnight and give them a quick squeeze. 'Pleaseeeee, Tereeee.'

Next day is bright and sunny. We are awakened by our nubile waitress with the tea trolley. What a luxury! She has nice legs and a wobbly bottom with the consistency of a Chivers jelly. Mulgrew lights his first cigarette of the day, has a fit of coughing that sounds like a plumber unblocking a sink. With a contused face and eyes watering, he says, 'Oh, lovely! Best fag of the day.' Then falls back exhausted on the pillow.

Toni has gone on the roof to sunbathe. 'I want brown all over,' she says. 'If you come up, make a noise.' I promise I will yodel like Tarzan. Ah! Some more mail has caught up with me and a parcel! My mother's letter is full of warnings about show business: 'It can ruin your health, and knock yourself up.' How does one knock oneself up?

Terry Pellici is leaving today to be demobbed. He asks us all
to have a farewell drink; so, I say farewell to my drink and
swallow it. I ask Terry was it awkward, being Italian by
descent, having to serve in the Allied Army and fight his
own people? 'That's the way the cookie crumbles. I'm an
Eyetie cockney. In a war you got to be on somebody's side,
so I was on somebody's side.'

'You got relatives living here?'

'Yer, in Cattolica. I went to visit them. It was funny –
most of 'em were in the Eyetie Army. I thought,' here he
started to laugh, 'one of them might say, you shoota my
uncle.' Terry had been in the 74 Mediums, a sister regiment
to the 56 Heavy. 'They used me as an interpreter. I did well
with Eyetie POWs: I tell them first thing they had to give
up was their watches. I made a bomb on them in Tunis.' He
brandishes an expensive chronometer: 'Eyetie colonel.'

He asks me for my home address and promises to contact
me when I return. He never did. In 1976 I phoned him. 'Is
that Pellici's Café?'

'Yer, 'oo is it?'

'You wouldn't know me. I was killed in the war.'

'Oo *is* that?'

'Gunner Milligan.'

'Spike! I've been meaning to write to you.' Thirty years
he's been meaning to write!

We finish the booze up and Terry gets on his Naples-
bound lorry. First, I take a posed picture of him sorrowing at
his departure.

Terry Pellici's farewell pose

Toni! She should be nude by now. I tiptoe up the stairs with Bornheim, my camera ready to click. She must have heard because by the time we got there she had her petticoat on. I got Bornheim to hold her while I took this memorable shot.

Toni resisting being snapped in her petticoat

That night, during the interval, Lieutenant Priest comes round with the wages or, as Hall called it, the Dibs. We sign the Dibs receipt. Hall puts his money in the rosin compartment of his violin case. I think Mulgrew put his on a chain in a money belt in his jockstrap.

After the show, I had planned for Toni and me to go out to dinner. First, a trip in a gondola on a clear starry night. The gondola man can see we are lovers, so he sings 'Lae That Piss Tub Dawn Bab'* ... It is midnight. Toni and I are at a corner table in the Restaurant Veneziana (alas, now defunct – possibly now the Plastic Pizzeria). It's all candles and Victoriana and dusty enough without being dirty. There are chandeliers with the odd tear-drop missing and white-aproned waiters lubricated by the growing tourism are grovelling and bowing at the going rate. A guitar and mandolin are trilling through Paolo Tosti and Puccini. I send a hundred lire with a request: 'Don't play "Lae That Piss Tub Dawn Bab".'

Toni and I are talking pre-dinner nothings. We watch the dancing calligraphy of the ruby in the wine on the tablecloth, we can hear the waters lap as gondolas pass the window. Please, God, let me die now! I am seeing Toni over a bowl of nodding roses, fallen petals tell of their demise, the sickly sweet smell courts the air. The waiter has held back to allow us our billing and cooing. He now advances with the menus as a shield. He recommends moules marinières: '*Fresche sta mattina, signorina,*' he tells Toni. Toni orders *vitello* (veal). Today, I'd have told her it was cruel; then, I was ignorant.

'This is very old restaurant, original home of Contessa de Rocabaldi. She die in 1900, some say she poisoned.' Oh? Did she eat here? 'Oh Terry, why you always talk crazy?' says my love. 'Here stay Greta Garbo.' Oh? I topped up our glasses only to have the bottle taken by the *sommelier*, smilingly outraged at the predation on his domain. He tells us that Valpolicella was the wine of Suetonius. I asked him did he come here? But the joke misfires and he says, no, you see Suetonius died two thousand years ago.

We were alone and eating. I looked across the roses at her and I said what I hadn't said to a girl since 1939. 'I think I love you.' She stopped eating, a *moule* in one hand. (There are no two-handed *moules*.)

She smiled. 'You *think* you love me?' I nodded. She raised her glass, I touched it with mine, they lingered together a moment. Then she said, 'When you are sure, you tell me

* 'Lay That Pistol Down, Babe'.

59

again.' And she elevated the glass, then sipped, her eyes on me as she drank. She called the waiter and rattled off something in Italian. He hurried to the duo which then played the 'Valzer di Candele', the version from the film *Waterloo Bridge* (with Robert Taylor and Vivien Leigh). She hummed the tune, a few rose petals fell. God, this was different from Reg's Café in Brockley! I reached out and held her hand and discovered how hard it was eating spaghetti one-handed. But what a romantic night!

It was past midnight when the waiter brought the bill, and two minutes past when I realized I'd left my money in the dressing-room at the theatre. I explain the circumstances, he calls the manager; I explain the circumstances, he calls the police; I explain the circumstances. It ends with me leaving my silver cigarette case and my watch. They were all returned the next night when I paid the bill, the manager now all effusive with smiles. The cigarette case was empty, the bastard had smoked the lot. Like my father said, 'Life is six to four against.'

THE CARNIVAL OF VENICE

Yes, tonight Venice is to have a carnival, the first one since 1939. Before the show, Toni and I sit at an outdoor café in the Piazza San Marco. The pigeons are wheeling in the sunset, and the light falls on the Ducal Palace and the Basilica, two different stories in stone. Around the square, beautiful buildings run cheek by jowl: soaring up is the great Bell Tower, whose doleful bells are ringing out the hour of six, sending more pigeons wheeling from their roosts. People stroll leisurely. One looks at St Mark's and is lost in wonder, its Byzantine-Gothic shapes catching the light to give a hologram effect. Alas, the four colossal bronze horses that had once graced some Roman quadriga were missing – still in store from the war.

Johnny Mulgrew joins us. 'Hello,' he says in stark Glaswegian tones. 'So you're going to buy me a drink?' He tells us Hall is missing again. Are we going to stay on for the carnival? Yes. I order a couple of Cognacs. May as well start the festivities.

'Here, wee Jock, drink this. It's awfur gude,' I said in mock-Scottish tones. Silently, Mulgrew holds it up then downs it in one, licks his lips, looks at us and grins. It doesn't take much to make a Scotsman happy.

The show over, we all make for the barge which has been stocked with drinks and food for the night. Our bargee has put little coloured bulbs in our awnings. There were 'ooos and ahhhs' as fireworks sprinkled the night sky. All the ferries and gondolas had coloured lanterns. In the Piazza San Marco, there was a municipal band and all the people in fancy dress, some quite fantastic with masks. Some waved handheld fizzers writing graffiti in the air. Gondoliers were outsinging each other, people waved and shouted from passing boats, rockets soar from the Isola di San Giorgio and it's a starry night!

We open the Asti Spumante and nibble fresh-cut sandwiches. It starts off quite civilized, but gradually the drunks start to manifest themselves. A gondola passes and tosses firecrackers into our boat. Screams and yells from us as they explode like miniature machine guns.

'We should have brought some grenades,' says Bornheim.

'You have anything like this in England?' says Toni to Bill Hall.

'Oh yes, Blackpool,' he says.

We had to stave off several British soldiers trying to board us from gondolas. 'Hey, you want Jig-a-Jig?' seems to be their contribution to the gaiety.

The trio plays for dancing. Swing, swing, swing, hot jazz, yeah Daddy! So I can dance with Toni, Bornheim relieves me on the accordion. I had never been relieved by an accordion before. Toni and I try to dance. It's a crush, but what the hell. It's nice just holding her. But now the drunks take over. Sergeant Chalky White thinks we need 'livening up': he is balancing a glass of beer on his forehead (Where

61

had I seen this all before?) and doing a Russian dance. Why, oh, why, is it always the most untalented that think they are entertaining? 'Eyeties can't fucking sing,' he says and makes us all sing 'Knees Up Mother Brown'. A barge full of people in Venice and it's 'Knees Up Mother Brown'. Then 'My Old Man Said Follow the Van'. Splash. Riccy Trowler has fallen in the water. We haul him out, he's giggling.

'He needs a towel.'

'No, I don't. I need a brandy.'

Toni and I sit it all out at the back of the barge. By 3.00 a.m., Life as we know it on this planet is over. The barge draws to the landing stage and they all stagger on to the Charabong. Chalky White is still manic with energy. 'Knocked 'em in the Old Kent Road,' he sings. Why God? At the Leone Bianco I say goodnight to Toni. Soon I'm in bed. Safe at last! No, with stifled laughter some low-life bastard is trying to fart through the keyhole. Yes, dear reader, FART THROUGH THE KEYHOLE.

I have a hangover. Someone has put a Lipton's tea chest in my head and the corners are expanding. I get up, someone is revolving the Lipton's tea chest. I look in the mirror, I am suffering a severe attack of face. My red eyes resemble sunset in Arabia; my tongue is a Van Gogh yellow, I have to push it back in by hand.

Bornheim enters. 'Someone's made a cock-up.'

'Then dismantle it. Here comes the Mother Superior,' I say.

The hotel in Trieste is full, so we are to move to Mestre just up the road. Someone is chopping up the Lipton's tea chest.

'What's up? says Bornheim.

'My head.'

'Yes, I *know* it's your head.'

'What time is the Charabong leaving?'

'Chinese Dentist.'

'What?'

'Chinese Dentist,* tooth hurtee!'

* Two-thirty.

62

'Please leave.'

I take two aspirins and a bath, feel a little better. I pack my suitcase with a man chopping up the Lipton's tea chest. It's nearly Chinese Dentist as I lug my case to the lift. Mulgrew is in it. 'First floor,' he says. 'Ladies underwear and drunks.'

I let you settle, and I took out a little leather-bound ... anyone to the nurse. Suppressing the thought, she must ... muss Gibbs. The first ... I im, by, see to a ... ... Dinners and first took home. Books and paper and drink.

MESTRE

MESTRE

It's a short fifteen minutes hop to Mestre and the Albergo Savoia, a large one-time country home. It's rectangular, very roomy with floral curtains and matching furniture. Along the back of the house are french windows which open on to what once was a garden, but is now concreted over. After a cup of tea Toni and I sit outside in the sun.

Toni and Spike – the back garden in Mestre, approximately 120 miles from where the Pope lives

Toni wants to know if I've told my parents about her. 'What they say, Terr-ee?'

'My mother say I must be careful of Italian girls.'

'For why?'

'She thinks all Italian girls are tarts.'

'What is tarts?'

'Prostitute.'

She bursts into a giggle. 'Me, prostitute?'

'No, no, she is just telling me to be careful.'

'You tell her I am a good girl?'

'Yes.'

'What she say?'

'I haven't had any reply yet, maybe in the next letter.'

I daren't tell her my mother thought all foreigners were ridden with disease and you caught it off lavatory seats. 'If you shake hands with them, try and wear gloves.' But then my mother thought that Mussolini was good for the Italians.

Bill Hall is in a playful mood. He drapes a curtain over his shoulder and plays salon music, 'Flowers in May', etc.

Bill Hall clowning in Mestre – a dismal failure

He is interrupted by the manager, Mr Marcini with his goatee beard and goatee moustache. In fact, he had a goatee head and goatee body. Bowing and nodding, he asks if we like to hear some folklore music. A chorus of ayes. He produces a mountain bagpiper. He's like a man from another age: he wears a Tyrolean hat, a red shirt with a brocade waistcoat, navy blue breeches to the knee, then leggings bound with goat hide strips. He plays his bagpipes, which sound like the sweet-sounding Northumbrian and gives us traditional tarantellas, marches, etc. It was an hour of great music and I realized that I was watching the last of the old Italy. The old Italy that was to be swamped with tourists, deafened by pop music and Lambrettas. Eventually, Bill Hall joined in on the violin. It was great stuff. When he'd finished, we had a whip-round for the piper and he departed well pleased. Mulgrew thinks he is a Scottish soldier on the run from the Military Police. 'It's a perfect disguise,' he says. 'I tell you the hills around here are full of squaddies on the trot from the police. You see those Italian women with hairy legs, they're squaddies on the trot.'

We are left to fossilize in Mestre while the powers that be plot our destiny. Meanwhile we live a sybaritic life, just mooching all day.

MOTHER: Where have you been at this time of night?
  SPIKE: I've been out mooching, Mother.

'I think they've forgotten us,' says Hall.
  'Forgotten us, FORGOTTEN?' says Bornheim. 'They've never *heard* of us.'

I break the boredom by trying to snog with Toni whenever the opportunity presents itself, which is only all the time, and that doesn't seem enough. Lieutenant Priest tries to find out what the score is. He phones Army Welfare Service in Naples and this is what it sounded like.

LT PRIEST: Yes, sir . . . yes, sir . . . Mestre, sir . . . but . . .
            yes, sir . . . yes, sir . . . yes, sir . . . very good, sir.

He hangs up. 'Christ,' he says. 'That was Colonel Ridge-way.'

'When do we go to Trieste?' says Hall.

'Everything is in order,' says Priest. 'We leave for Trieste tomorrow.'

The news is well received. I watch fascinated as a dewdrop runs along Hall's nose and extinguishes his dog-end. I suppose that somewhere someone loved him.

TRIESTE

TRIESTE

It's another bright sunny day as we board our, by now, dodgy Charabong. Lieutenant Priest has a quick roll call, and has a heart attack when Bill Hall answers his name.

Trieste is a combustible city on the Adriatic, the Allies have a large force there to deter combustible Marshal Tito who is claiming that Trieste is Yugoslavian. It's a hundred miles to go as we settle down for the trip. Our route runs across the Gulf of Venice – all agricultural land, very green, very lush. The cattle are fatter up here than their scrawny cousins in the Compagna.

Behind me, on the bench seat, Bornheim says, 'Who said "What the fuck was that?"' We don't know. 'The Lord Mayor of Hiroshima.'

'They should never have dropped it.'

'What else can you do with a bomb but drop it? Can't keep it in the fridge.'

'They asked for it.'

'Wot you mean *asked* for it? You think they phoned up Roosevelt and said please drop honourable bomb?'

'OK, what would you have done to end the war?'

'Well, something else.'

'I think we should have dropped Cold Collation on them,' I said. 'That, or watery custard. Can't you see the headlines?

Cold Collation destroys Hiroshima. Thousands flee Custard.

'If they'd have got it, you can be bloody sure they'd drop it on us.'

73

'It still wouldn't be right. What about us and Cassino?'

'What about us and Cassino?'

'We bombed it, didn't we?'

'There were Germans in it.'

'No, there wasn't.'

So the argument raged. From atom bombs to wages is a big jump, but that was what they were on about next. In a *sotto voce* Hall is telling Mulgrew and me that he thinks we should be on more money.

'Aren't you satisfied with ten pounds a week?'

'No, we are the hit of the show.'

'It's ten pounds a week all found,' I said.

'I've never found anything,' says Mulgrew.

'We should be on twenty-five pounds a week,' says Hall.

'If you're going on what it *should* be, why not fifty pounds?' says Mulgrew.

'Why stop at *should be* fifty?' I said. 'How about *should be* a hundred?'

And that was the end of the should bes. Bill Hall produces his violin and launches into an insane version of a very bad musician playing jazz. He crosses his eyes, puts on a fixed maniacal grin with his head shaking like a speeded-up metronome and plays 'Honeysuckle Rose'. Every note is exquisitely sharp or flat. To musicians, it's hysterically funny. He plays and sings Irving Berlin's tune.

> Wot'll I do, when you
> Are far away and I am blue
> Wot'll I do
> Kiss my bottle and glass*

Bornheim starts to conjure up tunes that have just missed being winners – like, 'That's Why the Lady Is a Trampolinist', or 'Honeysuckle Nose' again, 'Saint Louis Browns', 'Tea for One', 'We'll Meet Occasionally', 'On the Good Ship Lollibang' and so on. He reverts to his *Union Jack* newspaper. It has a report on Dachau. 'How can there be

* Bottle and glass (cockney slang) = arse.

74

places like this and there be a God?' I told him that my mother used to answer that question by saying God works in mysterious ways.

'Seven million Jews dead. That's not mysterious, that's bloody cruel,' says Bornheim.

Seven million Jews killed, I couldn't get it in perspective.

'Perhaps it *is* God's will,' says Hall.

'I never knew he left a will,' I said.

The coach comes to a halt in verdant countryside, we are just outside of a town called Portogruaro. 'We are here for an hour for lunch break,' says Lieutenant Priest. We carry our packed lunches and the thermos of tea to the verge that backs on to a vineyard that is delirious with grapes. In the field opposite, a plough with great white oxen: they are identical to the cattle I saw in Roman sculpture.

'They're bullocks,' says Bornheim, our deipnosophist (look it up).

'What exactly is a bullock?' inquires Mulgrew.

'It's when they had their knackers off,' says Bornheim.

'Who would do a job like that?' I said.

'Anyone on the farm. They do it when they are young.'

'Why do you have to be young to chop 'em off?' I said.

'Tsu, the bullocks, Milligan, the bullocks must be young.'

'Cor, what a job!' said Hall. 'I can see his card now: Jim Dungley, knackers neatly nipped. Two pounds a hundred.'

'Yes,' mused Mulgrew, 'but I wonder what he put in the shop window.'

The entire cast are now deep into sandwich munching, and it's amazing how bovine they look. John Angove, our character actor and vegetarian, is trying to swop his sandwiches. 'Anyone swop beef for cheese and tomato?' he shouts out. In those distant days a vegetarian was looked on like a freak – some of the cast are bleating and mooing at him.

'Don't worry, there's a lovely field of grass just waiting for you.'

Poor Angove, he specialized in make-up. He would spend up to two hours putting his old man make-up on. Alas, he didn't look a day older.

Mulgrew has a reddish stain around his lips. He appears to be drinking from a brown paper bag, the swine has got a bottle in there!! What's the idea? He tells us that Harry Lauder always drank from a bottle in a paper bag, it gave him an air of respectability.

'They're all bloody strange in Glasgow,' says Hall. 'As for 'Arry Lauder, he was a mean bugger. If he was a ghost, he'd be too mean to give you a fright.'

'He's still top of the bill, mate,' says Mulgrew.

Hall disagrees. 'I think he's bloody awful.'

'Well,' says Mulgrew, 'I saw him at the Glasgow Empire in *Highland Follies*. He was great.'

'The best thing I've seen him in was Woolworth's,' concluded Hall.

Bornheim asks Mulgrew for a swig of wine. Before giving him it, Mulgrew says, 'You haven't any disease of the mouth, have you?' Bornheim assures him he hasn't. 'Well,' said Mulgrew, 'I *have*.'

Toni has finished her birdlike eating. She waves a handkerchief near her face. '*Che stufa*,' she says. 'Oh Terr-ee, it so warm.'

A lorryload of soldiers drives past. At the sight of our females they whistle and wolfhowl and make certain signs.

'Oh no,' we all groan as Luigi the driver waves his arms in the air.

'*Una puntura*,' he says. He, who has holy pictures pinned to his dashboard and a rosary affixed to the steering wheel, has a puncture.

'He must be praying to the wrong saints,' said Lieutenant Priest.

We all lend a hand. Luigi is pumping the jack while, in time, the joker Bill Hall plays sea shanties. We manhandle the wheel into place, all the while singing along with Hall, 'What Shall We Do With The Drunken Sailor'.

'*Tutto bene*,' says Luigi as he screws the last nut into place.

'All aboard for turbulent Trieste,' calls Lieutenant Priest. We all troop into the Charabong with Mulgrew, Hall and Bornheim making mooing and bleating sounds.

'You've all been out here too long,' says Priest.

The journey is starting to drag. It's hot and dusty. 'Oh roll on demob,' says Bornheim. 'Roll on Civvy Street.' Through the afternoon there's considerable traffic of military vehicles, American and British, the American lorries ignoring the speed limit. They sport an upright broom tied to their vehicles.

'Wots that mean?' says Hall.

I explain it means they have swept all the opposition away. We pass a sign TRIESTE 20 CHILOMETRI. The Italian elections are coming up and the walls are daubed with signs – Partito Communisto or Christian Democrats.

'Won't it be a bugger if the Commies get in,' said Hall.

'What do you mean?' says Mulgrew.

'Well, after us fighting all the way up Italy – it would have been in vain, wouldn't it? It's like Poland: we went to bloody war for them and now the bloody Russians have got it.'

Toni has fallen asleep on my shoulder and my arm now has pins and needles. I try clenching and unclenching the fist, but she wakes up with a start. 'Where are we, Terr-ee?' I told her Italy. We now have the sea on our right – a cobalt blue, looks very inviting. We pass the ill-fated Castello Miramar, where some aristocrat shot himself – his ghost is seen on the battlements. As we enter the precincts of Trieste, lots of signs '*Abbasso con* Tito,' '*Trieste è Italiano*'. There are shrines to partisans murdered by Germans, faded bouquets hang on bullet-ridden walls, the partisans still strut the streets with great bandoliers of bullets and machine pistols. A Jon cartoon of the time sums it all up.

The town is shabby, the people shabby. There was the occasional non-shabby person; there were even the mildly shabby and those with just a touch of the shabbies. We are driven to the top of the town on a slight rise and stop at the Albergo Frederico, or Hotel Fred. It's another 1930s Mussolini modern, but turns out to be very comfortable. From my window the town is laid out like a carpet, with the tree-lined Via d'Annunzio stretching down to the waterfront. It's good news, I have a room on my own! No Mulgrew or Hall

77

'I say, old man, haven't you heard that the jolly old guerra is finito'

coming in late and pissed. I strip for a bath. I look at myself in the full-length mirror and scream. My God, I'm thin. I look like a Belsen victim. God knows I had tried hard to develop myself. I'd done weightlifting until I hurt my back, so the least I could do was give it a bath. I'm interrupted by a tap on the door. It's Mulgrew, he's out of fags again and gasping. 'You don't know what real suffering is,' he says. I gave him one of my Passing Cloud cigarettes that came in a parcel from my mother. 'My God, you're thin,' he said. 'Does it hurt?'

'If you mean I'm painfully thin.'

'Can't you take something for it?'

'Like what?'

'Like food.'

78

'I've tried everything – Sanatogen, cod liver oil and malt, even Mellins Baby Food.'

Mulgrew giggles. 'Let's see your biceps.'

I flex my arms. He starts to laugh at two protruberances that look like golf balls. 'Never mind,' I said. 'A good tailor can do wonders for a body like mine. There's padded shoulders for a start.'

'With your body, you need a padded suit.'

I repair to the bathroom, while Mulgrew lies on my bed blowing smoke rings. I scrub my body all the while singing like Bing Crosby. At the same time I am laundering my vest and underpants. I hear Mulgrew coughing his lungs up.

'Don't you bring that up in here,' I shout.

'I'm awa',' says Mulgrew. 'I'm taking four more cigarettes. I'll pay you back on NAAFI day.'

I'm really into Bing Crosby now. 'The bells of Saint Mary booboolum da did dee da,' I sing, refreshed. I towel down; next, I lacquer my hair with Brylcreem till it glistens like a fly trap. Now, a little read before tea. 'Boo boo da de dum de dee.' Yes, I was definitely as good as Bing Crosby. I lay abed reading a poem by Francis Thompson, 'To a Snowflake'.

> What heart could have thought you
> Past our devisal
> Oh filagree petal
> Fashioned so purely
> Fragilely, surely
> From what Paradisal
> Imagineless metal
> Too costly for cost

'Boo boo boo da de dum, the bells of Saint Mary.' Yes, there was no getting away from it, I was the equal of Crosby. I sing as I dress. Singing *and* dressing at one and the same time, ladies and gentlemen. I pick up the intercom.

'*Pronto*,' says the telephonist.

'*Possibile parlare con camera venti-due?*'

Soon Toni is on the phone, 'What you do, Terr-ee?'

'I'm reading poetry.'

'I come down. We both have tea, yes?'

'Yes, and Toni?'

'What?'

'Boo boo da de dum, the bells of Saint Mary.'

'Oh, very nice, Terr-ee. I come down now.'

When she arrives at my door, I have struck a Robert Taylor pose. 'Come in,' I say. It's not Toni, it's the chambermaid. Do I want my bed turned down? Blast, my Robert Taylor pose wasted. Toni arrives and we walk down to the dining-room, hand in hand. As we enter there is a great 'Awwwwwwwwwwwwww' from the cast. It was nice to get these unsolicited testimonials. An enterprising photographer has left his card on every table, a Signor Filippo Nenni. He can take photos during or after the show. Great! He can do my Robert Taylor profile and a couple of Humphrey Bogart with the cigarette in the mouth pose.

Today is Sunday. Back in England my mother will be on her knees before the altar of the Madonna praying that her son won't catch anything in Italy and save his money, that her son Desmond will get a commission and that my father will stop swearing.

After tea, Toni, Mulgrew, Marisa (one of the ballet girls) and I take a walk down the Via d'Annunzio. It's crowded with people in their best clothes on a 'monkey walk'. Down the centre of the Via is a wide pavement with chairs and tables. We choose a table and are immediately pounced on by an energetic young waiter. Holding his tray above his head, he threads his way through the crowds. As we sip chilled Orvieto, Toni is studying a map. Is she lost? The sun is setting on the heights above the town, oblique rays are shafting through the plane trees causing dappled dancing shadows. There is much fist waving and shouting as cars try to weave their way through the crowds. It's amazing how the Italians shriek at each other – one wouldn't be surprised if one exploded. Toni points to the heights. 'See Roman theatre.' There, silhouetted against the sun were the imposing ruins.

80

'Didn't they pick beautiful positions?' says Mulgrew, emptying his glass. Do we want another round? If so, can he borrow a hundred lire from muggins Milligan.

Lots of pretty girls are passing by, chaperoned by what look like Mafia bouncers. Mulgrew concludes that if you had an out of marriage shag in this town, you'd never see the next day. We indulge a few more wines and then wend our way home through the milling throng. At the hotel we discover Bornheim and some of the cast playing pontoon in the lounge.

'Winning?' I asked.

'At the moment, yes,' says Bornheim. 'Pontoons only,' he says and scoops the kitty.

By the earnest expression on their faces, I knew the stakes were high. Then I discover it's two lire a go. Mulgrew wants to play, can he borrow another hundred? I say no, but he goes on his knees. 'It's only a wee hundred,' he says. 'I mean all your money is doing at the moment is resting in your wallet.' OK. He is shit lucky, he wins five hundred, pays me back my two hundred.

Jimmy Molloy comes in. 'Ah Spike,' he shuffles through some mail and gives me a letter from home. It's Mother, she's still on about disease and says when I go to the toilet I must put paper on the seat; also, that Dad is finding the journey from Reigate to Fleet Street too wearing, so they are moving to Deptford. Dad and her are really proud that I am now a NAAFI star!

'How come you never get any mail, Bill?' I said to Hall.

'It's simple – the buggers don't bother to write.'

'Are they illiterate?'

'No, it's just that they have nuffink to say.'

'Do they know you're alive?'

'Think so, I mean they 'avent 'ad any notification from the War Office that I'm dead.'

I have dinner with Toni. What did my mother say about her in the letter? I told her not a word about her, but a warning about lavatory seats. 'You think that if I write that would be good?'

'Yes, I think so. Most important is you say you are a Roman Catholic.'

Dinner over, Toni says she is tired, she is going to bed. I accompany her in the lift and kiss her goodnight at the door. 'Can I come in?' She says, 'No.' Blast. I return to my room 'Boo boo dum de dum de dum.' Yes, definitely as good as Bing Crosby.

There is a general cast call at eleven o'clock, so into the Charabong. En route Italians keep banging angrily on the side. By looking out the window I see that some silly bugger has chalked VIVA TITO on the side of the bus. It was Mulgrew and his Scottish Highland sense of humour. I told him, 'We could all have been bloody killed.' He says that was the general idea.

As we de-bus at the stage door of the Theatre Fred, there's a loud explosion – a bomb has gone off. Civil and Military Police start whizzing by in jeeps, armed to the teeth – some were only armed to the throat, some to the knee. The theatre was built for opera, it has an excess of Italian kitsch. We are assembled on the stage and Jimmy Molloy says that parts of the show are slack so we are to run through those bits.

John Angove is not feeling well. He is taken to the Medical Officer who diagnoses that he has measles. Measles at twenty-five! He is put into a quarantine ward and is out of the show. I wonder if they are always caught in the plural?

PATIENT: What is it, doc?
   DOC: You've caught *a* measle.
PATIENT: Just one?

I mean, bronchitis is in the singular.

PATIENT: What is it, doc?
   DOC: You've caught bronchitises.

We try out a new gag for the show. I announce that I will fire the slowest bullet in the world. Mulgrew stands one side holding a water biscuit; I, from the other side, aim and fire.

There's a count of five and then Mulgrew crumples the biscuit manually with a cry of Hoi Up La.

In our dressing-room, there are signs of occupation scrawled on the wall: 'Harry Secombe was here', 'Norman Vaughan was here', 'Ken Platt was almost here'. We dutifully add our names. The manager, a voluble fat Italian, tells us many famous people have been here, including Elenora Duse. He tells us the story of how after she had had a leg amputated, she returned to the stage and people wondered how she would manage with an artificial wooden leg. On the first night, the theatre was crowded with the cognoscenti. It is French theatre custom to bang a mummer's pole thrice behind the curtain. When the audience heard 'boom boom boom', one said, 'My God, here she comes now!'

The first night was a packed theatre and a big success. The Town Major has invited the cast to the Officers' Club. Great. It turned out to be a large glass-fronted building overlooking the sea. Italian waiters move among us distributing drinks. An Italian quintet on a small rostrum is playing background music. I thought I had escaped it, but sure enough they played 'Lae That Piss Tub Dawn Bab'. All the girl dancers are pounced on by young officers; a Lieutenant Johnny Lee fancied Toni. He engaged her in conversation and even though I was standing next to her, he ignored me. I was furious, my skinny body trembled with jealousy: fool of a man, how could he compete with me? Boo boo da de de dum dum dee dee, and there was more where that came from! The swine has taken her on to the floor for a dance. Not for a moment did he realize that I was once the winner of the Valeta Contest at the Lady Florence Institute, Deptford! And the best crooner with the New Era Rhythm Boys at the New Cross Palais de Danse??? If he wanted credentials I had them! She'd come begging for me to take her back, you'd see.

The evening wears out and we are all on the Charabong back to the Hotel Fred.

'He want to see me again,' said Toni.

'Oh yes,' I said, as near to Humphrey Bogart as possible.

'Yes, I told him, no.'

'Of course, you told him no.'

There was no other answer. I mean I was a ten pounds a week man, with a great back-up of underwear.

It's late, we are flagged down by the Military Police. Who are we, where are our papers? Lieutenant Priest explains that we are the untouchables and are left to go our way. It's one o'clock as I stand snogging outside her bedroom door. 'Can I come in?' No I can't. Blast! Mulgrew or someone has struck again. As I pull back my bedcovers there in the middle is a replica Richard the Third with the message 'The phantom strikes again'. And so to bed.

The week followed with us going for walks, shopping for trinkets down on the waterfront and visits from Lieutenant J. Lee. He brings Toni flowers. The occasional bomb goes off somewhere in the city and on Thursday an Italian blows himself up and will soon be a Martyr. Soon people are putting flowers on the spot; scrawled on the wall is his epitaph, 'Luigi Sapone *mort per la patria*'. 'It beats me,' says Bornheim, 'how explosions and blowing up places advances a political cause.' He was right of course. There are other ways to draw attention to your cause. Standing naked outside tube stations would hit the media or anonymously posting people a bread pudding, with the warning 'Give up or you'll get another'. That, or nocturnally digging a fish pond stocked with goldfish in people's gardens with the same warning. Better still, attack political figures by sealing up their front door keyholes and letter box. Bornheim agrees. He suggests parking combine harvesters outside people's front doors.

Lieutenant Priest is warning us that we are to attend a VD lecture at the Medical Rooms on the sea front in Trieste. 'You've all got to attend. It's an order to all parties about to enter Austria.' Came the occasion, we were shown into a room of a requisitioned warehouse where chairs were arranged before a projector screen. A medical orderly is putting pamphlets on all the chairs. They warn of the horrors of VD and its related ailments. 'Eyes Front,' says Lieutenant

Priest as an MO enters. 'At Ease,' he said and made a sign to sit. The medical orderly activated the projector and as the MO spoke we were subjected to a series of men's genitals all in various stages of VD, from a small spot to a great red hanging blob. These were accompanied by cries of 'Hard luck, mate' and 'Stick to wanking'. It took about twenty minutes and we were then driven back to the hotel.

THE NIGHT OF THE PHOTOGRAPHS

After the show, one evening, Signor Nenni and his wife set up a huge box camera which swayed perilously as he placed it on a tripod. It looks like a monster from one of H.G. Wells's books, a Warlock. In a cracked voice he is instructing his wife in the placing of the floodlights. They are both over sixty and move with caution. *'Poco, poco,'* he says to her. She had curvature of the spine and in the gloom looks like Quasimodo. These are the results of his efforts.

Toni and Spike, posed photograph in Trieste

Johnny Bornheim, accordionist and furrier, on stage in Trieste

A DAY FOR SWIMMING

See, that means we've got to go near water. We are taken to
a beach adjacent the ill-fated Castello Miramar. Toni en-
lightens me about the legend. It was a duke and a broken
love affair that drove him to suicide. Ah broken romance.
There should be repair depots, like the A A.

A BROKEN MARRIAGE DEPOT.
THE PHONE RINGS.

OPERATOR: Broken Marriages Depot.
    VOICE: I wish to report a broken romance at
           the turn off 6 on the M1.
OPERATOR: Have you got all the pieces?
    VOICE: Yes, they're all over the verge.
OPERATOR: We'll send a solicitor right away.

We all lay out our towels and after a liberal application of
olive oil, we lay back and soak up the sun. Toni is next to
me, I hold her hand. I give it a squeeze but it's so lubricated
it pops out. I do it again, it's a turn-on.

Toni asks if I believe in ghosts.

'No.'

'You think we come back after we die?'

'Well none of my family have. I did have an Aunt Jane
Milligan who went to a spiritualist to contact her late husband. When he was contacted, the spiritualist asked did
Aunti Milligan want to ask him a question. She said, "Yes,
ask him wot 'e did with the fish knives.'''

Toni persists. 'Perhaps we come back different.'

'Like what?'

'Like tree or horse.'

'No, I don't want to come back as a horse.'

It's frightening. Suppose I come back as a tomcat and
have to have that terrible operation? Oh, no. Toni giggles,
'Suppose you come back as a woman, what you do?' I told
her I'd go for a walk and see what happened.

I'm starting to burn so I plunge into the waters of the
beckoning Adriatic. Mulgrew is standing waist-deep. 'Are
there any sharks in the Adriatic?' I assure him that there are
sharks in all warm waters. 'Oh Christ,' he says.

Greta Weingarten, our German girl, starts to swim out. I
follow her. We go about a fifth of a mile; she turns and says,
'You are gute swimmer.' How a German girl got into our
show was a mystery.

A FORCED LABOUR CAMP IN RUSSIA.
HITLER IS SHOVELLING SALT AND SHIT.

HITLER: It is not ein mystery! She is there as my
        personal representative of the Third Reich!!!

She always radiated a sense of aloofness. I suppose after the
macho attitude of wartime Germany she found this collection

87

of musicians and poofs a letdown, except that – ha! ha! – she was going around with our chief poof. All very strange: who did what to whom and how? We race each other back to the shore, I just beat her.

Bill Hall greets me. 'You put the shits up Johnny, telling him there were sharks here.'

Toni asks me, 'What is the shits up?' I roll over laughing, hearing this innocent voice. 'What is the shits up?' she says again. I explain, you know in French, *merde*? She does, 'So, it is rude?'

'Yes.'

The afternoon is one of running up and down the beach and splashing in the shallows, then lazing in the sun. At four o'clock we open our packed lunches, sit in the sun and masitcate our sandwiches, as eaten by the Earl of Sandwich. But who invented eating? Was it Tom Eating? What a breakthrough. Until then people kept dying of starvation. Then, Tom Eating discovered food! At first, the superstitious said, 'Nay, eating food is the devil's work.' Many eaters died for their beliefs, but in the end food won through and Tom Eating was beatified and became St Eating, Patron Saint of Food. So ended a lovely day out.

That night just after the show finished, BOOM! a bomb explodes near the theatre. We all rush out, some of us still in costume. A crowd has gathered, there are angry shouts, they suspect Yugoslavian extremists. Toni says to me, 'Did that give you shits up?' She knows it's rude and laughs. It's not as exciting as it should be. There's no blood, no dismembered bodies. An Italian partisan, smothered in bullets and a machine pistol, stands on one of the bomb-shattered tables and with veins standing out like whipcords makes an impassioned speech. He says no Yugoslav is going to take Trieste as long as he has breath in his body. The table collapses and he is pitched, still shouting, into the crowd. The American police arrive, the Italian police arrive and, true to form, last are the British police. They start to ask questions and are highly suspicious of all of us in costume. Lieutenant Priest explains that we are travelling mummers

88

and all is well. For all his patriotic utterances the partisan is taken into custody and is driven away in a jeep still declaiming that Trieste is Italian.

It had been quite a day, but there was still the night and, with it, Bill Hall's nocturnal desires. Somewhere in Trieste some old boiler of a woman will get his attention. 'Listen everybody,' says Lieutenant Priest. 'Tomorrow is a day off, the Charabong is going to Grado at ten for swimming.' We give him a cheer. This night Toni says I can come into her bedroom. Ha, ha. We start snogging on the bed. So far our affair has been quite innocent, but this time it starts to get serious. She pushes my fumbling hands away. 'You give me the shits,' she says and it doubles me up with laughter. But we were getting serious – all those little biological bugs inside us egging us on! Helppp! I'm on course to severely seduce Miss Fontana!

GRADO

Next day, we are all in the Charabong looking forward to the day at Grado. We are singing, 'Why Are We Waiting?'. In this instance, it's Bill Hall. He finally appears blinking in the unaccustomed sunlight. Luigi lets the clutch in and we are on our way.

Grado is a spit of land accessible by a causeway. It's apparently a fisherman's paradise. It's not much of a paradise for us. The beach is brown and so is the water. It's all due to a muddy bottom, of which I'd seen a few. However, it's a clear blue sky and hot. Toni and I hire a boatman who rows us to where the sea turns blue. We dive over the side. It's like swimming in champagne, you can see the bottom. We sun ourselves and take a few snaps.

We sit in silence, holding hands, watching the wake of the boat. The boatman smiles, he knows we're in love. '*Buona*, eh?' he smiles. Plimping (yes, *plimping*) on the sea are fishing

89

Toni taken by me in Grado   *Me taken by Toni, Grado*

boats, small two-men affairs – and, let's face it, in those days two-men affairs were not that frequent. It was all very stimulating – the salt water drying on your body, the tranquillity and being in love.

Our time is up; the boatman heads for the shore.

Mulgrew greets us. 'Ahoy, there. Welcome to Grado.'

'You're welcome to it, too,' I said.

Mulgrew has buried Bill Hall in the sand and shaped it like a woman's body, with huge boobs. Alas, I lost that photo. 'How much was the boat ride?' he says. I tell him a hundred lire for half an hour. 'A *hundred* lire,' he said, his Scots face wincing with pain. 'Why you can get three bottles of wine for that!' I agreed but said they wouldn't float as well as a boat.

There's a sort of beach café with a straw-matted roof. Toni and I sit on high stools sipping fresh orange juice. Mulgrew has lemon juice.

'It's got more vitamins in.'

'What is vitamin?' says Toni.

'You know, vitamins A, B, C, D.'

'That's a funny way to spell vitamins,' I said.

Marisa is coming out of the water saying, '*Aiuto! Aiuto!*' She's been stung on her bum by a jellyfish, who seemed to know what he was doing. From then on no one would venture into the water. Toni and I walked along the beach about a mile, stopping at any rock pools and looking for fish trapped by the tide. Sometimes, we'd splash our feet in the shallows. It was like being a child again.

The sun is getting the sea on fire as it lowers itself into the Adriatic. Dancing waves catch the deflected light and semaphore in silver gold flashes. It's been a wonderful day. The beach café wants to know do we want dinner. If so, they can make us sardines and rice. We ask the all-in price and Lieutenant Priest thinks it reasonable – so, OK. We sit eating it as a new moon like a lemon slice appears in the eastern night sky and, blow me, there's the sound of Bill Hall's violin. Soon the Italians are singing.

Vicino Mare
Vicino Amore

In the half-light, I lean over and kiss Toni on the shoulder. As I do so, she places a kiss in my hair – that hair that had lived with washing with Sunlight soap, Lifebuoy, Pears, Carbolic (never had a shampoo) and Brylcreem and Anzora hair goo. Yes, she kissed all that. We quaff white wine. Some of the boys collect driftwood and make a fire. We sit in a circle watching our dreams burn into embers. The tide rises and washes away our footprints in the sand. Sand from a shore that neither of us would see again. Already that sand was running out.

It was eleven when we drove back to the hotel, all pleasantly tired. Tomorrow? Who cared about tomorrow?

A FORCED LABOUR CAMP IN SIBERIA.
HITLER IS SHOVELLING SHIT AND SALT.

HITLER: I care about tomorrow. You see, Von
          Rundstedt and the Tenth Panzer Army will
          break through and rescue me.

I kiss Toni goodnight, *buona notte a domani*.

So passed the week in Trieste. This morning, we all embark for Austria. Austria, land of Strauss and the naughty waltz – men and women dancing face to face! Land of Franz Josef, the Hussars, the woods and the liver sausage! I massage my clothes into my suitcase, I sit on it and finally lock it. It looks pregnant. I've got half an hour to get breakfast. I dash down to the dining-room. Toni and the girls are at a table laughing and giggling. 'Oh, Terr-ee, you late. You must hurry.' I wolf down marmalade and toast and a cup of lemon tea.

KRUMPENDORF

KRUMPENDORF

'Oh Terr-ee,' says Toni. 'You choke yourself.' What a headline:

Man Strangled by Marmalade

Lieutenant Priest is rounding up the latecomers. 'Come on, we haven't got all day,' he fusses.

Aboard the Charabong, everyone is excited at the thought of Austria, especially Greta Weingarten. 'Now I vill be able to speak mein own language,' she says with an air of superiority.

Toni is in her drab khaki clothes, her hair in a bandana. She looks shapeless, but ah ha! I know what lies underneath, heh, heh, heh! She asks, 'In Vienna, we see Russian soldiers?'

'Yes, my dear.' But what's this Lieutenant Priest is saying? 'Before Vienna, we have to play Krumpendorf.' Krumpendorf? Isn't that a disease of the groin? He goes on, 'Then we play Graz and *then* Vienna.'

'You been in Austria before, Terr-ee?' No, I had travelled extensively in Catford, Lewisham and Brockley S E 26, but somehow never Austria. The trams didn't go that far.

Oh, no! The coach engine is faltering. We pull over and Luigi raises the bonnet. He is joined by Ricky Trowler who is a whizz kid at engines. He tells Lieutenant Priest, 'It's the distributor.'

'Wait until I see the bastard,' says Priest.

Trowler does some minor adjustments and we are on our way again. It's another sunny day with a few mare's-tails in the sky, where do they get such a name for clouds? Like mackerel – what was that poem?

> Mackerel sky, mackerel sky,
> Not long wet, not long dry.

To pass the time, we play noughts and crosses. I show Toni how to play noughts and crosses for idiots.

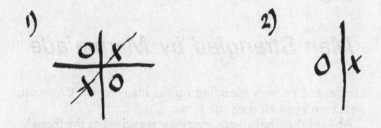

We are heading north and gradually climbing. On looking, we can see Trieste spread out below us with the Yugoslav coast disappearing in the morning haze. On one side, we have a sheer drop; on the other, vine terraces looking like giant steps. It reminds me of Doré's drawings from Milton's *Paradise Lost*. But then anything made me think of *Paradise Lost*. I remember in Lewisham where I was paying some money into my Post Office savings account, I was served by an old dear of sixty with huge ill-fitting false teeth and I thought, '*Paradise Lost!*' Another time I saw a mongrel sniffing a lamppost and I thought of *Paradise Lost*. What a good headline:

PARADISE LOST! POLICE AND ARMY IN SEARCH

We cross the border at Thorl. There is no customs barrier, we just motor straight through. 'Ladies and Gentlemen,' says Priest in mock German tones. 'Ve are now in Austria,' and gives the Nazi salute. We all give a cheer and Bill Hall, as though on cue, launches into 'The Blue Danube' and a selection of cloying German tunes ending with 'Grinzing' – that's another name I am baffled by. What or why is Grinzing?

MOTHER: Where have you been at this time of night?
   ME: I've been out Grinzing, Mother dear.

Mulgrew clips on a prop Hitler moustache, gives the *Sieg Heil* salute and says, 'Ve are now in zer Fatherland. From now, all Jews will haff their circumstances confiscated!'

Outside Thorl, the Charabong stops for lunch. We are surrounded by fir-tree covered hills. I climb up a hillock and get a wonderful view. I call to Toni to come up, then do a few yodels à la the von Trapp family. Toni starts to clamber up and I take yet another photo.

Toni climbing a hill to join me and the view, Austria

Mulgrew has heard me yodel, so he yodels back. Others join in and soon the hills are alive with the sound of yodels.

We are looking down on a valley with a torrent running through it. Anything done in this stream today will arrive in Italy tomorrow. It was very pretty, Toni and I stood enjoying the view. Helpppp! They are breaking out the lunch rations. If we don't get down, the bloody lot will be gone. They see us running down the hill; they are eating as fast as they can. But we manage to intercept some cheese and pickle sandwiches.

Lunch over, Lieutenant Priest herds us on to the Charabong – all bleating and mooing. The Charabong lurches off with a promise of further distributor trouble, but it doesn't materialize and the engine settles down as Luigi crosses himself with relief. Now we are seeing Austrians: some die-hards are wearing lederhosen (leather shorts). Greta Weingarten points them out, saying, 'Is *gut, ja*?'

'I bet they're all bloody ex-Nazis,' says Bill Hall rolling a cigarette.

'Zey are not all bloody Nazis,' assures Greta. 'Many people not like ser Nazis.'

A FORCED LABOUR CAMP IN SIBERIA.
HITLER IS SHOVELLING SHIT AND SALT.

HITLER: All lies! Everybody love *zer* Nazis.

We are trying to work out who the most disliked person in the cast is. 'It must be Chalky White,' said Hall.

'That's so,' said Mulgrew. 'Why do people take an instant dislike to him?'

'It saves time,' I said.

We are passing through Villach and see lots of British troops on route marches. We give them all a cheer. 'Bloody hell,' says Hall. 'Still marching. Don't they know the bloody war's over?' I tell him wars are never over. 'Wot you sayin',' said Hall.

Wörthersee

'They only have intervals and this is one of them,' I said. 'So take your partners for World War Three!'

'I tell you why we have wars,' said Bornheim, looking up from his *Union Jack* newspaper. 'Because men like it.'

'Ah, look, Terr-ee,' says Toni and points to the beautiful Lake Wörther with its bobbing boats and background of snowcapped mountains.

Priest is standing at the front peering out the window. 'Ah, this is it, folks,' he says as the Charabong pulls right off the road in front of a large guest house surrounded by chalets.

We troop into reception where a fierce German lady by the name of Frau Hitz welcomes us with penetrating blue eyes and a big nose. 'Velcom to zer Krumpendorf Guest House,' she says. 'Your rooms are all ready for you.'

'I wonder where the gas chamber is,' said Mulgrew, his shoulders heaving with silent mirth. 'She's a dead ringer for Bill Hall,' he said.

We all check in. Hall, Mulgrew and myself have a chalet to ourselves. We dash to it to get the best bed. Fleet-of-foot Milligan gets in first and bags the bed near the window which overlooks a rose garden. It's very simple furnishing, but very comfortable. No show tonight, so we relax. Toni has a room in the main guest house (BLAST, there go my knee tremblers again). From now on it's goodbye Italian cuisine and hello German. No more pasta, but meat and veg, dumplings and stodgy puddings. For dinner that night we had Wiener Schnitzel mit zer Sauerkraut, and it was delicious.

A SIBERIAN SALT MINE.
HITLER IS SHOVELLING SHIT AND SALT.

HITLER: You see, you Russian fools! Zey are already starting to like back us Germans! Soon zey will come begging to me for zer recipe!!

Our Italian cast don't like the food. Toni says it's all too heavy. She says no wonder they lost the war with food like this; you could lose everything, especially your appetite. She comforts herself with lots of German cheeses. We find the Austrian wines delicious and light.

After dinner we take our wine and sit overlooking what had been a lovely garden, now a little overgrown. It's just twilight time; small things are bumbling and buzzing in the late evening light. Wallop! Next to me Bornheim has flattened a midge on his arm. What did he do that for? It wasn't doing any harm. 'Another second an' it would have bit,' he says and Wallop! he exterminates another.

'Why not have pity and shoo them off?'

'Oh, no. It's not as much fun as flattening them,' he said with a grin. 'They've got a grand piano in the lounge,' he said. Wallop! Another midge dies. 'It's a Bechstein. Like to hear it?'

We follow him into the lounge, which is deserted. We sit on the couch and listen to him playing 'I Got It Bad and That Ain't Good', 'Summertime', 'Sophisticated Lady', 'Have You Met Miss Jones' and more – all songs that will remain fresh over the years.

'Do you know Ketelby's "Bells Across the Meadow"?'

'Yes,' he says. 'Good,' I say. 'Bring it in, it's getting rusty.'

Toni is tired and wants an early night. No, I can't come in – blast! We say goodnight and I retire to the chalet where I find Mulgrew in bed reading, with a bottle of wine to hand. I undress and ease myself between the sheets. Ah, bed! Soon I'm in the Land of Nod. I am awakened at about 1 a.m. by Hall tiptoeing into the room. I sit up.

'Oh,' he says. 'You still awake?'

'No, I always sleep sitting up.'

'I bin to the Garrison Cinema. Saw a Charles Boyer film where he drives his wife mad.'

'Oh, *Gaslight*.'

'Yes, *Gaslight and Coke* – something like that.'

'Well, goodnight.'

'Goodnight.'

From Mulgrew comes a low 'Thank Fuck'.

I had one of the strangest dreams. It's Oxford Circus in the rush hour and a man with Knicker Warden on his shoulders is holding a long stick with a mirror on it. He is looking up women's skirts and only lets those cross who are wearing knickers. I suppose Freud would have said something like it meant I wasn't getting enough carrots.

Next day is another fine one – a cloudless sky. After breakfast, Toni and I take a walk to the Wörthersee. I climb a tree to take a photo of the landscape and another of Toni. I'm not saying that you have to climb trees to take photographs, but it does make you look taller. The lake is heavily overgrown with bulrushes and it is difficult to get access to the water. 'Ahoy there young lovers!' It's Mulgrew and Angove and this should be fun – they have a fishing rod. We all stroll along looking for a break in the rushes. We finally find an

Mulgrew and Angove fishing from the leaky boat

old boat. 'Ah,' says Mulgrew. 'The gods are smiling on us.' I point out that the boat looks as though it's about to expire. They heed the warning not. With caution, Angove and Mulgrew get into the boat. With a plank of wood, Mulgrew propels the boat to the edge of the rushes and throws out their line. It remained thrown out for an hour while Toni and I sat on the verge.

'Caught anything yet?' I called.

'Sweet FA,' says Mulgrew.

'Here, let me try,' says Angove.

Very wobbly, they stand and change places. There is a shout and Mulgrew goes through the bottom of the boat. It sinks immediately and Angove joins Mulgrew up to their waists in water. They issue forth from the water with a mixture of swearing and laughter, with mud up to their knees and great cakes of mud on their feet.

'The gods have stopped smiling,' I said.

'Christ,' says Mulgrew. 'We better go back and get this lot off,' he added.

Toni clowning, Krumpendorf

Alone again, Toni wants to sunbathe. She strips down to her bathing costume; I get her to do a camp pose against the skyline.

'You no sunbathe?' said Toni.

'No, I'm still sunburnt from Grado.'

Apart from which, I was not wearing a bathing costume and the thought of stripping down to my underpants filled me with terror.

Toni wants to know more about England. I suppose it's on the assumption that one day I might marry her. 'Tell me, Terr-ee, you have what you call a Frog?'

'Frog? Ah, you mean fog. Yes.'

'All the time?'

'No, it just seems that way. No, we only get it in the winter.'

'Is it always cold?'

'No, in summer it's very nice.'

The morning passes. We are totally alone, almost like the last people left on earth. We snog in the warm grass. Time is meaningless. In a passionate embrace, Toni suddenly says 'It's time for lunch.' I swore I'd never get that hungry! Toni dresses and we walk back to the guest house.

Chalky White is in the lounge holding a housey-housey game. I get a card and play a few games. Italians and Austrians alike are baffled by the language. 'Number Nine, Doctors Orders, Legs Eleven, All the Sixes, Clickity Click, Kelly's Eye.' I don't win a thing so we go to lunch. A beaming, fat, bald Austrian in an ill-fitting suit greets us and shows us to our table. He introduces himself, 'Hi ham Ludwig zer Herr Ober.' We order a couple of salads. 'Tank you,' he says. He smells distantly of cod liver oil. He keeps checking the diners. '*Alles gut?*' he says and nods approval. After lunch, it's weekly NAAFI ration.

In Jimmy Molloy's room there's a lot of bartering – swopping sweets and chocolate for cigarettes. There are also toothpaste and bootlaces for sale and I don't see the connection. Why not toothpaste and potted shrimps? Or toothpaste and tinned carrots? Old debts are repaid but only after reminders.

'Come on Mulgrew, you owe me six cigarettes.'

'Six? I only borrowed five.'

'It's with interest.'

'I have no interest,' he said and gave me five cigarettes.

We carry all our goodies back to the chalet, where lovely Bill Hall is washing socks in the sink. 'NAAFI's up,' I tell him. He drops the socks and hurries from the chalet. Mulgrew sits by the window and writes letters.

'How do you spell sophisticated?' he says.

'I don't. I only say it.'

*Mulgrew cleaning his teeth at an open window,
Krumpendorf*

I spend the afternoon reading Edgar Allan Poe's mystery
stories, then have a doze. I awake at tea-time and meet Toni
in the dining-room.

'Hello, Terr-ee. You like my hair?' She revolves to show a
new hair style.

'Very nice,' I say. It's a good thing to say to women.

Cream buns and tea. Lovely. 'Theese make you fat, Terr-
ee.' If only they would. Oh, for a few ounces of fat on my
emaciated Belsen body.

That night, the show passed uneventfully except for a string on my guitar breaking in the middle of the act. Manfully, I played on the remaining five strings. After dinner, we sit in the lounge drinking coffee and listening to Bornheim play the piano. I am looking at Toni. Toni is looking at me. It's like electricity.

'What you think? she says.

'I think I love you,' I say. Love? I'm besotted with her!

Bornheim stops playing. 'Get this,' he announces – to the tune of 'The Girl That I Marry', sings:

The child that I carry will have to be
Dumped on the steps of a nunnery
The man I call my own
Has turned into a poofta and smells of cologne
He polishes his fingernails, tints his hair
He's known in the 'dilly as Old Doris Hare
'Stead of flittin', he sits knittin'
For a sailor who comes from Thames Ditton
I once had a lover, now he loves my brother, not me.

So much for Irving Berlin. Time for turning in. I accompany Toni to her chalet. A goodnight kiss in the shadows and I'm off to my own bed, bent double with erections. Down boy, down. Not tonight.

SUN, SNOW, SLEIGH

Next morning, I'm up first and it's down boy again. Mulgrew and Hall are both still asleep, both sharing what sounds like the same snore. Hall's laundered socks, now stiff as boards, swing gently in the breeze from the window. Ah, the poetry of an Austrian morning. I take a vigorous shower, singing boo boo boo da de dum dee dee. Ah, yes, as good as Crosby.

'Spike,' it's Mulgrew, 'we're trying to sleep.'

'What?' I said. 'How dare you try and sleep when I'm singing.'

I'm looking forward to breakfast and backward to sleep (Eh?). I leave the slumbering duo and make for Toni's chalet. I tap on the door. 'It's me, Toni. I'm coming in.' There are shrieks of No! No! from Toni. I push the door ajar and see Toni and her companions clutching towels to hide their nudity.

'I come very quickly,' she giggles.

Breakfast is very British: eggs and bacon. Toni joins me halfway through. 'You are very naughty boy,' she says, drawing to the table. She must have a coffee, she can't start the day without one. Toni sips it with a look of ecstasy on her face. What shall we do today? Today she can't see me, she has lots of washing and letters to write. My problems are solved! The Charabong will take those interested to the Consul Bhan, a skiing resort. Great!

We pile on the Charabong which threads its way up a mountain, or was it a hill? That's a point: at what height does a hill become a mountain? The sun is shining ferociously, even after we reach the snow line. We are met by a sergeant ski instructor. He fixes us up with skis and leaves us to it. So, it's fun on the slopes. There must be a world record for falling over, and I hold it. I strip to the waist – even in the snow, I'm perspiring. I rub my body with snow and feel exhilarated. The sergeant makes some tea for us in the out-of-season café. I notice lying among the trees spent cartridge shells. The sergeant tells us that this used to be a training depot for German ski troops. 'The lot that done Narvik trained here,' he says.

The afternoon passes with us falling down. Finally the sergeant lends us a two-man sleigh. 'This is more like it,' says Bornheim. The afternoon passes with us sliding down the mountain. No ski lift here, you have to schlep back up on foot. Plenty of tumbles on the overloaded sleigh.

'It was never meant for so many,' shouts Angove as five of us hurtle down into a tree. Great flurries of snow and tumbling bodies – sun, snow, sleigh, wonderful!

At six o'clock, Lieutenant Priest reminds us there's a show to do. I keep forgetting the show is the reason we are having all this fun. We arrive back sunburnt and shagged out, not looking forward to the show. A quick tea and a slice of cake, I collect my guitar and hurry to the waiting Charabong.

'Terr-ee! You all sunburn,' says Toni. I told her that all day I'd missed her and longed for her on skis next to me with the wind blowing through our hair as we raced down the mountain.

I stand up in the bus and start to declaim for all to hear, 'What a fool I was to leave you, darling, to do the laundry, while I, a young Celtic god, was coursing down the white mountain in a rapture of speed, wind and other things.' I kneel down and start kissing her arm. 'Oh, forgive me, my beloved, my little laundress. It will never happen again.' Toni is laughing with embarrassment and the cast give me a round of applause. Greta Weingarten is saying have we noticed how clean Austria is after Italy. I agree with her. 'I'll say this for Hitler: I bet before he shot himself he put on clean underpants!'

In the dressing-room, Hall and Mulgrew get into an argument about women.

'I look for women with experience,' says Hall. 'I choose women who make the act of love last.'

Mulgrew guffaws. 'Bloody hell,' he says. 'Some of the old boilers I've seen you with don't look like they'd last the walk home.'

'Looks aren't everything,' intones Hall. 'I mean, most of these young tarts – show 'em a prick and they'd faint.'

Mulgrew is laughing. 'No wonder. When I saw yours, *I* nearly fainted. For a start, it's got a bend in it.'

'It's not a bend. It's a slight curve,' says Hall.

'Curve?' laughs Mulgrew, 'it nearly goes round corners.'

I was crying with laughter. Barrack-room humour, there's nothing quite like it.

After the show Major Hardacre, the Town Major, comes backstage with two young officers. They congratulate us over the show. 'It was jolly good.' They seem interested in the girls whom the Major has a slight tendency to handle. He's very interested in Toni, *my* Toni. He shakes her hand

and holds it overlong. He'd better watch out or I'll have his Hardacre on a slab, sliced up like salami and stuffed up his married quarters! God, I was jealous! In love and jealous, it was like being on the rack.

After dinner, that night, we have a dance. The trio, plus Bornheim on the accordion, supply the music. Toni dances with Maxie. He dances splay-legged, as though he has messed himself. Toni, she was so doll-like. Strange – when I was a boy in India, up to the age of eight I liked dolls. My father was a worried man. Was it Toni's doll-like image that attracted me to her? Forward the resident analyst. I have the last waltz with Toni. Bornheim plays the 'Valzer di Candele'. He knows that it's 'our tune'. I hold Toni close and the room seems to go round and round – very difficult for a square room.

By midnight, the dance had broken up. Toni and I went and sat on a bench in the neglected rose garden. (Today's Special, Neglected Roses five shillings a bunch.) We talked about each other. Were we sure we were in love? The answer seemed to be yes. So, what to do? Do we get engaged? I think if I had asked her, she would have said yes. You see, I'd never thought about marriage. I was a day-by-day person. If at the end of day everything was OK, then we were set fair for tomorrow. Why ruin it by planning, say, six months ahead? I tell you, whoever planned my head should have *got* six months. I was a woolly thinker. Toni and I would go on for ever; there was no end to the tour, we would ride in the Charabong eternally and never grow old . . .

BLOODY AWFUL

Next day, after breakfast, it's a real hot day. I tell Toni we must try and get a swim in the Wörthersee. We take our costumes and make for the lake. But everywhere it's reeds, reeds, reeds and where there is access, it's mud, mud, mud. So, we settle for a sunbathe. Oh, the heat. Toni so close, covered in oil – it's almost frying her. 'Terr-ee, some more oil on my back, please.' So Terree obliges, taking his time to rub the oil on her satin skin. Ohhhh, the heat. Ohhhh, the oil. God, we all need a button on us that says SEX ON–OFF. Right now, I'm fumbling for the off switch. Through the lazy afternoon we talk with our eyes closed, sweet nothings that would bore any but us. Being in love, everything seems important. Small things. God, why did I have a small thing?

'What's going on here?' I open one eye to see Bornheim and Mulgrew; the latter, who hasn't learned his lesson, is holding a fishing rod. 'You know there's no mixed bathing allowed in the long grass,' he says.

'Go away, Mulgrew. Weren't you ever young?'

'Yes,' he says. 'It was on a Thursday.'

It is tea-time, so we give in and the four of us head back to the guest house. I need a shower to get the oil off and a cold one to reduce the swelling. Toni came down to tea in an all-white dress to show off her suntan, and lovely she looked.

The show that night was pretty hysterical. A lone drunk in the middle of the hall started to shout out, 'It's bloody awful, bloody awful.' It took a time to evict him. Then, in the second half he obviously somehow got back in because he shouted from the gallery, 'It's still bloody awful, bloody awful.' Again he was thrown out, only to reappear through a front row fire exit direct from the street. 'It's bloody awful from here, as well,' he shouted, before doing a bunk. It caused great laughter in the audience and the cast. It wasn't the last of him, my God. As we were about to drive back to the billets, he was thumping on the sides of the Charabong, 'You're all bloody awful, bloody awful.' Bill Hall rolled down a window and blew a thunderous saliva-draped raspberry at him, causing howls of glee in the truck.

'Perhaps we *are* bloody awful,' said Bornheim. 'I mean, how many of us would a West End audience come to see?' he went on. 'I mean, they'd pay to see the Bill Hall Trio. But the rest of us?'

This started a real row till we got to the hotel. Everybody was suddenly in star class. *Of course* the West End audiences would pay to see Chalky White hitting people, etc., etc. There was a lot of laughter as each artiste defended himself against the 'bloody awful' label. The fact is none of them were ever heard of again.

At dinner, the argument breaks out again. When Bornheim plays the piano, a shout of 'Bloody awful' goes up. From then on, no one could make a move without a shout of 'Here comes bloody awful'. The Italian artistes couldn't get the gist of it. But when they did, they too took up the cry. Toni asked me with a perfectly straight face, 'Tell me, Terr-ee. We are bludy awful, yes?'

The next morning broke sunny and warm. Across the road from us was a little Austrian beerhouse, so at lunchtime Bornheim and I toddled over and sat outside. We ordered a bottle of white wine and some cheese, then another bottle of white wine. Two Austrians in lederhosen with overmuscled legs and blue staring eyes asked us to join them for a 'drink of zer Schnapps' and my God we got pie-eyed. We wobbled back to our chalets. I was sick and crashed out groaning on the bed. Toni is horrified, I've never been drunk before. She sees the drunken wretch and says, 'Terr-ee, you, you, bludy awful,' bursts into tears and runs out. I stumbled after her and crashed to the floor where I was sick yet again. I now looked like a walking Irish stew on legs. By evening I was coming to and drank a lot of black coffee, brought in by faithful Mulgrew who knew drunkenness. That night on stage I *was* bloody awful. I muffed the announcements, got the wrong intros and generally buggered up the act. But we still went down well.

'Just bloody luck,' said Bill Hall.

'What did you get pissed for?' said Lieutenant Priest.

'About thirty Schillings,' I said. 'We were very economical.'

The weather stays divine. Up the road at the Wörthersee riviera Toni and I hire a rowboat and take a packed lunch. I row to the middle of the lake. It's one of those boats with a lounging double seat in the stern, so we snog while the boat drifts and drifts and drifts . . . Let it drift for ever, for we are lovers and the hands of the clock stopped the moment we met. We live in a time capsule called now. We can only think of each other. It is young and true love. The waters lapped the sides, lake birds flew hither and thither to their secret places and the day lay on us like a diaphanous dream . . .

Wake up, wake up! The boat is leaking. Blast, yes, there's three inches of water in the bottom. So I row the love wagon back to the boathouse and point out to the Austrian man what has happened. He just laughed and gave us half our money back. We walked back down the dusty road and arrived home for tea. Toni is giggling because somehow I have managed to wet the seat of my trousers, which looks like a giant ink stain. I hang my shirt out to cover it but that's wet as well. The hell with it! Wild poppies grow by the wayside. I pick some for Toni. Alas, the poor things start to die within a few minutes. Why can't we leave nature alone? Toni takes a photo of me. She wants me to turn my back to the camera. I refuse.

Spike Milligan, Krumpendorf. Quite a long way from where the Pope lives

Lieutenant Priest seeks me out. Tomorrow Bill Hall and I are to report to Villach Demob Camp to be issued with civilian clothes, how exciting! Next morning a 15 cwt truck takes us to the depot. Giant sheds loaded with military gear. We hand in our papers and discharge sheets, then we are given the choice of three suits – a grey double-breasted pinstripe suit, a dark blue ditto or a sports jacket and flannels. This photograph shows us with our chosen clobber.

Goodbye Soldier! Bill Hall, unknown twit and Spike

I had chosen clothes three times too large for me and Hall had chosen some three sizes too small. The distributing sergeant was pretty baffled. We duly signed our names and walked out. England's heroes were now free men. No more 'yes, sir, no, sir', no more parades. Back at the guest house, we have our first meal as civilians. As I remember it was spaghetti.

Milligan and Hall, their first meal as civilians

We had one more demob appointment. That was with the Army MO. This turns out to be a watery-eyed, red-nosed lout who was to medicine what Giotto was to fruit bottling.

'It's got you down here as B 1,' he says.

'That's right, I was downgraded at a medical board.'
'It says "battle fatigue".'
'Yes. "Battle fatigue, anxiety state, chronic".'
'Yes, but you're over it now, aren't you?'
'No, I still feel tired.'
'So, I'll put you down as A1.'
'Not unless I'm upgraded by a medical board.'
'Oh, all right. B1.'
He then asks me if my eyesight is all right.
'As far as I know.'
'You can see me, can't you?'
'Yes.'
'Then it's all right.'
It ended with him signing a couple of sheets of paper and
showing me the door. Why didn't he show me the window?
It was a nice view. To give you an idea of the creep, here is
his signature.

D. Fitness for further service.

Is the member fit for further service?
If so, in what medical category?
(If considered permanently unfit for further service he should be brought before a
medical board with a view to invaliding.)

E. Is the member a known or suspected carrier of infectious disease?

Date of Examination 20-8.46.   Signed
Place RS. MN1 Room   Personal No. and Rank 270921
    Klagenfurt   RANK

That was it. I was a civilian and B1.

Ah, Sunday, day of rest and something. On Monday we will
travel to Graz and do the show. In the morning I lie abed
smoking.

'What's it feel like to be a civvy?' says Mulgrew.
'Well, I've felt myself and it feels fine.'
'Lucky bugger. I've still got two months to go,' he said,
coughing his lungs up.

'You sound as if you're going now.'

Bill Hall stirs. 'Wot's the time?'

I tell him, 'It's time you bought a bloody watch.'

Lying in bed, Hall looks like an activated bundle of rags. Poor Bill – he, too, had been to the creep MO, who had passed him out as A 1. He didn't know it at the time but he had tuberculosis, which would one day kill him. So much for bloody Army doctors.

I take a shower and sing through the cascading waters. 'Boo boo da de dum, can it be the trees that fill the breeze with rare and magic perfume?' I sing. What a waste, singing in the shower. I should be with Tommy Dorsey or Harry James.

Mid-morning, Hall, Mulgrew and I agree to give a concert in the lounge. It is much enjoyed by the hotel staff. All blue-eyed, blond, yodelling Austrians, who have been starved of jazz during the Hitler régime. They have a request. Can we play 'Lay That Pistol Down Babe'? Oh, Christ, liberation had reached Austria. To appease them we play it. Hall plays it deliberately out of tune. 'I'll teach the bastards,' he says, *sotto voce con espressione*. They applaud wildly and ask for it again!! Hall can't believe it. 'They must have cloth ears,' he says and launches into 'Deutschland Über Alles' as a foxtrot. 'Take your partners for the National Anthem,' he says. Hitler must have turned in his grave.

HITLER: No, I'm not. I'm still shovelling
shit and salt in Siberia.

No sign of Toni so far, then Greta tells me she's in bed with tummy trouble. I go up to her room. She's asleep, but awakes as I come in. 'What's the matter, Toni?'

She is perspiring and looks very flushed. 'I think I eat something wrong,' she says. 'All night I be sick.' Oh dear, can I get her anything on a tray like the head of John the

Baptist? 'No, I just want sleep,' she says in a tiny voice. So, I leave her.

That afternoon, Lieutenant Priest has arranged a picture show just for us. We all go to the Garrison Cinema in Klagenfurt to see the film *Laura*, with George Sanders and Clifton Webb. It has that wonderful theme song 'Laura', after which I would one day name my daughter. We are admitted free under the banner of CSE. The cinema is empty, so we do a lot of barracking.

'Watch it, darling, 'ees going ter murder yes,' etc.

''ee wants to have it away with you, darlin'.'

'Look out, mister, watch yer ring! He's a poof!'

Having destroyed the film, we return home like well-pleased vandals.

Tea is waiting and Toni is up and dressed, she feels a lot better. No, she won't eat anything except a cup of coffee, so I get her a cup of coffee to eat. I light up my after-dinner fag and pollute the air. Toni flaps her hand. 'Oh, Terr-ee, why you smoke?' Doesn't she know that Humphrey Bogart never appears in a film without smoking? We spend the evening playing ludo with small bets on the side. Suddenly, *I* feel sick. It's the same as Toni. Soon, I have both ends going. I take to my bed and only drink water. That night, I have a temperature. What a drag! I fall into a feverish sleep.

GRAZ

GRAZ

Next morning, I'm still discharging both ends. Wrapped in a blanket, doused with Aspros, I board the Charabong.

'How you feel, Terree,' says Toni.

'Terrible.'

I semi-doze all the way to Graz, showing no interest in food or drink. When we arrive in Graz, I hurriedly book in and make for my room. It's a lovely hotel with double glazing and double doors to the room, so it's very quiet except for the noise of me going both ends. I take a hot bath and take to my sick bed. I get visits from everyone. Do I need a doctor? I say, no, a mortician. Will I be doing the show tomorrow? Not bloody likely. Bornheim will have to take my place on the squeeze box; I am delirious. Toni visits me and tells me she loves me. That's no bloody good. I love her too, but I've still got the shits. Can she hurry and leave the room as something explosive is coming on. I fall into a deep sleep. I awake in the wee hours to do a wee. I'm dripping with sweat. What's the time? 3 a.m. I take a swig at my half-bottle of whisky. When I awake in the morning, I seem to have broken the back of it – it feels as if I've also broken its legs and arms. Twenty-four hours had passed away but I hadn't. In two days I'm back to my normal, healthy, skinny, self. How did the act go with Bornheim deputizing for me? It was great! Curses. So I rejoin the fold.

The show is at the Theatre Hapsburg, a wonderful, small intimate theatre – one mass of gilded carvings of cherubim. This night the trio get rapturous applause from a mixed audience of Austrians and soldiers. Hall is stunned.

'Bloody hell,' he said. 'We weren't *that* good.'

'Rubbish,' says Mulgrew. '*They* weren't good enough!'

Dinner that night was a treat – first food for forty-eight hours. It's Austrian Irish stew. Bill Hall tells the waitress that his meat is very tough. She calls the chef, a large Kraut. He asks what's wrong.

'This meat is tough.'

'Oh,' says the Kraut. 'You are zer only von complaining.'

'That's 'cause I got all the 'ard bits, mate.'

'It's zer luck of the draw,' says the Kraut, who takes it away.

The waitress returns with a second portion.

'Yes, this is better,' says Hall. The excitement is un-bearable.

I'm convalescing, so I have an early-to-bed. I'm reading Elizabeth Gaskell's *The Life of Charlotte Brontë*. First, I'm delighted to find that the father was Irish. The interesting figure in the story is Branwell Brontë, the piss artist. He's amazing. He writes reams of poetry, can paint and also write with both hands at once. How's that for starters. Yet, he is the *failure* of the family. My eyelids are getting heavy. I lay the book aside and sleep peacefully until the morning when there's a birdlike tapping at my door. It's morning-fresh Toni. She kisses my eyes. 'You very lazee, hurry up. Breakfast nearly finished!' She will see me after breakfast in the hall. 'We go for nice walk.' It's cold but sunny; we are quite high high up.

I have a quick shit, shave and shampoo. I *just* make breakfast. I ask the waiter if I can have a boiled egg and toast. He looks at his watch. Is he going to time it? With an expression on his face as though his balls are being crushed in a vice, he says OK. Toni is waiting in the foyer. She is wearing a tweed coat with a fur collar and looks very pretty. We start our walk by strolling along the banks of the River Mur. Mur? How did it get a name like that? Our walk is lined with silver birch trees. We cross the Mur Bridge and I wonder how it got that name, Mur; through large iron gates into a park built on the side of a hill, called Der Mur Garten, and I wonder how it got that name, Mur. We walk up a slight gradient flanked by rose beds. It was then we did what must be timeless in the calendar of lovers: we carved our names on a tree, inside a heart.

> We carved our hearts
> On a tree in Graz
> And the hands of the clock stood still

Toni has found two heart-shaped leaves, stitched them together with a twig and scratched 'I love you Terry' on them. They still lie crumbling in the leaves of my diary. Ah, yesterday! Where did you go? I lean over and pick a rose only to get a shout, '*Oi, nicht gut!*' from a gardener. We climb higher to a lookout platform overlooking the Mur. How *did* it get that name? From here, we walk into the Feble Strasse, the Bond Street of Graz. As we cross the Mur Bridge, each of us tosses a coin into the river. 'That mean we come back,' said Toni. We never did. We never will.

We window-gazed. Why are women transfixed by jewellers, handbag and shoe shops? The moment Toni stops at a jeweller's, I feel that I should buy her a trinket.

'Isn't that beautiful?' she says, pointing to something like the Crown Jewels, priced thousands of schillings.

'Yes,' I said weakly, knowing that as I stood my entire worldly value, including ragged underwear, was ninety pounds.

The torture doesn't stop there. She points, 'Oh, look, Teree' – a fur coat valued at millions of schillings.

'Yes,' I say weakly, feeling like Scrooge.

'What lovely handbag,' she enthuses.

'Yes,' I say. Don't weaken, Milligan. As long as you can say yes, you're safe from bankruptcy. 'Look, Toni, isn't that beautiful?' I say, pointing to a small bar of chocolate for fifty groschen. Mur, how did it get that name? So, nibbling fifty-groschen chocolate, we walk back to the hotel.

During that night's show, Fulvio Pazzaglia and Tiola Silenzi have a row. Trained singers, their voices projecting can be heard on the stage. She empties a jug of red wine over Fulvio and his nice white jacket. Hurriedly, he borrows one that is miles too big. When he appears on stage, he looks like an amputee. On the way back in the Charabong, the row continues. She does all the shouting, he sits meekly in silence. It's something to do with money. She spends it and he objects when he can get a word in. We all sit in silence listening to the tirade. It is very entertaining and when she finally finishes, Bill Hall starts up a round of applause, shouting, 'Bravo! Encore!'' She is beside herself with anger.

It was one unforgettable night in Graz that Toni and I consummated our love. When it was over, we lay quite still in the dark. Neither of us spoke. I could hear her breathing, then she started to cry.

'What's the matter, Toni?'

'I am different now. I am not girl any more.'

'Are you sorry?'

'No.'

With one act, everything was changed. We had made an invisible bond. Only time would test its strength. I lay watching her dress in the half-light – every move was etched in my mind. I can still see it quite clearly.

Next morning, when we met at breakfast, everything seemed different. Yet, it was only us. We seemed speechless, but our hearts beat faster. It was as though we were caught in an invisible net, each a prisoner of the other. Primitive emotions held us in their timeless grasp.

That afternoon, the Trio met in Hall's room for a practice of some new numbers.

'You're bloody quiet these days,' he says.

'I'm in love, Bill. That's why.'

'Love, me arse. All you want is a good shag and you'll be right as rain.'

'I'll bear that in mind.'

'Are you thinking of marryin' this bird?'

'It crossed my mind and body, yes.'

'You'll see, she'll be fat as a pig at forty.'

'Don't listen to him,' says Mulgrew. 'He should talk, with all those old boilers he goes out with.'

'They're not old boilers,' says Hall. 'They are mature, experienced women, who know all the tricks of love.'

'Tricks,' guffaws Mulgrew, 'like cracking walnuts in the cheeks of their arse.'

The session over, I rose to leave the room. 'You'll see,' says Hall, who is now playing the Trout Quintet. 'At forty, you'll be able to roll her home.'

I am writing home asking my folks for more razor blades and pile ointment – at the same time, telling them that I'm considering marrying Toni. My mother's reply is full of advice. I musn't marry till I have a decent job and have 'settled down', whatever that means. Two *can't* live as cheaply as one. My ninety pounds' savings won't go far. I don't know, though; it's got as far as the Post Office in Lewisham. My mother should talk! In the days of the British Raj, her father was dead set against her marrying my father. He chased my father through the Poona Cantonments on a bicycle, my father escaping in a *tonga*.

Like all long-running shows, we are getting sloppy again. Lieutenant Priest assembles us all in the lounge. 'Look,' he says. 'It's getting to be like a private joke. It may be funny to us, but not the audience. We're going to have a full dress rehearsal tomorrow morning.' He is right, of course; we are all taking liberties. For instance, when Ricky Trowler is singing 'Let the Rest of the World Go By', he is barracked from the wings with raspberries and shouts of 'drink up!' In the 'Close the Shutters, Willy's Dead' number, numerous ping-pong balls are bounced on the stage from each side. I think it's funny; Priest doesn't. Bill Hall plays disturbing obligatos behind the curtain during the singers' spot, causing them to corpse.

It's a night with a hunter's moon. After dinner Toni and I go for a stroll down by the Mur. How *did* it get that name? We talked, the scenery drifted past unnoticed. We were now willing prisoners of each other. It had taken us by surprise; we were still in a state of amazement. Everything came through a rainbow-filtered haze. Toni was so childlike, I had a burning desire to look after her, to protect her. From

what? God knows. Elephants? 'This is lak a storybook,' she
said. 'We make it up as we go along.' Yes, one day the show
would stop but we would go on for ever. This is how the
story would go: the Bill Hall Trio would go back to the UK
and become rich, then I would send for Toni! I would
welcome her to England with a white Rolls-Royce, a glass of
champagne and a complete explanation as to why the river
was called the Mur!

We are finished in Graz and now to the dream city of
Vienna sausage!

> Call, call Vienna mine
> Sing night and day with your songs divine.

VIENNA

Ah yes, Vienna. 'Tales From the Vienna Woods', were they true or was it gossip? The Blue Danube, now called the Brown, the Emperor Franz Josef, Freud.

It's a crisp, misty, sunny morning as we board the Charabong in a state of excitement. Luigi crosses himself and starts the engine and crosses himself again when it starts. Bill Hall is on form and plays a terrible version of 'The Blue Danube' waltz. If only tape recorders had been invented! It was a masterpiece of bad intonation. I borrow Bornheim's *Union Jack* to see what's going on in the outside world.

Where is the Mufti of Jerusalem?

says the headline. What is a Mufti? Another headline:

Princess Nadija Braganca has thrown herself from the third floor of a London hospital

Well, it's cheaper than paying the bill. What else? General Milhailovitch is on trial for war crimes; his lawyer is claiming that his client is 'Ill and Mad'. Milhailovitch says he isn't which, says his lawyer, proves that he is.

The mist is lifting, giving way to sunshine. We are passing strange names. Knutcracken (it must be agony), Gloggnitz, Splatsputz and Pottyend. The Austrian countryside is neater than the Italian; the precise Teutonic mind had everything neat and tidy. Just after the village of Mürzzuschlag (How did it get that name?), we pull up alongside a daisy-spattled field complete with fat cows. We sit in the long grass dotted with scarlet poppies lusting for the sun. We are overlooking a valley that looks like a set for Walt Disney's *Snow White*.

'*Che carino*,' said Toni.

'This wet grass gives you piles,' said Chalky White, killing the ambience of the moment stone dead.

Bornheim is going to prove a theory. 'If you lie down in a field, cows will come up and lick you.'

'That's a lot of balls,' said the learned White.

So, Bornheim duly lies down. Gradually, the animals' curiosity makes them all approach Bornheim and, my God, they start licking him. 'All right, Clever Dick,' he says to White.

''Ow did you know that?' says White.

'I read it in a book.'

We are all munching our way through cheese and tomato sandwiches, and Lieutenant Priest wanders among us to see if we are all satisfied with the rations. It's very peaceful; very little traffic on the road save the occasional military vehicle.

'Watch, Toni,' I say.

I pluck a dandelion that has gone to seed. I blow the seed and like little parachutes they float away.

'You have to make a wish,' said Toni.

I make a secret wish that I'll become rich. It must have been a faulty dandelion. This is forty years on and I'm still not rich.

Lunch over, I lie back and light up a cigarette and watch the smoke curl heavenwards. What *is* up there in that blue vault? I'm looking into infinity and it's empty. What is it all about? What are we all about? Well, I was about twenty-nine. Chalky White has gone to the middle of the field to repeat Bornheim's experiment. It works except White has unwittingly lain in a cowpat, most of which has stuck to his back.

'That's lucky,' says Bornheim.

'What's lucky about cow shit?' moans White.

'It's lucky I didn't get it.'

'All right, let's be having you,' says Priest, mustering us back into the Charabong. We give off our customary bleating and mooing, only to be answered by the cows.

'I wonder,' says loony Bornheim. 'Do they moo in Austrian?'

A SIBERIAN SALT MINE.
HITLER IS SHOVELLING SHIT AND SALT.

HITLER: Of course zey moo in Austrian. Do you
         think zey would be unfaithful to der Führer?

The journey passes uneventfully. Hall and I occasionally break the monotony by playing some jazz and lead a few sing-songs. Towards late evening, we reach the outskirts of Vienna.

It's rush hour in Vienna; the streets are crammed with commuters all hurrying home. The city is unfolding itself. It is a bounty of grand and stately buildings, palaces and fountains. We pass in the shadow of St Stephen's. I tell Toni this is where Bach played the organ. She doesn't like Bach too much. 'He, too, how you say, mathmetica.' She likes *dolce* music like Puccini. 'You like Bach?' she said. I don't know, I've never met him.

Street lights are coming on. It's fun to see trams again. There's evidence of the quadrilateral occupation. American jeeps and the green-grey of Russian lorries with po-faced Russian soldiers. We pass the giant Ferris wheel that has survived the war – there had been a move to dismantle it as it was a focal point for bombers.

On we trundle through busy streets. We get lost several times, but no one notices the difference. We stop and Lieutenant Priest flags down a British Military Police patrol, which turns out to be lost itself. We are looking for the Franz Josef Hotel in Gustav Strasse.

'We're bloody lost,' moans Hall.

'No, we're not,' says Priest. 'I know exactly where we are.'

'Where,' says Hall.

'Here,' says Priest with a chuckle.

More by luck than judgement, we finally arrive, at which there is a dull cheer. But wait! Uniformed porters are coming out to *carry* our luggage. There's Bill Hall's bulging cardboard suitcase tied with knotted string. We trail behind them and are shown into a wood-panelled reception hall, all very, very chic. The receptionists are super-polite. There's lots of heel-clicking and '*jawohl*'s. They are all wearing gold-trimmed uniforms. 'I bet they're all ex-Nazis,' says Hall. It's a culture shock to see the smart porter carrying Hall's grotty luggage, followed by an even grottier Hall.

Toni is excited by the magnificence of the place. 'How beautiful, Terr-ee. *Che eleganza.*' My room looks like Madame du Barry's. It has a four-poster bed with velvet swags, a gold-plated chandelier, a burgundy carpet with fleur-de-lis motif. There must be some mistake. My phone is buzzing. It's Toni. She is in raptures over her room. She also says she loves me 'and you beautiful eyes'.

Bornheim visits me. He, too, is stunned by the opalescence of his room and has to tell someone. 'Well, enjoy it, Bornheim, because the day is not far off when you'll be back in Naples in a bare barrack room.' He says it's 'all a plot to lift you up and, wallop, bring you down'. We sit and smoke a cigarette and talk of the strange existence we are experiencing. Everyone is working for a living. In England, Mr Attlee is exhorting the nation to work harder, while we are in cloud-cuckoo-land, without a care in the world. 'We'll never have it as easy as this again.' It was a prophecy that came true. Bornheim departs saying, 'It's all a dream,' his hands clawing the air.

I bathe in my rose-coloured marble bath with gold-plated taps. I was disappointed when only water came out. The bath is twice normal size; should I dive in? I'm so thin, when I get in the bath it looks like someone's thrown a pair of braces in. My father always said, 'Don't worry, son. You'll fill out one day.' Did he think I was hollow? 'And there's nothing wrong with being thin. Look at Gandhi.' I didn't want to look at Gandhi; he reminded me of me. No! I wanted to look like Johnny Weissmuller and sing like Crosby. The combination would be infallible. I mean, swinging from tree to tree singing 'Love In Bloom' must be a winner. Who's that at the door? It's Lieutenant Priest with two letters, one from my father, one from my brother. The latter is now stationed in Cyprus.

Dear Hairy,
I'm in the land of Aphrodite, after Germany it's paradise, it's mostly guard duties. I'm a sergeant now stationed at Dekelhia, we are all under canvas and under a poofy O C. We're just outside Larnaca, the girls are heavily chaperoned. It's easier to lay eggs than lay one of them, some of them are beautiful, if things get worse the men will start to look beautiful. Dad seems settled back in Fleet Street and Mum is still boiling all his food to death. On my nights off we go to Larnaca, pulsating with twelve forty watt bulbs, a few smoky dens sell eggs and chips, a couple of Greek cinemas with sub-titles help to alleviate the monotony. They want me to put in for a commission, I'll see. Hope your new career goes well. What's this about you marrying an Italian bird?

Loving Brother Des.

So the news of Toni and me has reached as far as Cyprus. Well, well. Whereas my mother baulks at any reports of me marrying, my father is the reverse (there are not many reversed fathers). He says it's fine, and why don't we get married by the Pope!

I hurry down to the dining-hall, I hear the strains of a Strauss waltz. Wow, there's a quintet playing in the dining-hall, which is as sumptuous as the rest of the hotel – great chandeliers. It's very large and very busy. Toni, sitting small and petite at a distant table, waves to draw my attention. 'Oh, Terr-ee,' she says. 'What you think of this place?' I tell her it's marvellous. I'm as overwhelmed as she is. There's a menu a mile long. Mulgrew and Bornheim join our table. We enjoy a splendid repast of wienerbackhendl (chicken) and, after, we retire to the lounge where a pianist is playing Chopin. The waiter brings us coffee. We are all feeling rather splendid; I even order a cigar.

'Don't go mad, Milligan,' says Bornheim. 'We're all going to suffer withdrawal symptoms when we leave here.'

'We're only here four nights,' said Mulgrew, 'so make the best of it.'

We were doing just that.

The State Opera House is a two-thousand seater. When I think of all those bums making contact. The dressing-rooms? Well, you could have lived in them. 'This is better than the house my folks live in,' said an amazed Hall; but reflected that *anything* was better than the house his folks lived in. In London, Hall lived in a room with a gas ring that served as a) stove b) heater c) decoration.

Our first night had a very mixed audience: Americans, Russians, British, Austrians. The Russians are in a box and we are chuffed when they laugh uproariously at the Trio.

'If nothing else,' says Mulgrew, 'they've got a sense of humour.'

'Sense of humour?' said Hall. 'Have you read what they did to the women when they captured Berlin? Very funny.'

'They weren't the only ones,' said Mulgrew. 'I've seen some of our squaddies and GIs behaving pretty abominable.'

'You sayin' we're as bad as the Russians?'

'Given the opportunity, yes.'

'Listen, they raped everything from schoolgirls to grand-mothers.'

'Listen, mate. Some of the grandmothers were very grate-ful,' said Mulgrew with a sadistic chuckle.

These Hall vs. Mulgrew arguments never got anywhere; both were implacable. Their arguments ranged from who should turn out the light when neither bed was more than three paces from the switch, to why the Conservatives had lost the post-war election.

'Churchill was going gaga, that's why,' insisted Hall.

'Rubbish,' retorts Mulgrew. 'He's in his prime. Attlee has the personality of an overlaundered vest.'

Next day, Toni and I set out to see the sights. Toni has a small booklet in Italian telling what to see. Under her guidance, we visit Kärtnerstrasse. Helppppppp!!! It's the most expensive shopping centre in Austria, and me down to my last few schillings! Helppppppp!!

She stops at a window with a magnificent tulle white wedding dress. 'Oh, Terr-ee – look, how beautiful!'

'I couldn't wear it,' I said. 'It's the wrong colour.'

It was another one of my jokes that didn't register. If there was a graveyard for failed jokes, it would be overflowing with mine.

A JOKE MORTICIAN'S SHOP.

ME: I've come to bury a joke.
MORTICIAN: I'm sorry, sir, the graveyard is full. It's been a good year.
ME: What do you suggest?
MORTICIAN: Cremation, sir. You can have the ashes of your favourite joke in an urn. In moments of depression, you can take the lid off and have a good laugh.

After miles of shops, we repair to a coffee house. 'Schwi tass Kaffee, bitte,' I say in badly spelt German.

The place is crowded with people leaning forward and speaking in hushed tones, looking like trainee Balkan assassins. 'I like very much Vienna,' says Toni. 'I very hapee.' (I'm trying to spell like she talks.) The coffee arrives along with a cake only the Austrians can make, called Sachertorte – light as a feather, full of pure cream and caster sugar, topped with milk chocolate. With a balletic thumb and forefinger, Toni eats one with mincing mouth movements. I've crammed two, three into my mouth.

'You like Vienna, Terr-ee?'

'Yes, anytime is dancing time with you. But for drongles on the knees, we'd be waltzing now.'

'I no understand.'

MORTICIAN: I'm sorry, sir. I told you, the graveyard is full.

Next stop, the Spanish Riding School. I've always wanted to see Spaniards riding – something that's very hard to come by in Brockley SE 26. In a moment of transportation madness, I decide we should take a horse-drawn landau. I tell the driver, 'Mein Herr, Spanish riding school verstain?' He is not verstaining. I demonstrate and mime several well-known dressage movements. I prance back and forth. He still doesn't verstain. A small crowd gathers, thinking it is street entertainment. Then I remember – like Paul on the way to Damascus, I see the light. I remember the breed of the white horse.

'Lippizaner, verstain?'

A smile of recognition lights up a face that is nearly falling off. '*Ja, verstehe*,' he says, and we are on our clip-clop way.

Ah, driving through Vienna in a landau! How romantic, and how unromantic when the horse starts letting off. I am embarrassed; Toni is less self-conscious. She starts to giggle. How can she? We are down wind and getting the lot. Thank God, it's only a short distance. We pay the entrance fee and enter the famous place – very impressive with its white viewing galleries and forty-six columns. When did the horses come? When we are old we will remember this. Yes, where are the Lippizaner horses? 'Zorry, *mein Herr*. Zer Lippizaners do not appear in August. Zo sorry.' Good God, this was like early closing in Catford.

It's time to go home. I flag down a well-worn Mercedes taxi. We flop in and Toni says, 'Oh, I am soo tir-ed.' She slips off her shoes. I slide my arm round her and we explode in a long hot, passionate kiss. After that silence, what else? You can't say 'Thank you, madam. I'll be round tomorrow for the same. Here's a receipt.' There should be a light on all lovers that lights up when you reach breaking point. When it started to flash, you would know it was time to have it away.

The second night at the theatre, it's only half full. Still, that's a thousand; but there's something about masses of empty seats that lowers your morale. There is a sepulchral echo that makes us sound like we're doing a show in the Swiss Alps. However, the show is well received and afterwards we have to meet a Brigadier Fullwood and his retinue. He pumps my hand.

'Jolly good show. What part did you play?'

'I was in the Bill Hall Trio.'

'Oh yes, you played the banjo?'

'Yes, I play de banjo.'

'Are you a serving soldier?'

'Was. I'm now a serving civilian.'

One of his subalterns invites us to his party. 'Just round the corner from here,' he says.

Toni doesn't want to come. 'I tired,' she says.

The party is in the top floor of a block of prestige flats. This subaltern has it made, has got the lot – including a lovely Austrian mistress. 'I'd love to be in her class,' says Bornheim, making an appropriate sign. There's plenty to eat and drink. I am chatted up by a blonde Marlene Dietrich.

'Vy,' she says with heavily lidded eyes, 'vy are you not in zer uniform?'

'I'm not a soldier.'

'Oh, have you been in zer war?'

'Yes, I was with the artillery.'

'Ah, gut.' She draws longingly on a cigarette. 'Have you ever killed *einer Mann?*'

'No.'

'No one?'

'Well, I didn't fire the gun. I only gave the orders, I suppose. OK, yes, maybe I have killed some men.'

This seemed to cheer her up. 'So you haff drawn blood, *ja*?'

'Yes, I drew a pint every day from the stores for my Dracula impressions.'

'Please?'

MORTICIAN: I keep telling you sir, the graveyard's full.

She must have been a recruiting agent for the SS. Anyhow, she's taken to me and I get sloshed. People are leaving; not me, I get more sloshed. Wait, the place is empty. Mein host and his bird have gone to bed. 'Sit here,' says Marlene, patting the seat. The inevitable happened, I screwed her. I can't get out – the door is locked. I have to wake mein host for the key. I leave as the blonde temptress says, 'Gude night, soldier boy,' before she turned into a werewolf.

Comes the dawn! Toni suspects. She knows I stayed last night with a WOMAN, I can't get away with it. Being a Catholic, I confess the whole story. I feel better, she feels worse. She bursts into tears. 'I never talk to you again.' I tell her it's because I got drunk. That's even worse, drunk *and* screwing. She runs to her room and won't answer the door. She wouldn't even answer the windows. Soon, it's common gossip among the cast. '*Cattivo*,' says Tiola Silenzi.

'So you 'ad a shag,' says Hall, tuning his violin. 'Wots she worried about? There's worse things in life.'

'Why did you tell her?' says Mulgrew, lying back on his bed smoking a dog end.

'I *had* to. I'm a compulsive confessor.'

'There's no future for you,' chuckles Hall. 'You're going to go short.'

'What was it like?' says Mulgrew.

'I can't remember.'

'Oh, my! All that banging away with the sweat rolling off yer balls and you can't remember,' says Hall, and launches into playing 'Sweetheart, Sweetheart'.

He waltzes round the room to his own accompaniment. He's taking the piss out of me, I feel like a leper. Where will I get one at this time of night? Oh, Toni, Toni, what have I done? Rather, it's *who* have I done. Verily, I suffereth and there is a gnashing of teeth. Woe to me and Milligan is downcast and sacrificeth a lamb to the gods of pity and, lo, he layeth on his bed and smoketh a cigarette. But it easeth him not and he is sore afraid. Someone knocking on my door; it must be the Doppelgänger.

'Go away.'

'It's me, Toni.' I don't believe it. I leap and open the door. 'Can I come in?'

'Oh yes, yes, yes, Toni. Come in.' Come in, Toni. Yes, Toni, yes – you want to talk to me? Oh, yes, Toni anything you say. She is unbelievable.

'I come to ask you if you really sorry what you do.'

I tell her I am ashamed for what I did, but it was only because I got drunk. I still love her; I will never do it again, I swear. She pauses – the silence is unbearable. She walks to the window.

With her back to me, she says, 'All right, I forgive you and we forget all about it.' Of course, I'll forget all about it. Yes, yes, yes, Toni. We kiss and everything falls back into place. What a relief I can cancel the sackcloth and ashes. It's mid-morning, would I like to go out and see the Schönbrunn Palace? Yes, yes, yes, Toni – the Schönbrunn Palace, the very place I wanted to visit. No patched-up romance is complete without a Schönbrunn Palace. OK, she'll see me downstairs in half an hour. Yes, yes, half an hour, that's exactly what I would have said – half an hour, yes, Toni.

The setting was perfect for Toni and me. The Schönbrunn was such a romantic delight. Here Maria Theresa lived in her 'idyllic absolutism'. Here, in the Chinesisches Rund-kabinett, Mozart gave his first concert. The ballroom is baroque to the point of madness; it was a visit to this deserted

139

ballroom that inspired Ravel's fantasy 'La Valse', or so I was told. He might not have been inspired by the ballroom – no, he could have been inspired by his charlady hoovering the floor or a number 79a tram. There's no telling.

'What wonderful life they live here,' said Toni as we walked through the Hall of Mirrors or, in German, 'Spiegelsaal'. We were spiegelling ourselves in the mirrors and seeing ourselves reflected into numberless infinity. There were a thousand Spike Milligans and a thousand Tonis. She did a pirouette to see the effect of a myriad of ballerinas; not to be outdone, I did the same, jerking my hand up and down above my head. It was simple fun and very economical. I only stopped it when I realized one of the uniformed attendants was watching me. I gave him a grin and he grinned back – again, simple fun and very economical. I really am over the moon now that Toni has forgiven me. What a forgiving nature she had.

On, then, to the room that Napoleon occupied on his way to the Battle of Austerlitz. I didn't know the Hapsburgs rented out rooms! It's sad: this is the room that Napoleon's son died in. Had he seen the bill? The room contains his death mask and a stuffed pet bird. It has a pained expression as though it was stuffed before death. The evening hour grows late. While Viennese hurry home from work, we are going the other way – *to* work.

Bornheim had been at the fatal party. That evening, during the course of the show, he approaches me.

'You been having it away behind Toni's back? Well, well! Was it the good-looking one I saw you chatting up?'

'The same.'

'Cor, you must have enjoyed it.'

I round on him. 'Look here, Bornheim, I've had enough.'

'Oh, we know that,' he interrupted.

'I have no wish to discuss it further, it's over and done.'

'And you were the one that done it,' he laughs.

Please, God, stop the torture. Please, drop a vengeful Catholic mangle on Bornheim. I suppose now we are all a bit bored with the show and a bit blasé over its continuing success – there is never a night when we don't get an ovation. That's something you don't get tired of, applause.

That night, Toni and I are locked in each other's arms. I stay in her room all night. Still, that guilty Roman Catholic plagues me: should I be doing this to her????? I can still hear my mother's voice on the landing. 'Terry, where have you been at this time of night? It's one o'clock . . .'

Next morning I sneak out of her room, unobserved by the cast, back to my bath. After a bath and a vigorous shower, I meet Toni downstairs where we breakfast on fresh warm brioches with jam and tea. By now, of course, I only drink Russian tea.

Toni lays a hand on mine. 'Last night very beautiful,' she says, giving me a long steady gaze. I nod.

Tiola Silenzi, looking pneumatic, bears down on us. 'Ah,' she says, '*insieme ancora. Che carino.*' She smiles wickedly and wags a finger. God how the Italians love intrigue. Her husband Fulvio stands dwarfed behind her and nods in agreement to avoid assassination.

This morning is payday. The ghost walks, but not fast enough for me. It's in Lieutenant Priest's room, I sign for my hundred schillings and enjoy tucking the note inside my jacket. Today, Toni and I will ride the giant Ferris wheel! It's a short taxi ride. There it is, towering above us. We take our positions in the boxed cars; soon we are riding up and around, giving one an exhilarating feeling as one feels one's stomach come up into one's throat. 'Oh Terr-ee,' screams Toni as the wheel gathers speed. I put my arm around her and hold her tight. Enjoyment isn't the word; it's a feeling of secure fear (Eh?). Gradually it slows down and we emerge feeling slightly lightheaded.

Back at the hotel, it's NAAFI issue in Molloy's room. I draw my fifty free cigarettes in the vacuum-packed tin. I like piercing the tin seal with the opening prong in the lid and the hiss of escaping air brings the smell of tobacco. I lay on my bed eating my chocolate ration and smoking; life was good. Both Mulgrew and Bornheim visit to repay borrowed cigarettes.

That night, the most embarrassing night of my life, the act ends with my trousers falling down. OK, I hear you say, what's embarrassing about that? This night we arrive at the end of the act, I pull the string that drops my trousers – down they go. Then came the moment of truth: I had forgotten my underpants! My shirt *just* covered my willy, but people standing in the wings can see the lot. Two of the ballet girls, Luciana and Marisa call out, '*Bravo, Terr-ee, che bellino*' (well done, what a beauty) and who was I to disagree with experts? However, it was a near-run thing. That night Toni, Mulgrew, Bornheim and I dine together. It's Bornheim's birthday. He splashes out on a bottle of champagne. It's Austrian – called Schlocknut, which sounds like part of a diesel engine and almost tastes like it.

'Don't you like it?' he inquires.

'Not much, it's too dry for me.' Ugh, it has almost sucked my cheeks together.

How old is he now? Can we guess? He gets a selection: twenty-nine? twenty-six? twenty-seven? No, no, no, all wrong. One more guess – sixty? Silly bugger, Milligan, no. 'I am this day twenty-five.' We wish him *bon voyage* on his journey through life as a furrier in Leeds. What more can a man want of life?

We eat our dinner to the accompaniment of the quintet who are playing, as usual, waltzes. Bornheim orders another bottle of the diesel oil, then another, and I notice that Toni is getting squiffy. She is giggling into her food and missing her mouth. Enough is enough, I beg Bornheim not to give her any more.

'Just because you're falling behind, there's no need to persecute this poor girl.'

'Don't you listen to him, Toni,' says Mulgrew, who is himself starting to slur his words.

The evening ended with me helping her to her room a giggling female who was very unsteady on her feet. I retire to my room, where I'm suddenly awakened from a deep sleep by Mulgrew and Bornheim. Both are smashed out of their minds.

'Schpike, S C H P I K E! Cwan on hev a drink he he he he,' says Mulgrew trying to make me drink from his glass.

'Schjust hev hay liddle schippy poos,' says Bornheim standing or rather swaying behind him. I have to get up and gradually push the unintelligible lunatics out into the corridor, where I hear them stumbling along talking gibberish. What made it amazing was that they seemed to understand each other!! How I envied them in that blissful state.

Next morning, both Bornheim and Mulgrew are missing. They appear at midday in an Austrian police wagon. They had been found wandering the streets of Vienna and have spent the night pissed in a police cell. Lieutenant Priest has to sign for them to be released from police custody. They are both unshaven, bleary-eyed and, on their release, both take to their beds to sleep it off. Toni, too, doesn't appear until midday. 'Oh, Terr-ee, my head go bang, bang.' It's her own fault. I had warned her, I had tried to stop her. 'I am very soree,' she says. We sit in the lounge and have coffee. 'Oh, why, why I drink champagne?'

'It's too late now, my dear, and remember in your condition I *could* have taken advantage of you and had a "quickie".' As it was, I had only given them a quick squeeze.

Does she feel fit enough to go out? Yes, she thinks so. I want to see the Stephensdom (St Stephen's). We go, again, by horse-drawn landau – known here as a fiacre. The driver, a young man wearing a bowler, is the essence of politeness; he bows as he helps Toni in and clicks his heels. The building dominates the skyline as yet unsullied by tall buildings; its Romanesque western façade and Gothic tower loom above us. Fool, I've left my money behind. Never mind, Toni has some. She opens her handbag stuffed with schillings, the little miser!

The building is a marvellous example of the Viennese genius for harmonious compromise. We slog up the steps to the North Tower and are rewarded with what feels like a heart attack and a wonderful view of the city, as well as the huge Pummerin Bell cast from melted-down Turkish cannons captured in the great siege of 1683. It would take

143

pages to describe; let's say it was a masterpiece of Gothic creativity. We have nothing like it in Brockley SE 26 except St Cyprian's breeze-block church hall.

That visit over, we found a very up-market *Kaffeehaus* – das Café Sperl, where the inevitable string trio are playing Viennese salon music. They sell a great range of coffees. I glance down the bill of fare: ah, I'll have *ein Einspänner*.This is coffee with a touch of perversion – whipped cream. Toni has ein Kleiner Mokka – like Joe Louis, strong, pungent and black. Toni, avis-like, is sipping the scalding drink. I am looking at her and I am thinking, does she belong to me? This petite creature, is she really mine or on loan?

'Why you look like that?' she says.

'*Tu sei mio amore*,' I say in my best Italian.

She smiles. It's quite lovely – even lovelier, Toni paid the bill.

'*Danke, mein Herr*,' says the Herr Ober with a slight, stiff bow. How courteous they all were, not at all like English waiters who pick their noses when taking your order.

It's late afternoon when our fiacre drops us back at the hotel. Toni wants a lie-down: can I lie with her? No, no, no, she wants a sleep. I tell her I won't wake her up, she won't even know it's happened. No, no, no, I am very naughty. Never mind, I can hold out. While I'm holding it out, time is passing. I press on with the Mrs Gaskell book on the Brontës. I'm up to where Branwell Brontë, on his last night alive, is in a drugged state (laudanum); he's having dinner with a friend at his favourite piss-up pub, the Black Bull. He turns up 'wild-eyed and drugged and demanded a brandy'. Next day Branwell dies, something that the whole family specialized in. One by one, until only the Reverend Patrick Brontë survives. How lonely must have been his last years.

Immersed in the book, I forget the time. There's a thunderous Lieutenant Priest. 'Come on, we're all in the bloody Charabong. Don't tell me you're getting Hall's disease.' I grab my guitar case and follow him to the waiting vehicle. 'The new Bill Hall,' announces Priest as I board.

'Where you been, Terree?' says Toni. I explain. 'Ah, Brontë sisters, I know, I read in Italian book – very sad story.'

Bornheim walks up and leans over us. 'What you do today?' I told him; what did he do? He did three vests, three underpants and all his socks.

'Why didn't you give 'em to the laundry?'

Ah, he is trying to save money. Aren't we all?

It's a packed house again, great. I make sure I'm wearing underpants. That experience the previous night was to haunt me all my days I was with the Trio. Some girls stood hopefully in the wings, hoping for an encore. My God, in the front row it's that Marlene Dietrich that I screwed. After the show, she comes looking for me. She comes to the dressing-room; they hide me in the shower. I hear her saying this is her telephone number, will I phone her. Helppppp!! Thank God, Toni isn't around. Marlene isn't easily put off; Bornheim comes in and tells us that she's waiting outside the stage door!! I smuggle myself out the front of the theatre and get a taxi back to the hotel. How do I explain this to Toni? When I arrive everyone is at dinner.

'Terr-ee, where you been?' says Toni. Well, I tell her the truth. 'Why she come for you?' she inquires. I daren't tell her because I was very good at it; no, I say I don't know. 'You tell the truth?'

'Yes, Toni.'

She left it at that but the atmosphere was distinctly cool. I order: 'Herr Ober, ein Komenymag Leves Nokedival.' I don't know what it is, but it sounds magnificent. It turns out to be Caraway Seed Soup! There must be some mistake, I distinctly ordered Komenymag Leves Nokedival. What? That means Caraway Seed Soup? I should sue them through the Trade Descriptions Act! It's been a wearing day, so, after a fond goodnight at Toni's door, I go to bed, steaming with desire.

We come to our last day in Vienna sausage. It starts with a disaster for Johnny Bornheim: he left his shoes outside his room for the Boots to clean and someone has pinched them. 'The thieving bastards,' he rages. He reports the theft to the manager, a short, fat, bald, puffing Austrian with pebble-glass spectacles.

'Hi am zo zorry, *mein Herr*.'

He is full of profuse apologies and halitosis. He, in turn, phones the police and, duly, an Austrian plain-clothes police-man arrives and takes details. What colour were the shoes? Brown. How old were they? About seven years. The detective tries to stifle a laugh. Bornheim knows he hasn't a hope in hell of getting them back and, until he buys a new pair, has the embarrassment of wearing white plimsolls. He looked a real Charlie as he came down to breakfast. 'Anyone for tennis?' ribbed Mulgrew.

'They were my best pair,' moaned Bornheim. He could have fooled me.

He spends the morning along with me and Toni, shopping for a new pair. In post-war Vienna, there isn't much of a choice and the quality is very poor. Bornheim buys a cheap pair that seem to be made of reinforced brown paper with cardboard soles. To buy them, he has to borrow money from Mulgrew who goes faint at the thought. On this, our last day, Toni, Mulgrew and Bornheim, with his new shoes, decide to visit the Schatzkammer. It contains a dazzling display of the old Holy Roman Empire. I was stunned at the Imperial Crown of pure gold set with pearls and unpolished emeralds, sapphires and rubies – that, and the actual sword used by Charlemagne plus the lance that is supposed to have pierced Christ on the Cross. As I recall, this is about the tenth that I've seen! There was so much gold everything seemed to be made of it except Bornheim's new shoes, whose newness has started to hurt his feet. 'I must have a rest,' he says.

We repair to an adjacent coffee house and take refreshment. It's out on the street and we watch the passing of humans in concert, while busy Herr Obers move among the pavement tables. 'This is the life,' says Mulgrew, emitting a stream of smoke. Indeed, yes – it was a sunny day, I was in love,

Bornheim had new shoes and Mulgrew was going to charge him interest on the money he lent him.

'I tell you,' said Toni, nibbling a pastry, 'Austrians make better cake than Italy. Terr-ee, do you have places like this in England?'

'Oh, yes. There's Lyons Corner House with Welsh rarebits.'

I have to explain what Welsh rarebits are.

'They not sweet,' she says.

'No, they savoury.'

'What is savoury?'

'Well, the opposite of sweet.'

'Ah,' she says. '*Gustoso!*'

Yes, if she says so – gustoso.

Bornheim is feeling his new shoes.

'Are they hurting?' I said.

'Just a bit. They'll be all right when I've broken them in.'

Mulgrew warns him, 'Don't let water get on them, they'll melt.'

Bornheim shoots him a meaningful stare, whereof I'm sure Mulgrew knew not the meaning.

'Toni! That's the fourth cake you've had; you'll get fat.'

No, never, she says; she'll never get fat. 'No one in my family fat.' Dare I tell her that when she was forty I would be able to roll her home?

'*Wieviel kostet das?*' I say to the Herr Ober with the aid of a phrase book. With a grin he tots up the bill. I split it three ways: 'That's five schillings each.'

'I'm skint,' says Bornheim.

'He's had the last of my money,' says Mulgrew, so I am lumbered.

Dutifully, I pay up with a sickly grin. More expense is on the way: Bornheim can't walk back, his shoes hurt. No, no, we will have to take a taxi. I love the 'we' bit. So, 'we' get a taxi and 'we' all get in and 'we' drive to the hotel; 'we' get out, but 'I' pay.

Toni has some mending to do, so I spend the afternoon room-bound, reading the Brontës book, occasionally drifting into a shallow sleep. Bored, I put new strings on my guitar and practise some chords. I accompany myself: boo boo da de dum, love in bloom – all wasted on four hotel walls. Boredom should be a cardinal sin. I was bored. I lay on the bed, put my Brontës book aside, stared up at the ceiling. I stared at the wall opposite; I returned to the ceiling, fixing me gaze on the light fitting. I close one eye – this makes the light jump to the right. I close the other eye and it appears to jump to the left. I close eyes alternately, making the light jump back and forth. I cross my eyes and get two lights. So far, so good. By squinting, I make the light into a blur; by opening both eyes and swivelling my eyeballs left and right, I make the light move back and forth across the ceiling. Boo boo da de dum, love in bloom. I examine my fingernails; they don't need cutting, so I put them aside. I look down at my feet; I wiggle my toes. I give a giant yawn and nearly dislocate my jaw. By grinding my teeth, I can make the sound of a train on the inside of my eardrum. By wiggling my ears, I can make my scalp move backward and forward. Boo boo da de dum, love in bloom. By closing my eyes and pressing on them with my hands, I can see lots of different flashing lights and patterns. My house phone buzzes. It's Toni, what am I doing? I tell her I am pressing my eyes to see flashing lights. She doesn't understand. I tell her not to worry, neither can I. Do I want to come up and order tea in her room? Before she can put the phone down, I'm tapping on her door.

She's in the middle of her mending. 'We have nice tea, eh, Terr-ee?' Yes, but first embrace her and give her a head-swirling kiss. No, no, Terr-ee, not now. She orders tea and sandwiches. A very old waiter with watery blue eyes and a red nose brings in the tray and shakily puts it down. For his trouble, Toni gives him a tip.

He groaned '*Danke, Fräulein*' and went out – to die, I think.

The sandwiches are cut in small triangles, ten of them make one sandwich. I wolf down what I think is the requisite amount to stall hunger.

'Terr-ee, you eat lot of food but you always thin.'

'Yes, I am thin.'

'You must have some, how you say, *tonica*?'

Tonic, yes, I've tried it. I drank Horlicks and Sanatogen but nothing happened except the price of their shares went up. She feels my arm and shakes her head as if the sleeve is empty, which it nearly is. After tea I try to – but, no, no, Toni has more mending to do. I must leave without it.

It's not long to departure for the show-time. I seek out Bornheim, who has been trying to massage his shoes into a more pliable state. Sitting there on a magnificent four-poster bed with tapestry swags, massaging dubbin into his shoes is a culture shock. Have I heard? Lieutenant Priest has bought a radio! Great, must borrow it, I'm desperate to hear some jazz. I dash up to his room: yes, I can borrow it, but not just now – he's listening in for football results from the BBC General Forces programme. General Forces? Never heard of him. Priest says I can borrow it tonight. Great, I know from the *Union Jack* that there's Duke Ellington at half-ten tonight – just about the time we get back, goody! The thought of hearing Ellington was so exciting. In those days, was I that simple?

The last night, full house again – show goes extremely well. There is an after-the-show drink on stage with Lieutenant Priest. Chalky White and his helpers are starting to dismantle the set and load it on to lorries. Back to the hotel. It's half-past ten, I borrow Priest's little radio and take it to my room. Bornheim and Mulgrew join me. We sit and smoke as the programme is announced. 'A Date with the Duke,' says the announcer to the strains of 'The "A" Train'. I can't remember now the tunes he played after that, but it went on till eleven-thirty when the station closed down. I have missed dinner; I go down and inquire if there's anything to eat. Ahggggggggggg, Cold Collation!

PADUA YET AGAIN

PADUA YET AGAIN

The long journey back starts. We all board the Charabong at nine o'clock. Our destination is Rome, nearly nine hundred miles away. We will be staging tonight at Padua. It's going to be a long haul; none of us are looking forward to it. When we arrive in Rome, we are to do another week of the show at the Argentina Theatre. Toni says if I like, I can stay part of the time at her home in the Via Appennini.

We are now watching all the ground we travelled in reverse. There are occasional reminders of the war – the burnt-out tank or an abandoned artillery piece, fading military signs, DUST MEANS DEATH.

We journey throughout the day. As we travel south to a lower altitude, the weather gets warmer. Spirits are kept up by Hall and myself playing some jazz. Our Italians sing native songs and in between we talk in bursts, then sit silent. Some doze. By one o'clock, we are on the outskirts of Trieste. We pull over to the verge near a ruined castle. The sandwiches are distributed. Made back at the hotel, they are still these tiny triangular things. The lunch over, I and Toni explore the castle. Built of monumental stone blocks it is very haunting. Near the keep is a hole in the ground that I recognize as the oubliette. 'What is oubliette, Terr-ee?' I explain it means forget in French. This is where they dropped prisoners that were to be forgotten. Nasty! I wonder when archers last stood at these cruciform slits in the wall. All life would have been here: feasting, romance, battles, intrigue. What happened? Who was the last person to leave this place, and why? So many questions and no answers.

'Oi,' Priest is calling us from below. 'You two lovebirds come on down. We're leaving.'

We scramble back into the Charabong and take our customary seats.

'Wot you two been doin' up the castle, eh?' says Bill Hall, full of innuendo, and I think 'shit!'

We drive off into the city of Trieste. It's still got partisans walking round the streets. We see one or two agitators addressing a crowd. They are red in the face and gesticulating wildly.

'I don't know what they see in Communism,' says Hall. 'After all those bloody long-faced Russians we saw in Vienna, 'oo wants to be a Commie?'

'Ah,' says Mulgrew, 'they did laugh at our act.'

'Oh, yes,' said Hall, 'but they were generals. They can bloody well afford to laugh.'

Off they go on the merits of Communism. Both retire unbowed with Communism still safe in Russia.

'Oh, Terr-ee, it takes so long,' complains Toni about the journey. It is hot and dusty and I'm bloody bored as well. I give her hand a squeeze and give her an understanding smile, which is a lot of bloody help.

Toni has fallen asleep on my shoulder. All the morning exuberance has gone. Window-gazing, I take in the Italian countryside. I wonder what happened to my battery. It is, I know, somewhere in Holland. I wonder if they think of me. Do Harry Edgington, Alf Fildes and Doug Kidgell still play together, I wonder. I miss them; I miss playing in the band, I miss my pre-war days. What a convulsion in my life Hitler has caused. Mind you, it seemed to be for the better. Only time would tell.

Oh, Christ, this is all we need. We are slowing down as the radiator is boiling. We stop. With a rag, Luigi gingerly removes the radiator cap and lets forth a great gusher of steam. It was something I wished I could do when I got steamed up about Toni. Priest assures us it's not serious: 'We'll just have to wait till she cools down.' Meanwhile, Luigi has run across the road to some peasant's house and borrowed a bucket of water which he proceeds to pour over the radiator. He is obliterated in clouds of steam.

'For his next trick,' says Bornheim, 'he will appear as Ben Hur.'

We take the opportunity to get out and stretch our legs. It's now evening and much cooler. A rough calculation tells us we have another four hours to Padua. Luigi continues to pour buckets of cold water over the radiator. After about half an hour, which seemed like eternity, we are off again.

'Keep yer fingers crossed,' says Lieutenant Priest as we start.

The long journey continues with a fresh burst of energy from the Italians, who give off with a few Italian marching songs, including the banned 'Giovinezza' a Fascist hymn; then a long silence; then, without warning, Bill Hall sings:

> What is a dill doll, daddy,
> Said my little daughter aged nine.
> A dill doll, my chick,
> Is a property prick
> Six times the size of mine.
> Your mother bought one for Christmas,
> Straight off the Christmas tree.
> She's used it but twice,
> She's found it so nice,
> She's no bloody use for me.

All together! Those of us who knew it gave it another chorus. Not for a moment do the Italians know what we are on about (I was on about ten pounds a week).

'What this song?' says Toni. 'Why you laugh?' I have not the courage to tell her. 'Ah,' she suspects, 'it is something *cattivo*, yes?' Yes, it's *molto cattivo*.

This last effort, however, was the last effort during the trip. It's dark now and we've lapsed into silence. A great full moon appears on the skyline, looking – at this level – very big and the colour of custard. Finally we pass the city sign 'Padua 3 chilometri'. Thank God! We all give a cheer.

Toni wakes up, 'What's the cheering for?'

'It's for Padua, they are cheering Padua.'

At eight of the clock, our Charabong lurches to a halt outside the Leone Bianco and we wearily de-bus. All I want is a bath, some dinner and bed – preferably with Toni. We are all allocated to our rooms. By coincidence, I have the same one as previously. The hotel is pretty empty so we all have a room on our own. Ahhhh! I exclaim, as I dip myself into a hot bath. I had taken many baths in my time and this was one of them. Ahhhh! The bath has a shower attachment. The shower rose is in the shape of a blossom. People say a shower is cleaner than a bath – wrong! I turn this one on. The shower rose falls off and hits me square on the head. A lump appears on my head. I had had many lumps in my time and this was one of them. Dressing at speed, I hasten down to the dining-room, where everyone is tucking in. I order a double portion of spaghetti Neapolitan. In no time I had caught up with the rest of them, passed them and gone into the lead.

Bornheim is ogling a waitress. 'Cor, look at that,' he says, as a nubile waitress, all boobs and bum, passes the table, sending out coded sexual vibrations in all directions. I had seen many coded sexual vibrations in my time and these were some of them.

Everyone is travel-weary; most go up to their rooms. Toni and I finish off a coffee. 'Oh good,' she says, 'tomorrow Roma! *Grazie a Dio*.' Yes, I can, if I wish, stay with her at her mother's flat. But I realize that Toni won't be as available under Mother's eagle eye, so I give her a loose yes. When we get desperate, we can retire to the hotel as a second line of defence. So it's to bed. Ah, bed! It was not long before I was in the arms of the angel of sleep. Please don't drop me, dear.

ROME AGAIN

ROME AGAIN

I am awakened by the waitress and her morning tea trolley. 'Ah gratzia, signorina,' I say, as she pours the steaming liquid into my cup.

'*Piacere*,' she coos. She and her Chivers jelly bottom exit.

I sit up, sipping my tea. It's another bright day. Blast! My great gold obscene watch has stopped. I phone the porter. '*Scusi, che ora sono?*' It's otto o'clock, one hour to departure. A quick wash and shave with a very blunt razor that gives me a very blunt face – the beard isn't cut, it's pulled out hair by hair. My skin is a series of sore blotches.

I meet Toni at breakfast. Yes, she slept well. That's that out of the way. I eat my brioche and that's that out of the way. Lieutenant Priest leans over our table, how are we, did we sleep well? Yes, we both slept well. He also slept well – God, this is exciting news! Does he know anybody else who has slept well? We'd like to congratulate them.

The Charabong awaits. We board the bus, saying Buon Giorno to Luigi. Faithful Luigi has been to early Mass at St Anthony's and prayed for the success of the journey, and I wonder – as he didn't invent them – does God know about charabongs? That's the best part of the Catholic religion: you can pray for anything, your overdraft, the death of your mother-in-law, money. My prayers to be leader of a bit band had never materialized. I'd say God was deaf.

We have only travelled a kilometre outside Padua when there is a hold-up. Ahead, there has been an accident: two lorries have collided – one is a lorry containing chickens and now lies on its side, blocking the road. The two drivers are shouting at each other and gesticulating. Add to this a hundred chickens clucking. Some of their cages have broken open and chickens are running around, pecking by the road side or perching on the side of the lorry. A black mongrel dog has joined in and is chasing the chickens into the middle distance. It was chaos as a police patrol arrived and joined in the shouting.

Luigi backs up, turns round and finds another route.

'Why do Eyeties shout so bloody loud?' says Bill Hall.

'It's because they've slept well,' I said.

'What are you talking about?'

'I'm talking about twenty words a minute, which is the going rate.'

'The nearer the equator you are, the more hot-blooded,' says Professor Bornheim. 'In fact, people living *on* the equator actually explode.'

At the front of the coach, Tiola Silenzi and her husband Fulvio have been coaxed into singing a duet. They give us 'La Paloma'. Lovely, pure *bel canto* singing. They are warmly applauded for their efforts and nobody exploded.

Toni and I sit holding hands. Every now and then, we look at each other and grin. This is called looking without exposing the teeth.

Time for a British response to the Italians. 'Come on, Ricky,' says Lieutenant Priest, 'lead the singing or get off.'

Soon we are all singing 'You Are My Sunshine', 'We'll Meet Again', 'Blue Birds Over the White Cliffs of Dover'. This is followed by a short concert of jazz by Milligan and Hall. The Italians are mad about La Jazz. So pass the morning hours.

We stage on the sea at Riccione. We sit on the beach and eat our sandwiches, but are plagued by horseflies. Bornheim takes a delight in killing them with a rolled-up copy of the *Union Jack*. 'That's five of the buggers so far,' he boasts. Our costumes are all in our luggage, so no swim; but trousers-rolled-up paddling is being indulged in by a few of the more daring spirits. The sun is gloriously warm as I lie back on the sand with my eyes closed. A pleasant breeze is blowing from the Adriatic, a horsefly gets me on the ear. I lash out, miss him but nearly render myself unconscious. Why bite me? I'm not a horse.

'Number eight,' says Bornheim, gleefully flicking a corpse off his hand.

Mulgrew is up to his shins in the sea, occasionally throwing a flat pebble which skims the shining surface. What is it about the sea? It calls us all. Is it a prehistoric instinct? Were we once creatures from the sea? If you put a baby on the beach, it will instinctively crawl towards the water. Strange, eh?

On, on to Rome. We heave ourselves free of the beach and board the now very dusty Charabong. As we drive, Hall, Mulgrew and Bornheim play a game. Each one in turn has to sleep with the next living thing they see on the road. Hall gets a pretty village girl, Mulgrew gets an old toothless dear and Bornheim gets a horse. They soon tire of this and Hall produces his violin and plays Italian melodies. The Italians join in. I know this all may sound repetitive, but that's how it was. We were *all* very repetitive.

We are now in Tuscany: on our left the sea, on the right numerous vineyards, all looking uniform, neat and tidy, all heavy with grapes awaiting the gathering. I was reminded of Omar Khayyám's 'I wonder what the vintner buys, with stuff half as precious as that which they sell'. In another life, I would like to have been a vintner.

We are climbing into hilly country. It is getting overcast and so are we. Soon it starts to rain. 'This will do the garden good,' said Bornheim. I borrow his *Union Jack* newspaper. What was happening in the world apart from this tour?

Herbert Morrison promises full employment for many years ahead

Spanish Frontier Sealed

RUSSIA ASKS AMERICA FOR BIG LOAN

Nuremberg Defence Opening Delayed

Ah, here is the best one,

HITLER'S EX-SECRETARY ARRESTED

the copy reads. She is said to have lost none of her fanaticism for the Nazi cause and prays nightly beneath a picture of Hitler who, like God, appears to be deaf. Ah, a funny one: a blood donor in Australia had so much alcohol in his blood that the recipient got pissed. So, all that is going on in the world! What a jolly place it is.

The rain leaves off. Through the afternoon, we are getting travel-numb and I might say traveller's bum – there's a limit to how long a bum can be sat on. After three hours, there are cries of distress – people want to relieve themselves. Luigi pulls over by a wooded verge. The ladies disappear into the trees to the left and the men to the right, and never the twain shall meet. 'I think that I shall never see,' says Bornheim, 'A poem lovely as a tree.' So saying, he lets go against one. The floodgates are opened and we all return with satisfied smirks. (Are your smirks satisfied, dear reader?)

At Farno, we leave the sea and travel inland – two hundred miles to go. 'It's too bloody long,' complains Hall. 'We should have stayed at Riccione for the night.' For once we all agree with Hall. What a strange man he was: he looked permanently unshaven, he was six foot tall and even thinner than me. If anyone has seen an illustration of Paganini, then this man had the same deep-set burning eyes. I think he also had burning arms and legs. He was the epitome of the English eccentric. Why, why wouldn't he ever send his underpants and socks to the laundry? He would never say.

'I'll tell you why,' said Mulgrew. 'If he sent 'em to a laundry, they'd send them to a solicitor.'

'Anyone like a sweet?' says Lieutenant Priest, handing around a bag of bull's-eyes. Ah! My childhood favourite, black with thin white stripes. I used to wonder how they made the stripes. To this day, I don't know.

Ah! Luigi is slowing down, he's stopping for petrol! God, how exciting! We needed this to keep our morale up. Some of us get off. The petrol station sells bits and pieces. I buy a packet of nuts of unknown origin. I give some to Toni. They taste like almond-flavoured cardboard. *'Che bruto,'* she says, spitting them out. So did anybody want to buy a packet of carboard nuts? Only eaten once, must sell, owner going abroad. Toni wants to sleep. I put my arm around her and she drops off. I stick it until my arm goes numb. Wake up, Toni, it's arm back time. My circulation is worse than *Blackwood's Magazine.*

We are travelling through great vistas of farming land. They are still ploughing with great white oxen like the cattle we see on Roman statuary. It seems a timeless land – at places there are no signs of the twentieth century except our Charabong. It's like a journey through a time capsule. I light up cigarette number upteen.

'Ah, ah,' says Mulgrew, 'don't put them back.' He takes one with a sweet, forced smile.

'You're not out of them *again*,' I say.

''Tis better to give than receive,' he says, making the sign of an invisible cross.

Poor Johnny, one day this appalling habit would kill him.

John Angove, seated at the front, wobbles to the back of the coach. 'Anything exciting happening this end?' he said.

'No,' says Bornheim. 'Try the middle.'

Angove shrugs his shoulders, 'I'm bored to death.'

'It's no good you coming up here and moaning about being bored to death,' I said. 'If you must know, at this end we've been bored to death and then bored back to life again.'

163

Putting on a Groucho Marx demeanour, I added, 'So think youself lucky my man. When I was your age, I was seven, and, another thing, goodbye.'

Toni had never heard of Groucho Marx, but then she's never heard of Brockley SE 26! I have to explain what the Marx Brothers are like. It wasn't easy, it was like trying to convince Quasimodo that he ought to enter for the pole vault. I explain that Groucho always walks with his knees bent. 'Why?' says Toni. Why? For no reason at all, *that's* why! I'll say this, she *tried* to understand.

So we rumble on. By eight that night, we enter the northern suburbs of Rome down the Via Flamania. We all give a groan of relief, the Italians bravely strike up a song and Luigi pulls up outside the Albergo Universo. It's not over yet. There's the unloading of the baggage by two little porters and we all register at reception. And there is the lesbian manageress. 'Ahh, Terr-ee,' she says and seemed genuinely pleased to see me.

'Before we all break up,' announces Priest, 'the show is tomorrow at 7.30 p.m. Coach leaves here at 6 p.m. prompt – Bill Hall, please note.'

I'm in a room with Mulgrew again. He dumps his kit on the bed and hurries out for a drink in the vino bar next door. Would I like to join him, as he hasn't much money? Swine. OK, I'll be down when I've settled in. I lay out my clean pyjamas (laundered in Vienna) on the bed, then a quick wash, then to the vino bar to meet Mulgrew who is ahead by a couple of glasses. 'You're just in time,' he says, 'I've run out of money.' Wine is cheap, a few lire a glass, so Mulgrew and I down about four each and we go back for dinner. Toni and Marisa are at a table when we join them. Toni doesn't like me drinking.

She waves a finger at Mulgrew, 'You teach Terr-ee drink like you, you *cattivo* Johnny,' she says like a schoolmarm.

Mulgrew is totally bemused. 'Just hark at her,' he says.

I'm hungry and looking forward to my dinner and backwards to the trip (Eh?): minestrone, then lasagne washed down with Chianti. Great, that's better. I feel strong enough to go to sleep on my own. Tomorrow, Toni wants to take me to have lunch at her mother's flat. Fine, OK. I take Toni up to her room. Curses, she's sharing with Luciana, so it's a kiss goodnight and back to bed. Mulgrew has gone back to the vino bar having borrowed money off me. Still, he always pays me back. You have to take him by the throat, but he always pays back. So, I can enjoy the luxury of clean pyjamas. I take a quick bath and then don them. I love the smell of freshly laundered clothes. I read my Brontë book for a while and then drop off to sleep. At some time I distantly hear Mulgrew come in and racket around the room. He is humming a tune broken only by a smoker's cough. There's very little difference between the two.

Morning comes bright and sunny. Mulgrew and I lie in bed smoking.

'What you doing today?' he says. I tell him I think I'm having lunch with Toni and her mother. 'Getting your feet under the table, eh?'

'It's not like that. I have been genuinely accepted into the family, I am a *persona grata*.'

At this, he guffaws. There's no winning with him.

I must look my best for the lunch. I put aside my khaki travelling clothes and lay out my blue ensemble. I borrow a fresh razor blade from Mulgrew. It's strange, in those days people lent freely – soap, cigarettes, money. What happened, then? I shave very carefully, avoiding any nicks or cuts, have a shower, first testing the shower rose. I dress as far as shirt, trousers and tie, then Brylcreem my hair, all the while watched by the bemused Mulgrew. 'You're looking loverly, darling,' he says. And, though I say it, I was looking lovely. God, I've only got fifteen minutes to have breakfast. I dash downstairs to the dining-room. No Toni. I order toast and jam and tea. Still no Toni. I ask John Angove where she is. She had breakfast earlier; also, Lieutenant Priest has some mail for me. Lovely! I find Lieutenant Priest in the foyer. He is phoning Naples HQ. Still engaged on the phone he hands me two letters and a small parcel. I can tell by the over-cautious wrapping and endless knotted string that it is from my mother. As to the contents, it's marked socks. In the bedroom, I eagerly unwrap it. It contains chocolate, cigarettes and pile suppositories. Ah, how sweet, something for each orifice. The letters are from my mother and ex-girlfriend, Lily Dunford of 45 Revlon Road, Brockley SE 26. Mother harps on about not forgetting to go to church. She thanks me for the photo of Toni that I sent her, but feels she would rather have had a medical report. Don't forget to put paper on the toilet seat. If I can't, do it standing up, etc. Lily Dunford's letter is really just a progress report on her life. The man she had ditched me for had left her. But for Toni, I might have made it back with her again. Too late, 'the bird has flown and has but a little way to fly' (Omar Khayyám).

I break open the chocolate bar, giving some to Mulgrew. 'Fruit and Nut,' he mutters, 'my favourite.' But then, if it was free, *anything* was favourite with him. What is he going to do today? If he can get an advance of wages he'll go the vino bar and then the Alexander Club. Then? Then back to the vino bar.

I buzz Toni on the interphone. 'Good morning, Toni, *buon giorno*,' what time are we going to Mother's? *Mezzogiorno*. Good, that gives me time for a job long overdue – the cleaning of my trumpet and guitar. I dismantle the trumpet and run hot water through it. I dry and polish the valves, re-oil them and put them back in the cylinders. A general overall polish and that's that. The guitar, I give a thorough polishing and a set of new strings. What a busy little bee I am. Midday and Toni, all shining and new, is waiting in the foyer. We stroll out and flag down an ancient Fiat taxi. Toni gives him the address and we sit back and watch Rome flash by. It's a city of unending interest. We pass the great piazzas with their vibrant gushing fountains, the Colosseum, the National Monument, then into the suburbs.

Via Appennini is on a slight slope. The taxi stops at 53 but starts to roll back as his brakes are dodgy, so we have to leap out at the run. Mrs Fontana is at the window looking out for us. Gioia, the maid, opens the door, is all blushes and embarrassment.

Toni's mother greets us. 'Ah, Terr-ee, *come sta*?' I am *sta beni* and running out of Italian.

We are seated in the lounge where we are joined by her sister Lily. 'Ah, Terr-ee, *come sta*?' I am still *sta beni*.

Soon I am lost to view as Toni and her mother exchange all their news. I can understand bits of the conversation with words like, *si, no, buona*. Now and then Toni translates bits concerning me. Rather like discussing the dog with an occasional 'Good boy' and a pat on the head. Lily speaks broken English. She wants to come to the show. Neither she nor her mother have seen it. I promise two tickets. Toni's mother works in an Italian tourist agency called CIT which, when pronounced, sounds like shit. Lily works as a secretary and between the three of them they earn enough to live modestly well.

It's a splendid lunch: spaghetti then chicken liver risotto with white wine. Mrs Fontana asks about my family. I explain my brother is still in the Army and *almost* an officer. My father is in Fleet Street and *was* an officer. Only my mother has never been an officer. I plug the fact that my mother is a very good Catholic. This is well received as Mrs Fontana is herself a good Catholic. As yet, I haven't told her I am a bloody awful Catholic. When do I want to come and stay? Is tomorrow all right, *domani*? *Si si buona allora domani*.

Toni and I taxi back to the hotel. I want to write some letters, so retire to my room. I dash one off to Mother and another for Lily Dunford. I tell my mother that not only am I putting paper on the seat but, just in case, I do it standing up. Dear Lily Dunford, I commiserate with her over the loss of her husband (HA HA HA). After carrying the torch for her for nearly nine years, like an evil swine I felt some measure of revenge. I didn't tell her I was in love again, but said perhaps we could meet when I came back to London and see what happened. Good luck (HA HA HA). Yes, revenge is sweet but not fattening.

Maria Marini from Vol. 5 has turned up! I can't quite recall how she knew I was in Rome, but she did. I supply her with two seats for the show. Will I see her after? Yes, for a little while. Can I come home with her so she can be like 'A waf to you'? (See Vol. 5, p. 138 or ring the police.) So that I'm not trapped, I tell Toni about Maria and explain that we are 'just good friends from the waist up'. She accepts my story, but after my Vienna episode she is a little bit suspicious and, for that matter, so am I.

First night at the Teatro Argentina: very good show and a great first-night audience. Feel very good, feel lively, feel Toni. I'm healthy with lire, so I ask her if she'd like to go out to dinner. Yes, she knows a place I would like. Great. We grab a taxi with a driver who sings all the way, badly. The restaurant is the Trattoria San Carlo. It is small, bustling with waiters and pretty full. Nevertheless, we get a table in a corner near the resident accordion player. He plays, very *sostenuto*, Italian favourites.

'*Che desidera signore?*' says an *allegro* waiter.

I'm desperate for a drink to bring me down from my post-show 'high'. '*Una bottiglia di Orvieto abboccata, per favore,*' I say in ill-pronounced Italian.

It's to be a lovey-dovey evening. It's difficult for us two to be alone like this; now we are, and it's beautiful.

'You lak it here, Terr-ee?'

Yes, *si, si*, it's lovely and you are lovelier.

We spend a lot of time looking at each other. I won't try to describe the feeling in detail, but it caused vibration of the Swonnicles. *Allegro* waiter pours the wine. Toni and I touch glasses. All is sweetness and light. As I spill some down my shirt, in a flash the *allegro* waiter is at my side with a napkin. Toni giggles as he helps me mop up. We sit drinking, enjoying the music and the ambience. At this time of night Rome comes alive and takes you with it.

Time to order: I'm a sucker for it, spaghetti Neapolitan please! Chicken à la romane for Toni. This latter is baked in clay, the mould broken open at your table. 'You try,' she says, passing a piece on her fork. Mmmmm, delicious, but it can't seduce me from my spaghetti. Paradise would be to be buried under a mound of spaghetti, having to eat my way out. Toni complains, 'You eat much food but you never get like fat.' Who do I take after, my mother or father? For piles, I take after my father; for thinness, it's my mother. My mother has legs thinner than Gandhi. If my mother stands with her legs together, it looks like one normal leg.

I've had four glasses of wine and am feeling good. God, I fancy Toni like mad. Oh, for a room at the Grand, Brighton! I tell Toni, 'I want you very much.'

She gives a small understanding smile, which doesn't give any relief. 'Not possible, Terr-ee.'

There is the last resort, a secret knee-trembler – but no, I couldn't introduce her to that. That was for taller women. Of course, there was always the orange box. No! These were all sexual fantasies. I don't want the evening to end, but end it does and we take a taxi back to Albergo Universo. It's one o'clock. 'Good morning,' I say, as I kiss her goodnight.

Mulgrew is still awake. 'Did you get it?'

'Oh, Mulgrew, must you?'

'Yes, I must keep a check on the state of play.'

I undress, still with a warm glow from the evening with Toni.

'You know, I'm a better size for Toni,' says Mulgrew.

'What do you mean, better size?'

'I'm the right height.'

'Height? You haven't got any, you're doomed to be a short-arse.'

'Listen, Napoleon was short.'

'Napoleon never went short. There was Josephine for a start.'

'Well, he had to start somewhere.' Mulgrew giggles reflectively. 'He must have looked funny with his clothes off.'

It was a thought. Mind you, most of us look funny with our clothes off.

'Could he have conducted his battles nude?' said Mulgrew.

'Not unless he wore his sideways hat.' I pull the covers over me and turn off the light. 'Goodnight, Johnny.'

Another day in my life had ended. It was all going by so quick, but it was in the main very enjoyable. I didn't know it but these were to be among the most memorable days.

We awake to another sunny Roman morning. We mustn't waste the day. Johnny and I confer – the zoo, that's it we'd all go to the zoo. Is Toni interested? I buzz her room. Yes, she'd love to go to the zoo. She loves me and my beautiful eyes and can Luciana come to? Why, is she unconcious? O K then, *dopo prima colazione*. We all wear our khaki, messing-about clothes. After breakfast we meet in the foyer.

'Morning, Spike,' says Lieutenant Priest. 'Where did you disappear to last night?'

'Toni and I dined out.'

'Somewhere nice?'

'Yes.'

Then he lost interest. He is phoning CSE HQ Napoli. They want to know when I am returning to the UK, as they have to book my passage back. To date, I haven't made up my mind. I must give them a month's warning. O K. What's this noise I hear approaching, screaming, chattering and blowing raspberries? God, it's Secombe. It's a new show booking in. In his high-pitched nasal voice, he greets me with a rapid gabble. 'Hello Spike, hey ho hupla raspberry.' He dashes off to reception to baffle the receptionist with chattering, screaming and blowing raspberries. Norman Vaughan comes in; he's with Secombe in a new show. Forty years on, I can't for the life of me remember the name of the show; neither can Vaughan or Harry Secombe.

The zoo party assemble. We take a taxi. '*Giardino Zoologicao*,' we tell him and we lurch off. The taxi is like someone after a curry , prone to backfiring. At each explosion, we all give out an 'O H'. The driver is not amused. He crouches over the wheel while we do every bit of twenty-five miles an hour.

The Rome zoo is set in splendid gardens, with numerous flowerbeds all in summer bloom with a prolificacy of roses that leave a strong bouquet in the summer air. We wander through the cages, watching creatures which have been torn from their native land and imprisoned. In those days my conscience wasn't as awake as it is today and I enjoyed the sight of wild animals at close range.

We pass an ice-cream kiosk and buy four cornets, '*Quattro gelati*'. In a leisurely fashion we stroll, all immersed in licking our ice-creams like schoolkids.

In the chimpanzee cage, there are about a dozen specimens. We are witness to what Mulgrew finds hysterically funny. A male chimp is trying to screw a female, but two other jealous males are trying to stop him by hitting him. The chimp continues banging away under a rain of blows. 'My God,' says Mulgrew, 'I hope I never want it that bad.' The two girls haven't said anything but are convulsed with laughter, as are other spectators. They don't write shows like that any more.

Would anyone like a ride on the Indian elephant? Yes, four of us climb up to the mounting platform and get into the wicker howdah. It seems to sway perilously as the beast moves off. The girls scream with enjoyment. The driver asks Johnny and me to extinguish our cigarettes. I suppose travelling on a non-smoking elephant was a first. The elephant waddles on a circular route; the driver calls out instructions. Mulgrew wants to know how an Indian elephant understands Italian.

'Sitting on an elephant makes you look taller, Mulgrew.'

He agrees, he must get one when he gets back to Scotland. He tells me his father once owned an elephant hunting dog. When people inquired how it killed an elephant, he said 'He waits.' What do you mean he waits, they asked. 'Well,' he said, 'they got to die sometimes.'

I took a few photographs. Alas, over the passage of time they all got lost, except these two of Mulgrew and Luciana, me and Toni.

'Ah ha,' says Mulgrew as we reach the boa constrictor cage. 'Here's a good present for mother-in-laws.' Toni shudders at the sight of the thirty-foot-long creature. 'Just think,' says Mulgrew, 'there's thirty pairs of shoes there.' It's feeding-time and the keeper releases a live white rabbit into the cage. Before the grisly meal starts, we move on – into the cool of the aquarium, with its light diffused through the fish tanks.

'I like this,' says Toni, putting her face close to the glass of the octopus cage. 'Ah yes,' she realizes the meaning of the name, 'eight leg, yes?' Yes, Toni. Really, it only needs two. The rest are spares, I suppose. We watch as the octopus changes colours – it's a miracle, and those human eyes! The piranha are being fed! They attack the food like bullets from a gun. Several attack the same piece of food until it vanishes.

'*Che barbaro*,' says Luciana, putting her hand over her mouth.

In the carp tank, the keeper holds the food above the water line and they take from his hand – some hang on, and are lifted out of the water. 'What a turn on,' says Mulgrew.

So, on through the afternoon. Towards evening we seek relief for aching feet at the restaurant. We sit outside. What would we all like? Cold drink? Yes yes yes, four lemonades please. No no no, Mulgrew wants a red wine. Bacchus to the rescue. The girls chatter away in Italian. 'I think we've all had enough zoo, don't you?' says Mulgrew. Yes, agreed, so it's to the taxi rank and the journey back through rush-hour traffic. The noise! Italian drivers seem to live with their hands on the horn, plus they shout for the most trivial of reasons.

Luciana and Johnny at the Rome zoo

Spike and Toni in the zoological gardens, Rome, where the Pope lives

'I should say this is coronary country,' I said.

'*Che significa?*' says Luciana. I have to mime a heart attack. 'Ah, *capito*,' she says with a smile.

It was a bit embarrassing as, during my dramatic mime, the driver was watching me in his driving mirror and must have wondered.

We arrive, and it's Mulgrew to pay the fare and he mimes a heart attack. Unlocking his wallet, he pays with money that hasn't seen the light of day for months. He groans as the driver gives him change, he tips the taxi driver and *he* groans.

I return to my room to find a form with a note from Priest. It's for an application for a British passport which I need for return to the UK. I supposed at the end of this trip we'd call it a day in Italy, like Wednesday. Bill Hall, Johnny Mulgrew and I had discussed it and thought that, with the offer from Astor, the impresario in London and judging by the reaction of troop audiences, fame would soon be ours. But we were living in a cocoon of self-delusion. Italians also liked our act, but they had been denied jazz and were wildy enthusiastic about it now that it was being released into their society. So, then, what were my plans? First I would like to go somewhere alone with Toni for a holiday. The tour was to end in Rome and I was to be transported to Naples to live in the CSE hotel in the Vuomero until my ship sailed. That was as far ahead in my life as I could plan. Secombe, in between screaming, chattering and blowing raspberries, told me he would be released from the services in September when he hoped to audition for the Windmill Theatre in London.

I fill in the passport form, answer all the boring questions – is your father British, is your mother British, are you British, are your legs British, is your suit British, where was I born, etc., etc., etc. – and return it to Lieutenant Priest. 'You'll need a passport photo,' he says, 'one of those that make you look like a criminal.' Don't they all?

Tonight is the night Maria Marini is coming. I must be on my guard against her implorations. The show over, she comes backstage and I entertain her and her friend to a glass of wine. She says when I came on first to sing with the quartet, all of us wearing nightshirts, she was able to recognize me by 'you eyes' despite my false moustache. What's this Italian women have about my eyes? I mean, there were other important bits! Do I want to come back to her place? I'm sorry, no. My place, then. I'm sorry, no. I have an eating appointment with a dinner. She is downcast, I try to upcast her. She writes her phone number: can I phone her when I'm free? *Si, si,* yes, etc. I still have the number in case things get tough.

The Charabong is waiting. 'Come on, Milligan,' says Priest. 'We're waiting for you.'

I take my seat next to Toni.

'You see you ladyfriend,' she says in a slightly cool voice.

'Yes, and we're just good friends.'

'You see her again?'

'No, no.'

This is followed by a silence, then, 'You tell me truth.'

Of course, the fact she has a beautiful face, lovely boobs, long shapely legs mean absolutely nothing to me, absolutely nothing!

'What you say to her?'

'Goodbye!'

Toni gives me a long cold stare; I realize what I need is a good solicitor. At dinner, she is friendlier. I tell her, 'You are the one I love, you understand?'

Yes, she understands. 'But I no like you to see other pretty girl.' I tell her I can't go around blindfold. She smiles, 'All right, but I little *gelosa*, how you say?'

'Jealous.'

'Yes, I jealous.' She eats a few more mouthfuls of food. 'But now I all right.'

Good, the heat is off.

'Toni, when the show is finish, you like to come on holiday with me on Capri?'

She is surprised and bemused. 'Capri?'

'Yes.'

'Me an' you on Capri?'

'Yes.'

She's never done anything like this before. Neither have I. Yes, but we mustn't tell her mother. That's fine as long as she doesn't tell mine!

MOTHER: (On the landing) Terry? What time do you call this, where have you been to at this time of night?

ME: The Isle of Capri, Mum.

Toni is over the moon at the news. The Isle of Capri! She's never been there. Where will we stay? Don't worry, I'll fix a place. I'm going to cash in my Post-war Credits and my Post Office Savings – a grand total of eighty-six pounds!!! Rich as

To .... *Mr. S. A. Milligan* Nov 1946
P FORM R.16

RELEASE.

POST OFFICE SAVINGS BANK ACCOUNT No. *FO 166197* .

1 The amount of War Gratuity and Post War Credit as shown below is being deposited in your name in the Post Office Savings Bank :—

		£	s.	d.
WAR GRATUITY (Note—The period of Release and Overseas leave does NOT count as service for the assessment of War Gratuity)	*77* months at *12/-* per month *W/BUR*	46	4	–
	Less deductions (brief particulars)			
POST WAR CREDITS DUE	Balance of War Gratuity due			
	From *1.1.42* to *30.6.46*	40	14	–
OTHER CREDITS				
TOTAL AMOUNT DEPOSITED IN POST OFFICE SAVINGS BANK		£86	18	–

King Creosote!!!! Eighty-six pounds! Why, that was nearly eighty-seven pounds! Me, who had never had more than ten pounds in my hands. Oh, God, was I really that innocent? Yes, I was; why didn't I stay that way . . .

That night I go to bed with my head full of dreams about Capri. I can't believe that little old me who worked in Woolwich Arsenal dockyard as a semi-skilled fitter, little old me with one fifty-shilling suit, a sports coat and flannels, can afford to go to Capri with an attractive Italian ballerina. Little old me! The furthest I'd been from Brockley was on a school day trip to Hernia Bay on a rainy day! The galling part was I had to thank Adolf Hitler for this dramatic change in my life.

A CONCENTRATION CAMP IN SIBERIA.
HITLER IS SHOVELLING SHIT AND SALT.

HITLER: You see? You fools? If you had kept me on, zen EVERYONE would be going to Capri, nein?

Johnny Mulgrew and Johnny Bornheim come into the room. They've been drinking at the vino bar next door and are very merry. 'Ah, look at the little darling, in bed already,' says Mulgrew. Bornheim has a bottle of red wine which he holds up in front of me with a grin. What the hell! OK, I'll have a glass. The three of us sit drinking and yarning. All of us are yearning for our tomorrows to mature; we are all suspended in an exciting but unreal life. We realize that this is a post-war world with people still mourning the death of sons and husbands, and we are a band of Merry Andrews with absolutely nothing to worry about. We drink again and again, and get more and more morose.

'I'm going to bed,' lisps Bornheim, 'before I start to cry.'

Mulgrew takes off trousers and shirt and in a short vest that *just* covers his wedding tackle, climbs into the pit and, before I am, he is asleep with a long snore in the key of G.

177

How do I know? Like my mother I have perfect pitch. Back home, if I dropped a fork on the floor with a clang, my mother would say what key it was in. Apparently, if I remember rightly, I was eating my breakfast in E flat. I drift off into sleep as Mulgrew changes key.

'Ah,' says Mulgrew to the morning, 'it's a beautiful day.'

'It's raining,' I say.

'Ah, yes, but today,' he pauses and sings in a false opera voice 'it's Payyyyyyyyyy dayyyyyyyyyy.'

I sing back, 'Sooooooo it isssss and if I remember you owe me one thousand lireeeeeeeeeeee.'

'Ohhhhhhhhhhhh, buggerrrrrrrrrrrr.' Mulgrew disappears into the W C. His voice comes wafting, 'What's all this paper on the seat?' I tell him it's against deadly diseases. I'm sorry I forgot to flush it away – how embarrassing! 'What do you think you're going to catch?' he says, straining to his task.

'Leprosy, Shankers and the Clap.'

'The Holy Trinity of Scotland,' he says still straining.

I leap from my bed in my blue pyjamas in which all the dye has run. I take a hot shower, singing all the while: 'When I sing my serenade, our big love scene will be played, boo boo da de da de dum.' I watch the water cascade down my body making it shine as though I had been varnished. I quickly turn the shower to cold, giving off screams of shock.

'Have you caught something?' strains Mulgrew.

'Yes. Pneumonia,' I scream and sing 'Pneumonia a Bird in a Gilded Cage'.

It's a good morning, we feel good. Mulgrew has his shit, shave and shampoo and we toddle down for breakfast. We meet Toni and Luciana on the stairs. *'Buon giorno, mio tesoro,'* I say to her. Today would we like to go to the Vatican? What a splendid idea. Who knows, we might see the Pope. 'Hello Pope,' I'll say, 'I'm a Catholic, too! Can I have a piece of the True Cross for my mother? And can you bless my Bing Crosby voice?' First, I visit our Lieutenant to draw my ten pounds wage which came to twelve thousand lire –

twelve *thousand*, it sounded so rich. Well set up, I meet Toni and we hail a taxi.

'Hail Taxi,' I call, doing the Hitler salute.

'Wot you do, Terr-ee?' says Toni, laughing.

'La Vaticino,' I tell the driver. My God, I'm speaking the lingo well.

Sitting back and holding hands, I can't resist a tender morning kiss. Oh, sentimental old me! Toni's lips are soft and velvety; mine are ever so slightly chapped, but she doesn't complain. It shows you what can be obtained with second-hand equipment. Where are we? We're on the Corso Vittorio Emanuele and about to cross the River Tiber. On the right riverbank is the great Castle San Angelo. On, to the Via Conciliazione which runs directly into the great St Peter's Square with its great semi-circular colonnade by Bernini. The whole place is teeming with visitors and numerous vendors of holy relics, pictures of Pope Pius, rosaries, etc. The taxi sets us down, and we walk up to the Sistine Chapel with the Swiss Guards outside in their blue and yellow uniforms designed by Michelangelo.

Now, dear reader, to try and describe the treasures on view would fill six volumes. I'm not going to put you to that expense – no, suffice it to say that there were so many master-pieces they made you giddy. I was moved by one particular piece: that was the Pietà by Michelangelo. It was like a song in stone. Toni and I wander round the great Basilica of St Peter's, totally overawed. All I can think of is that God is very, very rich. I don't think I've ever seen such a concentration of creative art. Toni keeps saying, '*Che fantastico*, Terr-ee.'

The morning passes and by lunchtime we've had enough. Outside, I decide to buy a rosary in a small container embossed with the image of Pope Pius. My mother will love it as it has apparently been blessed by the Pope. '*Benedetto dallo papa*,' says the lying vendor. What shall we do now, Toni? She would like to sit down. We walk back across the great square and just outside find a small coffee house where we order two small coffees. We sit outside. Tides of the faithful are going back and forth to the Vatican with a mixture of nuns and clerics in black hats and schoolchildren buzzing with excitement – it's THE VATICAN SHOW! Toni laments that we haven't seen the Pope.

'*Mi dispiace*,' she says, pulling a wry face.

Don't worry, dear, he didn't see us either and when you've seen one pope you've seen 'em all.

We discuss what to do when the show finally finishes on Saturday. Toni will, of course, stay at home; her mother can't understand why her daughter stays at a hotel when her home is in Rome. What will I do? Can I stay on? No, I have a better idea. We go back with the company, go to the Isle of Capri, spend a week there, then come back to Rome and stay until my ship sails. She agrees. There are a few problems, like how do I get my wages when I come back to Rome, but I'll try and fix that with the CSE cashier – that, or a bank robbery should suffice. I can always sell the rosary. I light up an after-tea cigarette. 'What it taste like?' says Toni. 'I like to try.' She takes a puff, starts coughing with eyes watering. 'How can you smoke like that thing? *Sono terribili*,' she splutters. Serves her right; cigarettes are man's work.

It's a very hot day and we decide to go back to the hotel. Again, we take a taxi. It's but a twenty-minute journey to the hotel. Once there, Toni wants to wash her hair. I retire to my bed and read Mrs Gaskell's book on the Brontës. What a family! All the children literally burn with creative talent. Oh, for just a day in their company. I have a siesta (that means sleeping in Italian) until tea-time when I am awakened by Scotland's gift to the world, Johnny Mulgrew, bass player extraordinary to the House of Johnnie Walker. He's been to the pictures: 'Saw a bloody awful film.' Oh? You interest me Mulgrew, what was this bloody awful film? Betty Grable and her legs in *The Dolly Sisters*. 'The dialogue was an insult to the intelligence,' he said, flopping on his bed. Insult to the intelligence, eh? I didn't know he'd taken that with him. Never, never take your intelligence to a Betty Grable movie. It's best viewed from the waist down. Had he been paid yet? Yes.

'Two thousand lire, please,' I said.

That hurts him, his Scottish soul is on the rack. He pulls the amount from his padlocked wallet and, with a look of anguish, hands me the money.

I buzz room service and order tea for myself and my Scottish banking friend. A blue-chinned waiter with a slight stoop brings it in. I give him a tip.

'How much you tip him?' says Mulgrew.

'Ten lire.'

Mulgrew groans. 'What a waste. That's five cigarettes.'

I pour him a tea and drink my Russian one.

'What's that taste like?' he says.

I tell him I never knew the real taste of tea until Toni got me on to lemon tea. Would he like a sip? No, he wouldn't. I like a man who knows his own mind.

I take some of my clothes to the washing lady and ask her to '*stirare*' (iron) them. She'll have them by tomorrow morning. She's a big, fat, voluble Italian lady who, you feel, would do anything for anybody. She smiles and nods her head – such dexterity! Coming up the stairs with his suit is one of our chorus boys, Teddy Grant. 'Ah, ha! Teddy, how's the romance with Greta Weingarten?' It's platonic; they're just good friends. As Teddy is gay, that makes sense – not much though. To me, it's an enigma.

Back in the room, I have a little practice on my guitar, trying to remember Eddy Lang's* solo 'April Kisses'. Mulgrew listens, then says it's one of the most mediocre renderings he's ever heard. I keep practising. At the end of an hour he says, 'It's the most mediocre rendering I've ever heard.' Never mind, I had it over him – *he* couldn't tell what key forks were in when they hit the ground.

The show that night is held up; the electric front curtain has fused. The stagehands try the manual lift, but that doesn't work either. However, suddenly, when the electrician is tinkering with the mechanism, it shoots up revealing the set and several stagehands who run off as though being seen on a stage meant instant death. Otherwise, the show runs as per

* Popular jazz guitarist of the twenties and thirties.

usual. In the dressing-room, the three of us discuss when we should be getting together in the UK to start our fabulous stage career. I tell them I won't be home until late October; Johnny isn't discharged until December, so we decide to start afresh in the New Year.

Jimmy Molloy comes round with a book of raffle tickets. It's for two bottles of scotch, ten lire a ticket. I take ten, Johnny takes one, Bill doesn't drink whisky – he's not interested. The draw is after the show in Molloy's dressing-room. At the appointed hour we all cram into his room. Luciana draws the tickets from a top hat. Mulgrew, with one measly ticket, wins! He is very generous. That night, after dinner, we gather in the lounge and he gives us all a measure – the toast is 'Scotland for ever'!! Toni wants to try some; she sips mine, has a coughing fit with watering eyes. Serves her right! Whisky is man's work.

It's my lucky night: Luciana is staying with her parents, so Toni is alone. We spend a lovely night together and the devil take the hindmost. Awake, for morning in a bowl of light has put the stars to flight! So I awake, with Toni still sleeping soundly. I dress quickly so she doesn't have to see my skinny body at such close range. Don't willies look silly in the morning light? I tippy-toe out, seeing no one sees me, and make my way back to my room.

'Good morning, little lover boy,' says Mulgrew in the middle of shaving; 'naughty, naughty, naughty,' wagging a finger like some old crone at the guillotine.

Soon my night of bliss will be all round the company. He tells me that Jimmy Molloy is holding housey-housey in the lounge at eleven o'clock. Right, I'll try me luck. After breakfast we all settle down with our little cards. It's twenty lire a go and there's about fifteen of us. Jimmy starts calling, 'Clickety click, sixty-six, Doctor's Orders, number nine, Legs Eleven, number eleven and another little dip.' I played until lunchtime and didn't win a bloody thing. Mulgrew comes down for the last round and wins five hundred lire! And, lo, he falleth in the shit and cometh up smelling of roses.

Toni missed breakfast and I missed Toni. She makes an appearance at lunchtime. There's a knowing look between us that echoes last night. 'I sleep so longgg,' she says; then, in a quieter voice, 'Oh, you terrible man, tsu, tsu tsu.' And then a wicked smile. She holds out her tiny hand and leads me like a lost sheep to the lunch table.

'You win money?' she says.

'No, I'm not lucky; I'm *never* lucky.'

I remembered that the last time I won anything was in Poona in the mid-twenties: I had drawn a horse called Brienz in a Derby sweepstake and won seventy-five rupees. I never forget the wondrous joy of having enough money to go and buy several boxes of lead soldiers in the Poona bazaar. What golden days they were, bursting with sun and quietude. Do I have any idea as to what to do this afternoon? Yes, Toni. I'm going to have a good night's sleep! After my night as Casanova, I was knackered. She gives me an impish smile then holds her hand over it, a peculiarity of hers. O K, will I phone her when I wake up? If I'm strong enough. I doze through the long hot afternoon, interrupted once by Mulgrew.

'Shagged out, eh?'

'Yes, Mulgrew. Shagged out.'

'I bet it's cleared all that custard off your chest,' he says.

Go away, Mulgrew, go a *long, long* way away. Go and play on a cliff edge. God, it was lovely last night – overlong, but lovely. Would it always be like this? If so, I must go on a course of vitamins. The sleep restores me to my normal febrile self; in future, I must do it less.

Enter a Bill Hall rampant on a field of khaki. 'You seen Mulgrew?'

'Yes.'

'Well, tell us where he is for Christ's sake.'

O K, for His sake, I think Mulgrew is in the wine bar next door, spending my hard-earned money. Hall lingers, then says, 'Can I borrow some fags?' How many? 'Have you got a packet?' I tell him no, the last time I caught a packet was in North Africa. Hall doesn't laugh at joke. I lend him a packet of twenty Passing Cloud. He's never seen this brand before and turns the packet round and round. 'Where you get these?' he says, taking one from the packet. My parents send them. 'I never see 'em before' and I'll never see them again. He takes one out and starts patting his pockets. ''Ave you got a match?' he says. Get on my back, Hall, and I'll carry you around. ''Ave you heard about Chalky White?' he says. No, I can't wait to hear. Chalky White has assaulted an Italian civilian and is in prison.

'That's a splendid setting for him,' I said.

Apparently, Lieutenant Priest is at the prison now with the man from the British Consulate, trying to get him released. With that exciting news, Hall, rampant on a field of khaki, is gone. I phone Toni: what is she doing? She is doing some mending. Do I need anything mended or buttons sewn? No, but my underpants need a transplant. Joke. She doesn't laugh at joke. No no no, I mustn't come up. It will distract her. What am I doing? I tell her, recovering. She'll see me in the Charabong. By Mulgrew's bed are a few well-worn magazines – *Titbits*, *Lilliput* and *Picture Post*. I thumb through them all; particularly poignant is a German doctor's description of conditions for war refugees in Europe. Even under Allied administration many are starving, people are still being moved around in cattle trucks. The doctor has attended the birth of a child to a starving woman. It made you realize the war wasn't over; a war is never over, there is just an interval. In *Lilliput*, there's a story referring to a death mask taken from a girl who committed suicide by drowning in the Seine. The amazing part of her death mask is that she is smiling. How do you do that when you are inhaling a river?

Towards show-time, I start to feel shivery. Am I sickening? Some people had said so. By the time the show was over that night I knew I had a temperature. I don't have any dinner; I take to my bed and douse myself with the magic medicine, aspirins. I start to sweat. Toni brings me up a hot cup of tea which I lace with Mulgrew's whisky.

'You wouldn't deny a sick man a nip,' I said.

'Not too much,' he cautions, 'it's bad for me.'

My temperature stays up. That night I'm a bit delirious and I sweat like a pig. Lieutenant Priest visits me.

'How are we this morning?'

'Well, this part of "we" feels bloody awful.'

'Have you got a temperature?'

'Yes.'

'Can you manage the show tonight?'

'No, but I can manage to stay in bed.'

'OK, we'll get Bornheim to dep. for you. I'll leave you to make a will,' he says grinning, and departs.

Through the day I doze and sweat. Toni ministers to me, bringing up hot soup and drinks.

'I hope to Christ it's nothing catching,' says Mulgrew.

'So do I,' I say with a fit of sneezing.

'That's it, spread it all round the bloody room.'

I was doing my best to.

That night my temperature goes up again and I feel like death. Alas, it's not forthcoming. Next day Priest says I should be in hospital. Oh, no, not that – not a military hospital with bedpans and bottles. Toni says she will get her doctor to come. At midday he arrives and does all the 'Say, ah', the listening to the chest, the back tapping to see if you're hollow. He presses his fingers into my stomach displacing my liver. Finally he gives me an injection in the bum. 'It bring you fever down,' translates Toni. I explain that I don't have fever in the bum. His fee is two thousand lire! I feel worse; I'm sickening for bankruptcy. I feel an overdraught coming under the door. I fall into a feverish sleep. When I awake, it's night-time. The room is dark; Mulgrew is snoring. I switch my bedside light on; it's 2 a.m. My temperature seems to be down. Has it gone to the bum? I get up to do a Jimmy, have a glass of water. Ridiculous, empty one end and fill up the other. Back to sleep.

By morning I am much improved. I get regular visitors; no, I'm not doing the show tonight, I am convalescing! Through the day my nurse Toni brings up drinks and snacks, which I nearly bring up, too. I'm still not cured. Do I want her doctor again? No, I say and am two thousand lire better off. Mulgrew tells me that when I was delirious, I was talking in my sleep. Did I say anything significant? 'Yes, you kept saying we must get to the woods before the trees get there.' Yes, that sounds like me.

I borrow Priest's radio and tune into the Allied Forces Network, Rome. What a treat! I lay back to a day's listening. There was Debroy Summers and the world's corniest band, 'Organ Parade' with Reginald Fort, 'Forces Favourites', 'String Along with Sandy Powell' (can you hear me, Mother?), then high notes and rupture with Richard Tauber, then cricket, Sussex vs. Essex, Joe Loss and his orchestra – he was the man who would give me my first stage break as a comic – then ITMA which, I am afraid, I didn't find funny (my humour was more Marx Brothers and W. C. Fields) and 'Parade for Swing' with Harry Parry and his Quintet. Occasionally, I'd switch to the BBC General Forces programme which gave long boring news bulletins telling us that the price of butter had gone up and that food rationing would continue for the time being. Poor bloody Britain! Here, in Italy, eat as much as you like; but win the war, and you are rationed! I was still enjoying the radio by the time people were back from the show. They were all laughing – apparently, Eddy Garvey, the lead trumpet player, had had a disaster. He was washing his false teeth in his dressing-room when he dropped them and broke them. The result was a trumpet player who was a disaster. The whole evening was full of cracked notes and bad intonation which, though it baffled the audience, had the cast in fits. He is now walking around with his face folded, uttering gummy oaths.

Toni rushes up to see me. ''Ow are you, my love?' she says. I tell her her love is better and will be up tomorrow night, knocking on her bedroom door. Is there anything I want? Yes, will she take her clothes off and get into bed for an hour's sabbatical. 'You much better,' she said with an impish grin.

So I was. Next morning I joined the human race again and was running last. I enjoyed my breakfast of boiled eggs. Two of them were being boiled and one said what a terrible life being boiled like this was. The other one said this is nothing, wait till you get out; they bash your bloody head in.

What shall we do this sunny but very windy day? We all settle to see the Colosseum. The four of us share a taxi – Mulgrew, Toni, Luciana and myself. The taxi drops us off in the shadow of the great edifice. We ascend the stairs to get to the top. It's a bit hairy with the wind blowing up the girls' skirts with constant double exposure of knickers. Other splendid views were the Great Arch of Constantine and the monument to the unknown soldier. He was possibly very well-known as a banker or a solicitor, but totally unknown as a soldier. The chambers beneath the floor of the Colosseum are exposed.

'It's hard to believe,' said Mulgrew, 'they actually threw living people to the lions here.'

'Yes,' I said, 'it kept the food bills down.'

The wind blows Mulgrew's hat off; he dashes after it.

'Che vento,' exclaims Toni.

Indeed, what a wind. If they thought this was bad they should have heard my father; he was jet-propelled.

Mulgrew's hat has gone spiralling into the arena. He appears below, a minuscule figure climbing over crumbling walls where he finally finds his hat. I give him the Roman thumbs-up sign; he gives me the British up yours.

'Terr-ee, too much wind here. We go down,' says Toni, clasping her skirts around her.

We descend to meet Mulgrew coming up. 'Oh, Christ,' he groans, 'all this way up for nothing.'

A great gust of wind, more knickers. The girls give a mixture of screams and giggles. This is no day for sightseeing unless you are a voyeur. Despite the gales whistling up our trouserlegs, I still have time to take in the incredible durability of a place started in 72 AD and still standing. What it must have looked like before it was stripped of its marble.

On the way down, we come to the Royal Box where Caesars sat. Mulgrew sits on the seat. 'It suits you, Johnny; a ruined colosseum suits you,' I said. We continue down the timeless steps of history to the ground level. Another great gust, more knickers on display. Across the road is a coffee house where we settle. We sit in the shadow of the great edifice. I can imagine a Roman holiday and the great crowds flocking to the games, the sweetmeat vendors, chariots bearing important personages, attendants shouting 'Hurry along, please, take your seats', the great roar as a favourite gladiator enters the arena. There's no denying man has a bloody lust.

Toni is saying how could people watch such cruelty. 'Och,' says Mulgrew, 'it's no worse than Celtic versus Rangers; you should see the punch-ups.'

This reminded me of a story of two ancient Picts being captured by the Romans and condemned to be thrown to the lions. As they await this, they are talking about the women they were allowed as a last request. 'Och, she was great,' says the Pict, 'she had huge boobs. I'll tell you more later, here come the lions.' I tried to explain the joke to the girls, but speaking in Italian with a Scots accent had its limitations – plus the fact there was no Italian word for the word 'boobs'. 'Booso' was the nearest I could get. But my mime succeeds.

Oh, dear, this wind is too much for the ladies, their hair is becoming windblown. So we take a taxi back to the hotel. En route, Johnny suggests we go to the ENSA Supercinema. Yes, yes, yes. We redirect the taxi to the Via Depretis, which means passing the great Quirinal Palace. It seems that Roma is an unending vista of historical buildings.

'All king of Italy live here sometime,' says Toni.

'Very nice,' says Mulgrew of the magnificent edifice.

The cinema is showing *Hanover Square* with Laird Cregar. It's basically the story of murder on Guy Fawkes night when Cregar, the murderer, dumps the body on a great bonfire. All through, Mulgrew makes remarks like 'You'll never get away with it, Jimmy', 'Fools! It's a body not a dummy.' It is a film with unending background music. Nobody can move without musical accompaniment, giving a vision of a great orchestra just off screen following the actors wherever they go. It's all monumentally boring. Cregar sweats profusely through the film and spends most of his time flattened against walls, avoiding the police. Hollywood films – when I think that all my emotional development was based on them! For me, the real world didn't exist, so I grew up emotionally deformed. As I rode on those early workmen's trams to Woolwich, filled with hunched people in workmen's caps, I was still wrapped up in the aura of the last film I had seen at the Wasdale Road Astoria. Forest Hill. The tram, the fog-ridden cold morning outside were all imaginary. They would all disappear when I saw my next Bing Crosby film. Most of my middle life would be spent trying to escape from their cloying influence. The final nail in the coffin was a book by Bing Crosby's son, Gary, in which Bing was anything but like what his films were. That's when my past life sank without trace. Hollywood of the thirties and forties has a lot to answer for. It wasn't until I saw *The Grapes of Wrath* that I saw a *real* film. Then, I thought it rotten because it didn't have a happy ending. But now, I'm in Rome, taking a taxi back to the hotel. Unlike films, the first taxi you flag down doesn't stop. They stop for Bing Crosby!

'God, we're spending a fortune on taxis,' moans Mulgrew.

Correction. '*I* am spending a fortune on taxis.'

'True,' he says, 'you are living beyond my means,' and makes like Groucho Marx, eyebrows wiggling, inane grin.

Toni wants to know why I'm laughing. To explain, I would have to describe again what the Marx Brothers are like. It's rather like trying to teach the theory of relativity to a Chinese peasant – not that Miss Fontana has the mind of a Chinese peasant, but in this case she might as well have. I just say that they are American comedians. 'Worse,' says the evil Mulgrew, 'they're Jewish.'

At the hotel, there is little sign of anybody so the girls withdraw to their room to do whatever girls do in rooms. Mulgrew heads for the wine bar next door. In the absence of any other interesting direction I follow him, sheeplike. I have a brandy and coffee to stiffen the sinews and vibrate the Swonnicles.

'I think I've had enough of this tour,' ventures Mulgrew; then, with great feeling, 'I want to go home.' Though his body was in Rome, his eyes were in Glasgow – but! His gullet was in a wine bar. He downs wine like a thirsty camel at an oasis. After one I've had enough. 'Deserting a sinking alcoholic, eh?' he says.

In my room, I write a long overdue letter to my pal in the Battery, Harry Edgington. I tell him of my new-found fame and ten pounds a week wages. I take great pride in the last-mentioned because I think I am in the top wage-earning bracket. I miss the boys in the Battery and especially playing the trumpet with the Battery dance band, the Boys of Battery D, as we were called. That, too, would never happen again – another stepping stone in life that I would never tread again. What was it like being stationed in Holland? Had he married Peg, his childhood sweetheart? Perhaps, when we were both back in England, we'd play together again; perhaps ... I write to Mother, acknowledging the parcel she sent, and pose the question as to why she labelled a parcel containing suppositories and cigarettes 'socks'. I presume it was a ploy to deter thieves. Why not mark the parcel 'Live Snakes' or 'Rancid Meat'? I write to my dear, romantic father, urging him to start on his autobiography. He has a title, *Saddle, Sabre and Spur*, that's been on his typewriter for ten years. It was still on it when he died.

Mulgrew returns. Either they've run out of drink, or he's run out of money. He flops on his bed and lights a cigarette. He doesn't speak; he is gazing at the ceiling and blowing the smoke heavenwards. He still doesn't speak.

'Let me guess,' I say. 'You have taken the vow of silence and are on your way to a monastery.'

He smiles. 'No, Jimmy, I'm a bit low today.'

'You're low every day; it's the curse of duck's disease.'

He doesn't answer but continues staring at the ceiling. In case there's anything up there I'm missing I have a look. No, there's nothing up there. I wonder what he sees in it. We all have our quirks; perhaps ceilings are a turn-on for him. I finish off the letter to my father, reminding him that I am on ten pounds a week. Despite this, I am still his loving son.

On my way downstairs to the postbox, I meet Bornheim coming up. 'Halt, who goes there?' he says. Why has he got his hat on? Let me guess, he's been out or he's Jewish. Yes, he, too, has been to see bloody awful Laird Cregar in *Hanover Square*. He laughs as he recalls the huge overweight Cregar humping the dead body over his shoulder to sling it on the bonfire, when it was painfully obvious that the stiff was a badly made dummy. 'Did you see it start to slide off the bonfire when they cut?' he laughed. Glad he enjoyed it, but then Bornheim would laugh if his grandmother was run over by a steamroller. I think, with his name, there was a touch of the Hun.

Do I want to come to his room? He's written a new tune. Right away, massa boss. Letters posted, I hie me to his room. He gets out his 'squeeze box' and plays his composition. It's very Tchaikovsky – yes, he admits to that influence, do I like it? Yes, it's a splendid tune; it's the best one I've heard this afternoon. Has it any words? No. Does he mind if I have a try? It's a long time ago, but I remember the opening lines:

> Wonderful night on Capri
> We threw a kiss to the sea
> Her lips met mine
> That were wet with the wine
> Of that wonderful night on Capri

As I have pointed out, all Hollywood slurp. Today I would write:

> Wonderful night on Capri
> I felt a pain in the knee
> I counted till nine
> Then cried rotten swine!
> Hi diddle Hi diddle Hi dee

Bill Hall has heard the music and comes in with his fiddle. What the hell, I go and get my guitar and we all try out Bornheim's new number. It develops into a jam session.

Lieutenant Priest pops his head round the door. 'Guess what,' he says.

'It's time to go,' we all chorus.

Two more shows and this life style will be over. All chattering like monkeys we board the Charabong for the penultimate show.

'Listen, everybody. Attention!' says Priest. 'Tomorrow night, after the show, there will be a wine and cheese party on stage. Everyone allowed to bring one guest.'

I stand up and in a twit voice say, 'On behalf of me an' my friends we would like to thank you for this generous offer, made possible by the money you bloody swindled us out of in the NAAFI.'

Priest grins and waves me away.

Another good attendance. For a two thousand seater, we are getting the sort of audiences that London impresarios would like. 'Mind you,' says Bill Hall, 'compared with the box office takings, we get peanuts. Someone's getting a good rake-off.' To this day, I often wonder if somebody was. It was so easy to fiddle during the war. Fortunes were made by soldiers who had sterling posted to them which they exchanged, at inflated rates, on the black market, then changed back into sterling at a profit. But *I* didn't have to do that; *I* was on ten pounds a week!

During tonight's show, I take time to watch Toni in her 'Dance of the Hours'. She had been the start of my love affair with ballet. I love the grace, the posturing, the elegance. I see her spinning like a top around the stage, my ballerina. Aw, shucks.

To boose our ego, we find a splendid write-up in the *Rome Police News*.

Naples where they were forced to hang out the 'House Full' sign every night.

Speaking with Raymond Agoult before the show I was informed that one of the objects of good producing is to send your audience away with a feeling that they want some more, if that is the case then 'Barbary Coast' is an example of good producing on that score alone, because the audience certainly wanted more, much more in fact.

The most popular with the audience was the evergreen 'Bill Hall Trio' with their clowning and music in the best slapstic style. In order to be able to clown on a violin, I was once told by a famous English violinist, you must first of all become a master of your instrument. Bill Hall shows how true this statement is, his handling of the violin throughout all the clowning had the touch of the master throughout and when he started into the 'Flight of the Bumblebee' it was evident that he had his technique 'at his fingertips'. The trio were without Johnnie Mulgrew, their Double Bass player who is in hospital, tonight and Johnny Bornhiem, who is one of the singing waiters, stepped into the breach with his accordian in such an expert manner that one had to know the trio to realise the alteration. Spike Milligan was able to demonstrate all the horrors of drink - being without it - and at the same time maintain a steady flow of music from his guitar. Here are three boys who are going to be top liners in Blighty, I understand they have already received offers to appear in 'Ridgway Parade' and at the London Windmill Theatre, and I am looking forward to seeing them there.

'That's bloody good for coppers,' says Mulgrew.

'You see, they're not all bastards,' says Hall.

'Well, this lot aren't,' concludes Mulgrew.

'I say, I say, I say,' I said, 'what do you do with bent coppers? Don't know? I'll tell you, send 'em back to the Mint.'

Neither of them wish to know that.

Priest comes backstage to tell us that our favourite, Gracie Fields, is in tonight.

'She's in a box,' he says.

'Well, screw the fucking lid on,' says Hall, who can't stand her singing.

'She wants to come backstage after the show,' says Priest.

'Oh, Christ,' says Hall, 'she's not going to sing, is she?'

Priest laughs: no, she wants to say hello to the cast.

During our act, I can see Gracie who laughs and applauds with enthusiasm. She's not a bad old stick, if only she didn't sing. After the show we dutifully await her visit. Finally it comes to us.

''Ow do, lads,' she says. ''Aven't seen you since the C M F Arts Festival.'

She then introduces us to an old dear, a Mrs Biddick of E N S A Welfare, who is 'frightfully pleased to meet us'. She is *very* interested in Bill Hall. 'I say, you play your fiddle frightfully well.' Hall mumbles something like 'Ta'. A few more boring pleasantries and Miss Fields and Mrs Biddick leave our sphere of influence.

Our chorus girls liked her. 'She speak little Italian,' said Toni, who herself is a little Italian. 'She says if we go Capri, she like to see us.'

With that threat hanging over us, we board the returning Charabong. Luigi, our driver, is very happy. He has heard from his wife who has, this day, given birth to his seventh child. *'Una ragazza.'* At dinner, we open a bottle of Asti Spumante and wet the baby's head. Mulgrew goes on to wet the arms, the body and the legs.

'Christ,' says Hall, 'they don't 'arf have big families.'

'It's very simple,' says Mulgrew. 'They do it more often.'

Hall shakes his head, but no noise comes from it. Toni is telling her friend Luciana about our proposed Capri holiday. Of *course*, she won't tell anyone else – except the entire company.

The javelin-throwing champion, lesbian manageress of the hotel asks Mulgrew and me to have a goodbye drink in her flat. She doesn't invite Hall as she freely admits she thinks he's got leprosy. I can vouchsafe that his underwear has. We take the lift to the top floor and press the buzzer. A very tall, willowy blonde answers the door. She's the sister, Claudia. She leads us down the hall into the lounge, beautifully furnished with modern furniture – very Mussolini-modern.

'*Si accomodino,*' says lesbian manageress. We settle for wine. Yes, she had enjoyed our show and loved our 'jizz'. She gives us little nibbly snacks. Her radio is tuned into the American Forces Network with unending big bands playing. Right now, it's Ray Ventura. It was all so accessible those days. Nowadays, I have to journey to Ronnie Scott's to hear any.

We don't stay long. She won't be here on Sunday morning when we leave, so she'll say goodbye now. So we all say, 'Goodbye now.'

As we go down in the lift, Mulgrew makes a certain sign. 'Oh, her sister, 'ow!'

'Ah, more's the pity, Johnny,' I said. 'I know you could have given her four inches. The trouble is she could give you six.'

On that note, we ended the evening.

SATURDAY

I slept late and missed breakfast. Never mind, folks; across the road from the hotel is a splendid coffee bar, where I order *caffelatte* and a rum baba which I dunk in the coffee – all delicious, gooey, decadent. When in Rome . . .! It's a scorching hot day. It would be a wonderful day for a swim, but where? Back at the hotel, the porter tells me there is a *bagno municipale*, Via Catania. I don't want to go alone; I'm so thin people won't know I'm there. Where is Toni? Gone to Mother's. Ah, here comes innocent, whistling-the-while Bornheim. Does he want to swim? OK, the easiest way is a taxi. We arrive at the baths: it's a huge complex, a multi-sports place. We pay our admission fee, are given a ticket and a key – No. 56 Downstairs, to the changing area: my God, the crowds. The cubicle is minuscule. If we both change together, we'll have to get into the same bathing suit. Bornheim waits while I change and vice versa.

It's a covered pool; the echo of the noise is deafening. Worse the pool is crowded to the point of combustion: you can jump in when you see a space, and then you only have room to jump up and down. There are no other variations, so we dry off and leave.

'What a bloody waste of time,' said Bornheim.

'I'm sorry, I had no idea it was like this,' I said.

So that our legs don't totally atrophy from taxi travel, we decide to walk away. We walk about a mile and Bornheim says 'Enough is enough. Taxi!' We arrive back at the hotel, I'll see him later. To my room, phone room service: can I have an iced lemonade? *Si, signor, pronto.* A smiling doe-eyed, bewitchingly dark-haired waitress brings it in. Help, Toni; hurry back, darling! The temptation left the room, I felt, with a certain amount of reluctance. It was a hot afternoon; it was the best of times, it was the worst of times. I was reminded of a Military Police case, of a soldier and a girl caught *in flagrante* in a Bradford doorway. At the trial, the magistrate gave the man three months. Had he anything to say? 'Yes,' he said, 'you'll never stop fucking in Bradford.'

I lay on the bed slurping iced lemonade, followed by a Passing Cloud that tasted of pile suppositories. I'd asked my mother so many times never to parcel them up together, to no avail. I buzz Toni's room; she's back. Why didn't she tell me she was seeing her mother? I was asleep. That's no excuse, you could have still told me. Shall she come down? Yes, yes. It's not long before I bolt the door and we start snogging. We were both about to get there when, blast, someone's trying to get in. Who is it? It's Mulgrew. Can he wait a minute? Why? Toni and I hustle into our clothes and let Mulgrew in. In a flash he senses all. 'Ah,' he says, 'your clothes don't fool me.' They'd fooled me: I had my Y-fronts on back to front and all my arrangements were screwed up. Toni is blushing, but then she's new at this game! There is nothing so indicting as silence and Mulgrew gives us yards of it, laced with a knowing grin. How dare he think that we've had it away, even though it's true? How dare he think it. I know that he personally fancies Toni, but well, poor fool, look at the competition he has. Glasgow fool, how can he compete with a Brockley S E 26 boy? Toni leaves the room in a state of confusion; I stay and face it out. Mulgrew says, 'I can't have my bedroom used for immoral purposes.' Immoral? This was true love, white as the driven snow. His shoulders are shaking with silent laughter. So ended a chapter in the love story of Toni and me.

I lay back and took my ease on the bed. 'Well,' I said, 'last show tonight.'

'Thank God,' he replies, 'rather sad in a way, but I think we've had enough.'

Would I like a cigarette? Is he out of his mind? Could he say that again! Yes, he is definitely offering me a cigarette. I remember it was a classy cigarette, Churchmans No. 1. Ah, it's all clear: *he*, too, has had a parcel from home.

Time for the last show. We gather chattering in the foyer, then board the Charabong through the Roman cacophony of motor horns. Toni has recovered her demeanour and I have put my Y-fronts back on the right way, and the Swonnicles are revolving normally. Tonight our strong man, Maxie, will try and break his own weightlifting record of umpteen pounds. We all watch from the wings as the dwarf-like strong man strains to get the weights above his head. The silence is broken by his grunts and strains, the veins stand out on his head. Finally, with a gasp, he gets them above his head. He takes the applause.

'What a way to make a bloody living,' says Hall. 'I bet one day 'e'll get a double rupture.'

There's a sense of sadness in the air. This company has been together every day for three months; it has become as familiar as a family. As the Trio are taking an ensore, I think well that's it; the next time we play will be in England. Then what? I can still hear that applause on the last night . . .

The stage party is very good. Chalky White and his helpers erect trestle tables which are loaded with cheese, wine and biscuits. We help ourselves. Johnny Bornheim plays the piano. The Italians have invited members of their families, big fat mommas and kids. It's a very jolly affair. Before we finish, Lieutenant Priest thanks us for our efforts and says the show is the most successful one that Combined Services Entertainment have put on. We drink and eat our fill. We stand in circles, chatting and laughing, recalling moments that have highlighted our tour, and then the evening has run out. Time for home. Some of the Italian cast will be leaving us at Rome; there are tearful goodbyes, a lot of red eyes and red noses. Mulgrew's nose is going red for an entirely different reason. In dribs and drabs we board the old Charabong where patient Luigi waits. The engine is running, but no one else is. Finally, we set off for the hotel. We all start slightly inebriated singing: 'You are my sunshine, my only sunshine, you make me happy when skies are grey' echoes along the now empty Roman streets. It's nearly 2 a.m. by the time we get back; yawning, stretching and farting we climb wearily into bed. I can't sleep, my mind starts to revolve around the things I have to do when we get back to naughty Napoli. I must collect all my kit from the CSE barracks, get a passport, an advance of money, presents to take home, fix the boat trip home – all this, and fix a week on Capri. Gradually I fall into fitful sleep to the sound of Mulgrew's snoring in Scottish, plus a few postern blasts.

NAPLES

A SUNDAY

Yet another glorious, sunny Roman day. I draw the curtains; the light falls on the slumbering Mulgrew, who stirs with a few mouthy sounds like 'Abregibera'. I have a quick shower, singing 'Love thy neighbour, wake up and say how be yer boo boo da de dum.'

Oh, what a waste! Mulgrew is awake; he calls out, 'While you're there, have one for me.'

The packing, and I'm baffled as to why each time I do it, there seems to be more stuff than last time. 'The suitcase is shrinking,' says Mulgrew, having the same trouble. We lug the cases down to the care of the porter.

Toni is in the dining-room; she's not eating. 'No I wait for you, my love,' she says with a morning-bright smile. I mouth the words 'I love you.' She smiles again, her head inclined to one side. Was her neck giving way? No, it's just a posture of hers, ha ha. Lovely hot toast, melting butter and conserve – there *is* a God.

We are all wearing our rather shapeless travelling clothes. Toni's are too big for her, while I'm too thin for mine. People keep knocking on my shirt to see if I'm in. Lieutenant Priest looms large. 'Are you all packed?' he says. 'We board in ten minutes. All hurry along.' Dutifully, we mount our motorized steed for the haul to naughty Naples. This journey will be interesting to me as we will be passing over ground that my regiment has fought over.

We leave Rome by the Via Appia Nuova, flanked on the left side by the Roman aqueduct that once fed Rome its water. Despite the ravages of time, lots of it is intact, rather like Bill Hall's body. We pass tall cypress trees and the occasional Roman tomb, where occasional Romans were buried. 'I suppose the bombin' did all that,' said Hall, referring to the ruins. That's right, Bill; these are specially bombed Roman ruins. Somewhere along this road would one day live Sophia Loren, who once squeezed my hand at a dinner table. But more of that in the future.

We are passing through the great frascati vineyards where the grapes are being harvested. Peasants with coloured clothes are speckled in the fields. We are on Route Six which will take us through Cassino. It's a quieter coachload than normal; there's a sense of anticlimax (why anybody should be anticlimax, I don't know). Nobody talks much. Toni breaks the silence, 'I so excited to go Capri,' she said and squeezed my hand extra hard.

The warmth, the rumbling along, the scenery flashing past; I nod off to sleep, waking up with a start when my head starts to fall off. 'You tired, Terr-ee?' No, just sleepy. 'Tell me, Terr-ee, you lak opera, Italian opera?' Yes, I love it. Good, if and when we go back to Rome, she will take me to one. 'Which one you lak?' I lak *Madam Butterfly*, *Aida*, any romantic ones. 'You lak *La Bohème*?' Yes, *mi piace molto*. Good we will go and see all of them; after, we'll have dinner and I can sleep at her mother's place. Good, now I can go back to sleep again.

I nod on and off until in the early afternoon we pull over under the shadow of the now ruined monastery at Cassino. I carry the sandwich box on to the grass verge while John Angove brings up the vacuum tea container. We arrange ourselves on the grass and help ourselves to the sandwiches. Toni and I sit in the shade of a tree. I lean against the trunk and look up at the sad spectacle of the ruined monastery. Bornheim sees me and reflects, 'Bloody madness, eh?' Yes, bloody madness.

'You fight here, Terr-ee?' says Toni, with a full mouth.

'No, I was over that side.' I point behind me. Was it as bad as Cassino? Bad enough.

Luigi is walking round the Charabong, looking at the tyres. They are like Bill Hall, starting to go bald and will just about last the journey. I wonder if I will.

After an uneventful lunch, we are back on board. We turn left round a bend and there ahead is the skeleton of the town of Cassino, looking like a First World War setting. A road has been bulldozed through the rubble, but that is all. There are people in the ruins, but where they live, God only knows. Here and there are a few street stalls selling vegetables and fruit – how resilient is the human race.

Bornheim is reading his *Union Jack*. 'You're Irish, aren't you, Milligan?' he says.

'I couldn't afford anything else,' I said. 'Why?'

'Well, it says here, in the human race today, the Irish came last.'

Bloody cheek. It must have been the first of the Irish jokes.

'Remember this, mate: General Montgomery and Alexander were both Irish. Till they took charge, the English were having the shit knocked out of 'em, ha!'

We pass through the ghost of Cassino and travel down what had been called the Royal Mile. This was the road used by the Allies to reach the obliterated town. By day it was constantly shelled by the Germans, who liked that sort of thing; vehicles had to go like hell to avoid being hit. We are bumping along its heavily pitted surface, all of us bouncing up and down like a trampoline. When we hit a deep pothole, the whole lot of us give a great 'OHHHHHHHH'.

'I wonder why we always use the letter "O" to express surprise,' I said.

'Wot you mean?' says Hall, his tiny mind set ablaze by the question.

'Well, why always choose "O"; why not use "X" or "K" or "Z"? Like, "I'm sorry your cat has been run over." "X!" Or a combination of letters: "I'm sorry your cat has been run over again." "XGHYZLP!"'

Hall looks blankly at me. ''Ow long were you in the Army?' he says.

'Same as I am now, five foot eleven.'

'You downgraded to B1, weren't you?' Yes. 'Ah,' he says and shakes his head sympathetically.

On, on, then. We reach the ancient town of Capua, at one time captured by Hannibal and his elephants. We cross the

River Volturno by the same Bailey bridge that I crossed as the Fifth Army fought its way north in the mud. Ah, memories, nostalgia and goodbye yesterdays. I have been smoking cigarettes at a rate; my mouth feels like the inside of an Arab wrestler's jockstrap. Ugh, yuck, splutter, I decide to give up smoking until the next one.

It seems such a long journey. 'Someone's moved Naples away,' says Mulgrew who is smoking a dog end so short that it's really fumigating his nose.

'*Che tedioso,*' says Toni, resettling her bottom on the seat.

''Ow many mile 'ave we got to go?' inquires Hall.

Bornheim tells him, 'We aren't travelling in miles; we are travelling in kilometres. It's shorter that way.'

A weak cheer goes up when Priest points out a roadsign 'Napoli 10 chilometri'. To raise our morale like the 12th Cavalry coming to the rescue, Hall unleashes his violin and plays Italian pop songs. Fulvio sings them and the Italians join in.

'They're happy now,' grins Mulgrew; 'they can smell spaghetti.'

'This could mean the OBE for you, Bill: violinist saves demoralized passengers!' I said.

Activated by the praise, he waggles his head, crosses his eyes and plays a wobbly version of 'God Save the King'.

Mulgrew rises to his feet and salutes. 'The toast and marmalade is the King,' he says and is jerked back into his seat as the Charabong lurches forward.

In the early evening we are entering the northern outskirts of Napoli. '*Grazie a Dio,*' says Toni, yawning and stretching but not getting any longer. On to the Via Roma with its bustling life and traffic, Luigi weaves in and out, shouting and blowing his horn. He's happy. Soon he'll be setting up his wife for *bambino* no. 8; he has already loosened his trousers. Finally we pull up at the Albergo Rabicino, where all the Italian artistes disembark. I kiss Toni goodbye; I'll see her tomorrow morning. We wave goodbye as we turn off in the direction of the CSE barracks. It's only ten minutes later when we draw up to the grotty façade of the barracks. I go to the Q stores and pick up my belongings, and back on the bus. Hall and I are to go to the Army Welfare Hotel in the Vumero.

'Fancy you two lucky buggers staying at a hotel,' says Mulgrew.

I remind him that Mr Hall and I are now officer status and that they are still soldiers in service of the Crown and are thus khaki minions serving their time, and good luck with the food.

'I'd forgotten how grotty these barracks are,' said Bornheim.

'Yes, it's amazing how they suit you,' I said. 'Just stand there and I'll record your picture for posterity.'

From somewhere, he gets a hammer and strikes this pose.

Private J. Bornheim – soldier, friend and twit

This fragrant moment in time over, Hall and I re-bus and are taken to our hotel. It's a middle-class affair, called Albergo Corsica in the Vomero. It's run by the WVS with Italian staff. A Mrs Laws is the manageress, a portly matron in the tweed uniform of the WVS. She hopes we'll be comfortable; so do we. A terribly weak little Italian porter with a trolley takes our luggage to the lift, or tries to. It takes his entire energy. In the lift, sweating, he leans against the wall, giving a sickly grin that only normally comes on deathbeds.

I am shown to a room on the second floor. It is at the back and therefore, though the room is high up and the hotel overlooks the bay, I overlook the rear streets. Bill Hall is next door, not for long – what's my room like? It's as the matron said, comfortable, just about – a bed, a table, a cupboard, a dressing table, the standard quartet of furnishings. Bill Hall sits on my bed. What's he going to do?

'I think I'll hang around a couple of weeks, sort of holiday.'

Holiday?

'We've been on one long holiday,' I said.

'There's some friends here I want to visit.'

We both go down for dinner. The dining-hall is crowded with ENSA and AWS bods, all no doubt having a bloody good time at the expense of the taxpayer. My God, they were good days for skiving. As the apparition of Hall enters, the buzz of conversation stops, rather like when a gunman enters a saloon bar. I order minestrone and pasta. 'I'll 'ave the same,' says Hall, mainly because he can't pronounce the Italian names himself.

We discuss things we have to do and both agree to visit the British Consulate on the morrow to collect our passports. It's too late and I'm too tired for any activity save bed. When I return to my room, the maid is turning down my bed and I hadn't even offered it to her. '*Mi scusi*,' she smiles, showing those magnificent white teeth, and that's all she was going to show me. '*Buona notte, dorma bene*,' she says and leaves. I survey my ex-Army kit: there's a big pack, small pack and my big stencilled kitbag. I'll attend to that on the morrow. I fall asleep to the distant sounds of the streets.

I awake at nine of the clock. I have much to do; I do some in the WC and some in the bathroom. My toilet complete, I knock on Hall's door to be greeted by a stunning silence. I push the door open. The curtains are closed and so are Hall's eyes. I awake him as gently as an 'OI WAKE UP!' will allow. He gradually comes to; I count him down to consciousness, 7, 6, 5, 4, 3, 2, 1! Wide awake now, Hall; hands off cocks, on socks! He'll see me in the foyer in half an hour. Yes, but will I see him? I take breakfast in my stride.

'Is anybody sitting here?' It's an English rose of a woman. No, nobody is sitting there. 'Mind if I join you?' she says. She is blonde, blue-eyed, nicely filled out, oven-ready, I'd say. She is a singer and has come to join CSE. As there's nobody else to do it, I introduce myself – DIY. She wants to know what there is to see. I tell her there's Pompeii. What's that? It's a dead city. No, thanks, she says; she's just come from one, Birmingham. She is satisfied when I say there is extensive shopping on the Via Roma. Will she excuse me? I have an appointment with the British Consul.

Hall is *not* in the foyer. I phone up to his room. Yes, yes, he's coming. Together we get a taxi, I tell the driver Via Roma. We are looking for a passport photographer. Hall looks out the left side and I look out the right. Hall has the eye of an eagle and legs to match. He spots one.

'There, over there,' he says, rapping on the driver's window.

'*Fermare!*' I shout.

'Ah, *si, capito*,' says our photographer, a tall Italian with slick black hair parted in the middle, a little pencilled-over moustache and a grey tight chalk-striped suit. He looked the ideal co-respondent in a divorce case. Yes, si, si, he can have the photographs ready in '*un'ora*'. So, after presenting our visages we have an hour to kill.

'Let's kill a policeman,' I say.

We pass the time window-shopping and having a cup of coffee at the big NAAFI in the Via Roma. We duly collect our photos, which aren't as bad as some.

Passport photo of the bearer

It looks as if I've been on drugs. Hall looks as if he's been dead a month. Thus supplied, we take a taxi to His Majesty's Britannic Consul in the Piazza Bagnoli. At a desk with a 'Ring Bell for Service', we attract a middle-aged, slightly balding, thin, pale-faced Englishman wearing pebbled glasses that make his eyes stand out like organ stops. Ah, yes, he has received our applications. Have we the photographs? We present them. He looks at them at arm's length, drawing them towards him then away again. Finally, he says 'Which is which?' I point out me; he writes my name on the back. If we come back in a week, they will be ready. Bring five thousand lire each.

Now Hall and I split, me to the cashier at CSE barracks to sort my finances out. Another taxi. The cashier is a corporal in the Queen's. Have I the CSE contract? I produce it from other papers. Yes, I'm in CSE for another six weeks; yes, I can have it all in advance. God, I'll be so rich! It's almost 72,000 lire! I must be careful; Naples is full of thieves, commonly known as the British Army.

I taxi to Toni's hotel. It's lunchtime and I find her in the dining-room, which abounds with the smell of garlic. Toni greets me; it's all coming from her – yes, she just had scampi with garlic sauce. What a sauce! She's anxious to know what day and garlic are we going to Capri? I tell her possibly the day after tomorrow. Only, she will only be allowed to stay at this hotel and garlic for another five days. Don't worry, I will save her and garlic long before then. That evening would she like to go to the Bellini Theatre where they are showing *Night Must Fall*? Oh, she and her garlic would love to. OK, I will pick her up at seven and put her down again at one minute past. What am I talking about? Only time will tell. So saying, I catch taxi number three and take me and my 72,000 lire back to my hotel.

I inquire from the hotel porter about the ferry to Capri. Oh, yes, there are four a day: two in the morning and two in the afternoon. He shows me a printed brochure with times and prices, so I am set fair for the romantic isle where dwells the goddess Gracie Fields. In my bedroom, I lock the door then do an hour's gloating over my 72,000 lire. I lay it on the bed next to me to have a rest. I shut my eyes. When I open them, the money is still there; the room appears to be safe. Aloud, I say seventy-two thousand lire. It sounds good. I carefully fold the money and place it in my jacket pocket to see if it makes a bulge. No, it doesn't look like 72,000 lire. I take it out again and it does. I hold it up to the mirror, where it now looks like 144,000 lire! So, I spend a pleasant afternoon's gloating.

Comes evening and I pick Toni up in a taxi and we drive up the Via Roma to the Theatre Bellini. Good heavens, Captain O'List is the manager for the show. 'How nice to see you again, Spike,' he gushes. 'I hear that the tour went very well.' Pay for seats? No, no, no, we can have complimentaries. Obviously this man doesn't know that I'm carrying 72,000 lire. What posh! Captain O'List gives us a box for two. 'See you in the interval for a drink in my ofice,' are his parting words.

Night Must Fall. Toni cannot follow the dialogue, I am constantly having to translate in a hushed whisper. True to his word, Captain O'List is waiting for us during the interval and we have 'drinky-poos'. Are we going steady? Yes, Toni and I are going steady.

'We're going for a week on Capri,' I tell him.

'Oh,' he says, and lets it hang in the air like the Sword of Damocles. 'Oh, Capri, eh? Ha, ha,' he says, the whole shot through with innuendo. Why, oh, why doesn't he ask me how much money I'm carrying? 'I'm due for demob in four weeks,' he says.

'Are you going back to the Windmill?'

'Yes, Vyvyan van Damn has kept the job open.'

'Do all those wankers who come to the Windmill to see naked birds listen to him singing?'

'Not many, but it's a living.'

The second half puzzles Toni even further, especially the head in the hatbox.

'What he got in the box?'

'A head.'

'Head?'

'Yes, *una testa*.'

'Ah, *testa*.'

I enjoyed the play in which Miss Fontana took a leading part.

At the exit, Captain O'List wishes us goodbye and 'Have a nice time on Capri!' Taxi? No, it's a warm night so we walk down the Via Roma hand in hand and I unravel the play for Toni. By the time we get to the bottom of the Via I have done all the play again and, though I say it, played all the parts better than the actors managed. I flag down one of Napoli's fleet of decaying taxis.

'Where we go?' says Toni.

'Ah ha,' I say, 'somewhere nice – Zia Teresa.'

The driver nods.

In the taxi, I give Toni a long, lingering, burning kiss causing steam in my trousers. We arrive at the restaurant on the waterfront at Santa Lucia and walk down the side facing on to the bay. Zia Teresa is over a hundred years old; the roof is made of raffia-like straw with rough wooden poles as support. In the centre of the restaurant is the cooking area with a metal cowling over the top. I give the maître d' a thousand lire note. *'Una tavola viacinal mare, per favore,'* I say, and we get a table directly on to the sea. As we sit down, night fishermen are hoving to, selling fresh fish to the chef. At the back of the restaurant are a guitar and a violin player plus a singer. *'O, mare lucido'* he sings.

'Theese is lovelee, Terr-ee,' says Toni, beaming with happiness.

We have an entire fish meal: fresh mussels and scampi. The wine was one of my favourites: Est Est Est. All this and tomorrow, Capri; walking on clouds wasn't in it. What a view! At the end of a pier, on the right, the ancient Castello del Ovo, where I believe Cicero once had a villa; then, the broad sweep of the bay circling to our left, its winking lights following the curve to distant Sorrento; out in the crepuscular night, a ghostly image of Capri; above us all, the giant shape of Vesuvius, now black and silent but always threatening.

'How you find theese place?' she says. Well, before *Barbary Coast* one night we asked a taxi driver for a good restaurant and he brought us here. 'How lucky,' she said. *'Che roman-tico.'*

Yes, how romantic, and the wine fortifies that feeling.

Midnight: the singer and the duo are visiting the tables. He reaches us; I ask him for 'Vicino Mare'. We sit back sipping wine as the silvery voice floats on the balmy night air. After this, I call for the bill. When it arrives I flourish the

72,000 lire, peeling off the notes in time to the music. A very impressive performance enjoyed by the waiter. I give him a handsome tip and turn a normal human being into a subservient, grovelling hulk.

On the way home, I tell Toni about the arrangements for the morrow. I'll pick her up at ten and we'll catch the eleven o'clock ferry. 'I don't think I sleep tonight,' she said as she kissed me goodnight, causing more trouser steam. It's one o'clock by the time I turn my light out. I close my eyes, undress Toni and fall asleep.

CAPRI

CAPRI

Lovely! It's a sunny day, nice and warm with a cool breeze. I pack my suitcase, only taking the bare essentials – like me. I'm too excited to eat breakfast, so I have a cup of tea. I buzz the porter and ask him to get me a taxi. When it arrives, he buzzes me: '*Taxi pronto, signore!*' Toni is waiting in the foyer of her hotel; she is all beaming and giggles. She lights up when she sees me; she must know that I'm carrying what *was* 72,000 lire. Our taxi turns into numerous buzzing backstreets on the way to the Porto Grande. There, waiting for us, is our dream boat – *Spirito del Mare.*

At the quayside ticket office, I buy our two returns and we board. We go into the airy saloon bar: we are early, the saloon is empty save for the barman. Can we have two coffees? '*Si accomodino.*' We sit at a window overlooking the deck; we hear the engines start up. There are only a few passengers carrying bundles. All of them appear to be peasants who have come to Naples to shop or collect something. They are all much more sunburnt than the mainland Italians.

We hear the bell on the ship's telegraph; there are shouts as the hawsers are slipped and the donkey engine takes them in. Expertly we move away from the quay; Tony and I finish the coffee and go to the ship's rail. We turn slowly; clear of the harbour wall, we increase speed and the ship vibrates to the engines. There is that gorgeous sound of a ship slicing through warm waters. We leave the brown waters behind and soon are into the clear blue waters of the Bay of Naples. The city starts to recede, is gradually obscured by the heat haze. Capri lies about twenty-five kilometres ahead.

A few vest-clad crewmen are moving about the ship, all looking rough and unshaved. They shout their conversations

215

even when face to face. I always thought it made you go blind; apparently, it makes you go deaf.

'What did you say, Toni?'

'I feel sick.'

Oh, my God, she's allergic to sea travel. She runs to the ladies and is in and out of there for the whole trip. What bloody luck. I breathe a sigh of relief as we pull up to the Marina Grande. We disembark, with me carrying Toni's case and mine and Toni holding a handkerchief over her mouth. I ask a tourist guide for the nearest hotel; he points to one five minutes away.

'Albergo Grotta Azzurra, *signore*.'

'*Grazie, grazie.*'

We walk uphill to the hotel. Up a few steps in reception, a smiling old Italian greeted us. Are there any vacancies? *O, si, si, molto.* Would we like 'una camera matrimonia?' No no no, I say; we would like separate rooms with adjoining doors. '*Ah, si, si.*' We register in our own names, killing any breath of scandal. They are modest, old-fashioned, unpretentious rooms with a view of the sea. We didn't know it, were totally

Befogged photo of Toni outside the Albergo Grotta Azzurra

216

ignorant, that this was the 'poor' part of the island. Further up on the far side, was where it was all happening, which we would in time find out – only, too late.

Toni is still feeling queasy, so she'll have a lie-down. OK. I repair to my room, unpack my few belongings and read Mrs Gaskell's *Life of Charlotte Brontë*. Will I never finish? I'm taking longer to read it than she lived. From my window I can see down to the Marina Grande, which is primarily a fisherman's port. Little boats are beached on a laticlave of sand; painted on each prow is an eye to ward off evil. They all appear to be looking at me. At about four o'clock Toni comes into my room; she's feeling a lot better. What would she like to do? Why not a swim? OK, we change into our costumes and walk down to a small beach this side of the Marina. No one else is in the water. We have a good hour's swimming.

Milligan the human skeleton escaping from jellyfish, Capri

Toni swimming in sewage-ridden water, Capri

Then a little sunbathe. It's so peaceful; in the distance, we can hear the chatter of the fishermen's wives and their children. We decide that we will have dinner at our hotel and really start exploring the island tomorrow. Toni says she is feeling much better now; *I* am feeling much better now. We *both* feel so much better that we get back into bed, which is even better than better. We watch the twilight approach.

'I think I'll have a bath, Toni – wash all the salt water off.'

She laughs a little. What is it?

She says, 'I think you wash you self away.'

She's referring, I think, to my thinness.

I return to my room and turn the light on. It is a very low voltage bulb that just about illuminates the room. The same bulb in the bathroom. I have a lovely long hot bath in braille. I get out before I pull out the plug, just in case. All together, now:

> SING: Your baby has gone down the plug 'ole
> Your baby has gone down the plug
> The poor little mite
> Was so thin and so slight
> He should have been washed in a jug.

Toni and I are the only couple in the dining-room. The waiter says the season is *passato*. It's a fixed menu, under celluloid: potato soup, vermicelli, then fish and the wine of the island, Vino Capri Scala, Grotta Azzurra – a light white, very fruity. We eat in silence with three unemployed waiters and a waitress standing in attendance. 'Food very nice,' says Toni. When we've finished, we are bowed out of the room.

We decide to take the funicular up to the piazza. We wait as the little box car descends and climb in. It's a slow ascent to the top. The view is a night setting: in the distance, we can see the lights of Naples and the bay winking in the dark. It's a clear night, cool with a starry sky; the air is like velvet. We reach the top and usher out into the piazza. All is brightness with the shops around still open. We sit ourselves at a table outside the Caffè al Vermouth di Torino. A few

American officers and their wives/birds are in evidence. It's two coffees and two Sambuccas, that daring drink that they set on fire. Our waiter speaks English.

'You here on holiday?' he said.

'Yes.'

'Ah, good time – not many people on the island.'

In the square, a few landaus with sorry-looking horses wait for customers. Around us, at other cafés, people are partaking of the night. Among them are the élite of Capri, well-dressed, haughty, never looking left or right as though the rest of the world doesn't exist, and on Capri, it doesn't. The waiter puts a match to our Sambuccas, a blue flame appears. We watch it whisper on the surface as they burn the coffee beans. It's the first time Toni has had one. We blow out the flames, wait for the glasses to cool; we clink them together.

'To us, Toni.'

'Yes,' she says and clinks again. 'To us,' which she pronounces 'to hus'. (I'd better explain that Toni spoke with a pronounced accent, which I have straightened out for the benefit of the reader.)

She sips it rather like a food taster at the court of the Borgias.

'Ummm!' she says, closing her eyes. 'Very good. What they make it with?'

I tell her it's Strega, a drink that can revive dead horses and cause Brongles to rise earlier than normal. 'I no understand.'

'What a pity. I was hoping you'd tell me.'

She knows I'm out of my mind and it's showing.

We don't want to go to bed; the air is so invigorating. Let's have another two Sambuccas. Yes, why not? The night is young even if I'm not. Again the two flames burn in the night; shall *we* blow them out or call the fire brigade? Toni says, 'You mad, Terr-ee!' As an inspired guess that was pretty accurate. After the second Sambucca, Toni says she feels really fine and I say that I am really fine. So we go back to the hotel, get into bed and have a fine time, bearing in mind that my mother would say, 'You are ruining your health.'

The morning breaks fine and clear. It's going to be another hot day. I peer out the window; it's quite early and the fishing boats are coming in from their dawn excursions. The sky is a clear light blue. Bath, shower, shave, teeth, hair, clothes. I tap on Toni's door.

'Oo is eet?' she says.

'It's me, your tesoro.'

She comes to the door in a dressing gown.

'Oh, I sleep too long, Terr-ee.'

Too long? How could she? She's only five foot four. She has delusions of grandeur. Then she says she *won't* be long, shall we have breakfast on the terrace? Splendid, I'll see her there.

The terrace is on the south side of the hotel. Alas, it doesn't get the morning sun but it gets the flies. Mario, for that is the name of our waiter, attends me. *'Signore, buon giorno. Che desidera?'* Not yet, Mario! I'm awaiting the tiny love of my life. Would I like a tea while I'm waiting? Yes, Mario. Why not. I'm looking at an azure sea through pots of pink and scarlet geraniums. The colours are heady with vibrancy. It's the light, the Capri light, clear like fine Venetian glass. Ah ah! Here comes Toni in her white dress showing off her lovely bronze limbs. She walks with the upright carriage of a true ballerina. I pull back her chair, she sits and gestures a small hand towards the sea. 'Beautiful, eh?' she says. She looks so attractive I could eat her. Now, where would I start? Mario looms forth smiling. Holding his tray at head-height, he swings it down professionally and places my lemon tea before me.

'Ecco,' he says.

The menu: we'll have hot bread rolls and *conserva*. What is that perfume? Ah! Behind us, growing up the wall is jasmine with small yellow and white flowers. Toni inhales the fragrance with her eyes closed, 'What nice, how you say, *profumo?*' Perfume, yes, that's it. Where shall we go? says Toni.

I'm for the Grotto Azzurra; she'll get seasick. No no no, it's very calm today and it's only a quick boat ride. '*Sicuro?*' she says. Yes, I'm *sicuro*.

After breakfast we walk down to the Marina Grande. The sun is hot but pleasantly so. We go to the place where the skiffs are waiting to ply their trade; we are besieged by boatmen offering their services. They all shout in Capri dialect. Standing back, I say to Toni, 'Choose one.' She points to one with a peaked sailor's cap; we fight our way to him and climb into the skiff. The shouting abates. We sit on a double seat in the back; the boat pulls away on the calm, delightful, champagne sea. The water here is clear though heavy with sea-stars and, to my horror, jellyfish. I point them out to Toni.

'Ah, *la medusa*,' she says. We'll have to watch it next time we swim.

We loll back in our seats, my arm around Toni. She lets her hand trail in the sea. It was an image I was never to forget and forty years later I wrote this poem.

> White hand washing in a stream.
> What then does my lady dream?
> Down and down in cooling deep.
> Is your mind at ebb or neap?
>
> Fingers whisting in a pool.
> Are they pointing at a fool
> Drowning in the greening deep
> Of your blind and endless sleep?

We are rowing along the base of the precipitous rocky shore. Flowers abound among the rocks. They were too far away for identification, but I think they were wild nasturtiums in their hundreds, yellow and red intermixed. Here and there, where purchase affords, stately cypress trees stand like green fingers against a powder-blue heaven.

'I don't believe this,' says Toni.

I don't believe it either. The only time I believe it is when the boatman says, 'That will be a thousand lire,' thus eroding my fabulous wealth of lire. But that's all to come. Now it's us approaching the tunnel that leads to the grotto. The boatman waits for the rise and fall of the surge, as it goes down he deftly gives a mighty pull on his oars that propels us through while we duck our heads. Then, miracle! we are inside a sea-girt cavern. The roof is about fifty foot high by about a hundred foot in width. What was blue sea is now translucent; we appear to be floating on air. The effect of the blue refraction of the light is indescribable and at first completely dazzles and disorientates the eyes. Toni is stunned. She gasps, 'I don't believe.' Inside, we see that there is a lad in a boat whose ploy is to dive in to show the effect. He wants fifty lire. Agreed. He dives in and his body turns to silver. He gives a few underwater turns and spins; he looks like some godlike child covered in gilt. He surfaces with a smile.

'*Buona? Si, buona.* Fifty lire, please.'

We are only allowed five minutes as other boatmen are shouting to come in. We exit with the surge of the sea and are out into the white-hot sunlight.

Toni clasps her hands: 'I never see like that before, Terree!'

Halfway back, the boatman points out the ruins of the Baths of Tiberius. Did he really have to come all this way for a bath? He must have been desperate. We are soaking up the sun; the only sounds are the dipping oars and the squeaking rowlocks. Not mine, the boatman's. Toni has her head back; she's letting the sun fall on her face with her eyes closed.

'Ah! *che bello*,' she breathes and opens her eyes.

I can't help but say, 'I love you very much, Toni!'

Her reply is to smile and lay her small hand on mine. '*Anche tu sei mi amore*, you understand?' she says, inclining her head on one side.

Could life be better? Yes, life becomes much better. I'll tell you how. We arrive back at the Marina Grande, walk back to the hotel and get into bed with each other and, indeed, life becomes much, much better. But perhaps my mother is right. Am I ruining my health? Will I go blind?

All this before lunch. I tell you what – by God, it gives you a good appetite.

We have a huge pasta lunch in the inside dining-room. I feel stuffed. We decide to have an after-lunch nap; after that, we can go swimming again. We ziz for a couple of hours. I awake with Toni looking round the door. 'You ready, Terr-ee?' Does she mean swimming or the other? Blast! It's swimming. Killjoy! We make our way to our little beach and, keeping an eye out for jellyfish, enjoy a late-afternoon swim.

'Look, Toni,' I say.

I dive down and stand on my hands with legs poking out of the water, what a little Clever Dick I am. I then show her how I can dive underwater through her legs. Is there no end to my aquatic ingenuity? More to come: I show how I can dive between her legs, get her on my shoulders, then stand up and toss her into the sea. I then swim on my back with my legs doubled up so when my feet break the surface, I look like a midget. It's all good clean fun and what a pain in the arse I am.

The afternoon wears on and I wear out. I've really enjoyed my little self. How much better than the Lewisham Public Baths this was. We lie on the beach taking in the evening sun, which is just right. Toni takes her bathing cap off, shaking her head to loosen her hair. She wants to know how the 'Valzer di Candele' goes. I sing 'Should old acquaintance be forgot and never brought to light.' Ah yes, she remembers it and tra la las the rest of it. But no way could she compete with my Bing Crosby voice, oh no.

From Signor Brinati, the hotel manager, we hear that tonight a team of Neapolitans will be giving a demonstration of tarantella dancing in the Taverna Salto di Tiberio. Where's that? He tells us we can get a guide or take a donkey – it's only ten minutes from the piazza, but you have to know the way. Good, that takes care of the evening's entertainment. After dinner we ascend to the piazza. After a coffee at the Caffè al Vermouth di Torino we approach the donkey man: *si*, *si*, he knows the taverna. I climb aboard a donkey. Toni has one with side-saddle and, embarrassingly, a huge erection. With it swinging like a pendulum, we set off. 'Aiiiiieeeee,' shouts the dragoman and off we clop through an archway drunk with clematis on to the old Corso di Tiberio. It is now dark and, as we leave the lights of the piazza, darker still.

'You all right, Toni?' I shout.

'Yes, Terr-ee,' she replies in a gleeful voice.

We are ascending a slight slope, passing an old ruined light-house that went out of business when the keeper fitted blinds to the lights so the neighbours couldn't see in; along a dark, winding path, past a whitewashed church and to our right is the sea, in this light purple-dark. We appear to be about seven hundred feet up. The tavern is near to the rock edge; it's a long, low building, quite old, very simple. There's one big room with wood tables and rush seats; it's quite full. We pay the donkey driver. Do we want him to wait? If so, there's a standing-waiting fee. *Si, si,* we'll see him after the dance.

A waitress shows us to a table. When are the dancers coming? Just starting, what good timing. On come a guitarist and a mandolinist and a violin player. They strike up a tarantella and from behind a curtain a pair of dancers in traditional seventeenth-century costume emerge. They go into an exhausting dance full of exuberance. With clapping and shouts, they stomp the flagged floor; they get an enthusiastic reception. An old man goes round with a bag to collect donations. Exhausted the dancers are replaced by a fresh pair who perform an even faster tarantella. The girl dancer's red skirt is whirling and whirling like a dervish – the Moorish and Spanish influence in the dance is very, very strong. Toni and I are sipping a nameless local white wine and nibbling mozzarella cheese. It's all a most enjoyable evening and a thousand miles away from my jazz-oriented life, but this is very Hollywood and I'm on top of the world – just wait till I fall off!

After an hour and three sets of dancers alternating, the show is over. We all applaud wildly. With their departure, the tavern is quiet, save for the buzz of conversation. We drink a little more wine and then to our donkeys! They are waiting faithfully outside, eating a grass verge. I'm relieved to see that the huge erection has gone. Thank God Toni hadn't noticed it, it would have made me feel so inadequate. Back along the dark path with cypress trees looming like portents of doom; under this sky they look like Van Gogh's 'Starry Night Over Arles'. The dragoman starts to sing. All Italians have a natural aptitude for singing; ours doesn't. He has what jazz musicians call a 'cloth ear'. It wasn't helped by my donkey starting to bray. Behind me, I can hear Toni laughing.

We arrive back at the piazza, still alive with people. I pay the donkey man from my diminishing 72,000 lire. A drink before we retire, Toni? *Si*. We get the same waiter as last night. How are we enjoying the holiday? Very much. Would Toni like a Sambucco? No, she found out what that leads to last night. No, a lemonade please. And me? A half-bottle of Asti Spumante, my good man. I watch it being poured and frothing up in my glass. Can Toni have just a sip? Yes, a little sippy-poos then. Oh! She likes it! Another glass, please, waiter, and take this silly lemonade away.

I love watching people and here there were plenty to see, creatures that only emerge at night – they have a certain feline aura and use lots of brilliantine on their hair. At a table opposite is a man in a white suit, a heavy tan and patent leather hair. You can tell that he's spent all day getting ready, the crease in his trousers says he doesn't wear them for long periods. He drinks very slowly to conserve money. The woman with him looks like she's been sprayed in varnish. She, too, has a powerful tan – hours spent slobbed out in the sun to show off at night. I feel that they are both skint but they keep up a front. Toni and I pick everybody to pieces. It's great fun fantasizing over people. Are they doing it to us? They don't appear to.

A church steeple clock strikes midnight; Toni and I drink up, and make our way on to the funicular down to the Marina Grande. Fisherfolk are sitting outside their houses chatting, some are preparing for night fishing, putting pressure lights on the prow to attract fish. The night porter lets us in. 'Thank you for nice day,' says Toni. Never mind that. I grab her, weld our bodies together and kiss her. If I'd had glass eyes, they'd have steamed up. Despite the steam, she is going to bed alone, understand? Me and my steaming trousers bid her goodnight. I'm soon locked in the great empty space called sleep.

I awake on the third morning of our holiday. Through the window, I can see that it's another day with a clear blue sky. I yawn, stretch and make all those morning noises that men make. In the bathroom I can hear Toni's bath running. I tap on the wall, she taps back. What a pity she doesn't read morse code. I could tell her I love her: . . . . – . – – – . . . – . . – . . – – – . . –! I soap myself all over, giving the wedding tackle an extra soap for pleasure. Then I try the rickety shower; it just about works. I sing, Boo Boo 'twas on the Isle of Capri that I found her. Toni gives a furious tapping on her wall. Ah! why aren't we bathing and wall tapping together . . . I wonder which part she is washing. Ohhh helppppp. A brisk towelling down, then into my English gentleman's 'I'm-on-holiday' kit. Grey flannels, white shirt and brown sensible lace-up shoes. There's no doubting it, I look like a young nobleman on holiday. I collect Toni and we breakfast on the terrace. This morning it's fresh orange juice. I give Toni's upper thigh a squeeze – yes, it's fresh Milligan as well. Toni smacks my hand. 'You naughty, naughty, naughty boy,' she smacks in tempo to the words. A few rounds of hot toast and jam, a lemon tea and we are ready for the day.

I have consulted my Baedeker and have decided on a nice long walk to the Faraglioni. We board the funicular, empty save a peasant mother and her little girl. The child's eyes are like a doe's, giant brown things that tear your heart out. Like all children, though dressed poorly, she is scrubbed clean with her hair in a careful pigtail. Out of the box car and into the piazza where the cafés are setting up their tables and chairs for the day, and a few colourful sunshades. A street cleaner is sweeping the square. '*Buon giorno*,' he says as we pass. How nice, how different from those glum bastards on the workmen's tram to Woolwich Arsenal.

Off the piazza, we enter a vaulted tunnel. Then there's a small sign with an arrow, 'Faraglioni'. We hold hands and wander the flower-strewn path with this incredible light in the warmth of the morning sun. Flowers! Flowers! Flowers! Wild nasturtiums are going insane among the grasses. Columbine, campanula, yellow green arum, tall asters, little alkanet blue flowers, myrtle – the list was endless. There is the occasional villa staring out at that enticing sea. We pass a few explainable ruins – no doubt from the masonry that they are Roman. We don't talk much, nature is talking for us. A few words to point something out, that is all. Along the path, at intervals, are stone seats. We sit and enjoy the magic silence of a place with no motor cars. The path zigzags lazily on. One thing I notice is the total absence of birds due, I presume, to the islanders killing them either for sport or to eat – both an abomination. We reach a point with a railed lookout. Here we stop and take a photo of each other.

Spike, Capri

Toni, Capri

227

The magic walk continues. There seems to be nobody else in the world. I remember well how we stopped every now and then to embrace. It was nice to be able to do it outdoors without the neighbours looking on. 'I never forget this walk,' said Toni, 'I always, always remember.' We turn a corner and a new vista opens up to us, we can see to the top of the point where the remains of the villa of Tiberius are. Two white butterflies volute above us and dance on the wind. 'Ah,' says Toni, '*farfalle*.' Oh! So they are *farfallas*. I thought they were butterflies.

We have been ambling along for half an hour when we turn another sharp corner and there is the majestic view of the Faraglioni, this great rock ejecting from the cobalt blue water. We both oo and ahh. This is photograph country, partner! I take one of Toni and she one of me. What a pity we can't have one together! But wait, the superb brain of the young Milligan burns with inventive creativity. All I really need to do is place the camera on the wall, then with a long stick press the release button. As you can see below, it worked perfectly. Toni is totally bemused by her lover's audacity. 'You so clever,' she says and by God, I am *and* I'm still worth 68,000 lire.

*DIY photo of
Toni and me*

The ascent becomes fairly steep – a mixture of steps and paths and we reach what has been the villa of Tiberius, now down to a few bits of masonry. Who in their right mind would vandalize a magnificent Roman villa built for an emperor and leave nothing to show for their efforts? From the point, we see a sheer drop into the Tyrrhenian Sea. I let a stone fall; it seems an eternity till it hits the water. You felt that you could leap off into space and, like a bird, swoop over the waters. Looking down is hypnotic. 'It make me giddy,' says Toni, shaking her head.

We've been away a couple of hours and would dearly like tea or coffee, so we return to the piazza. It's a hot afternoon, so along with lemon tea we order two ice-creams. When they arrive, we are overwhelmed by the size. They are in tall champagne glasses, each layer a different garish colour, topped by a mountain of cream that ascends in a conical spiral. 'Oh,' says Toni with a child's delight. They look so beautiful, it's a shame to eat them. So we eat them with shame. I do everything except lick the glass – how I'd love to do it! We wander over to a low-key souvenir shop; we are looking for postcards. I want to send them off to all those poor buggers I know in England and wish I could be there when they see the Capri postmark! I'd make 'em suffer. This done we decide to return to the hotel and fill them in.

We sit on the hotel terrace. I send my parents a postcard telling them I'm here on Capri to stop me ruining my health. If my mother knew the truth, she would be having a mass said for my redemption and the death of Toni. We drop them all into the hotel postbox where we meet Signor Brinati. He is happy because he has some new arrivals. They turn out to be an English officer and his wife, whom we would meet later. Right now it's very hot and it's time to immerse ourselves in the Bay of Naples. To our little beach then and that amazing display of Milligan's water-sport tricks, a male Esther Williams. It all come to an inglorious end when a jellyfish stings me on the back of my thigh; it stings like mad. Toni says to put vinegar on it. Very good, Miss Fontana, now where is my usual supply of vinegar? What? I never carry any? You fool, no swimmer is complete without vinegar. So, no vinegar and not a vinegar shop in sight. I have to lump it and the bite just happens to turn into a red lump. Now Toni won't enter the water – it's silly when you haven't any vinegar. We sunbathe and talk a little. Only four more days; it's going so quickly, what a pity time hasn't got a brake on it. I'm getting a very fine tan that I hope will last till I get to my parents' new home in Dismal Deptford. I am going to keep the date of my return secret from them; I want to surprise them. Little did I know they would surprise me. More of that later.

Toni thinks it's time we went for tea. Thinks! It's time for tea! To the hotel, where I did sport under the shower and admire my appendages. We take tea on the terrace where we meet the young English officer and his wife, Lieutenant and Mrs Foster. I nod a good evening to them and they are pleased to hear their native tongue. We talk across to them; they are here for a week prior to posting back to the UK. He was in the Buffs regiment and she wasn't. Yes, he was in Tunisia. I'm quick to let him know that he was not alone – I was there, too. He says which part and I say all of me.

He laughs. 'Do you know Longstop?'

'Personally,' I say.

It terminates there, as they leave. They are going to have an evening swim. I warn them about the jellyfish and vinegar; they are grateful.

Toni wants a little lie-down. We retire to our rooms. Is she sure she wants to lie down alone? 'Yes, go away, Terr-ee.' I continue the *Life of Charlotte Brontë*. Oh, hurry and die, Charlotte. I want to finish with the book. The sun, sea and air have their effect – I fall asleep with Charlotte far from dead, she'll have to wait. It's a nice little doze, ended by Toni leaning over me and kissing my eyes. 'You sleep looong time,' she says, 'nearly eight o'clock!' I'll be ready in a flash and we'll dine out tonight. I put on a cardigan to keep the chill of the night from my emaciated body.

In the piazza, I hire a horse and landau to take us to Anacapri, the other village on the island. It's a half-hour gentle drive through undulating landscape on one of the few made-up roads on the island. Even in the dark, the visibility is good. The night flowers are giving off the end of day wafts of scent, lovely. The lights of Anacapri grow closer and closer till we drive into a delightful little square dominated by a church, Saint Sofia. In the corner of the square, I spot a very nice little restaurant, the Caffè Bitter – sounds German. (Listen, darling, can you hear a German-sounding café?) A young waiter with a fierce expression and an immaculate white jacket attends us. He smiles, the menu? *Si, si,* a drink while we're waiting? Two white wines.

The piazza is slightly larger than the Capri one, but a bit more down-market. At a table, some old men are playing dominoes. Here and there, sticking out like sore thumbs, are a few tourists rubbernecking. None of your *haute couture* Caprians here, this is more like the Scunthorpe-end of the island. Nevertheless, the menu promises a feast: they specialize in fish, and so do I. Was I not this very day bitten by one? Is there jellyfish on the menu? We both plump for Zuppa di Mare and Spaghetti Marinara. The latter they cook by the table with a great display of bunsen burner and flames leaping up, hoisting it from the pan with pincers and setting it down on the plates like an overhead crane. Ah! Music has started. A guitar and a mandolin tour the tables round the square.

'Toni, do you have any work when you go back to Rome?'

'I not know, we wait for work if start again Royal Ballet Company.'

'You want to dance again?'

'Oh, yes, I like. If you not dance, you soon lose practice.'

Yes, that's what ruined my ballet career; I never practised. A lady flower seller comes to our table and I buy Toni a posy of small red roses. It's our turn for the music. No, they don't know 'Valzer di Candele', but they know 'Lae That Piss Tub Dawn Bab'. No thanks, not that *or* the 'Warsaw Concerto'. We get 'Torna Sorrento'. Under the table, I press my foot on to Toni's just to let her know the fire hasn't gone out. She looks at me like a fireman.

I finally push my plate away, bloated. 'Oh, I eat too much,' says Toni, dabbing her lips with a napkin. Oh, lucky, lucky napkin. I've drunk too much wine and I'm lusting after her. Please, God, explain what sex is all about! Waiter, waiter, there's a fly in my ointment! Paying the bill, we catch a horse and landau back to Capri; we snog on the way. By the time we arrive at the piazza we need stabilizing. Any moment now someone will chuck a bucket of water over us. Who do we meet in the funicular but Lieutenant and Mrs Foster, who have had a 'jolly good dinner' and 'bai jove it's cheap here,' he says.

'Yes,' says Mrs Foster, 'we think it's cheaper here than in Naples', and he agrees with her.

I want to ask them why they are persecuting us like this. Would we like to join them for a drink on the terrace? Why not, says Toni. The four of us sit on the terrace. The night porter asks us, in a surprised voice, what we want. Would he settle for a bottle of wine? He's not very happy as it's gone midnight and he should be fast asleep, guarding the hotel. He goes away mumbling. 'I don't think we're very popular,' said Lieutenant Foster. Well, if he must know, he's not very popular with me. But for this, I'd be safely tucked up in bed with Toni. The porter returns with a bottle and four glasses. He can't get the cork out of the bottle. 'Here, let me try, old chap,' says Lieutenant Foster, a man of action. He pulls the cork with a self-satisfied grin as though he'd captured an enemy machine-gun nest.

'Where do you live in London?' he asks.

I tell him I live in Deptford. Oh, well, he lives in Chelsea. The excitement is unbearable.

'We used to live in Esher,' says Mrs Foster.

Dare I tell her that *I* used to live in Brockley S E 26? I put on a few false yawns – get the message, Toni? Toni doesn't get the message. Thank God, *they* are going to bed. Can I come with them? 'We've got an early start in the morning,' says Lieutenant Foster. One o'clock, soon *I'll* be trying to make an early start.

We get back to our rooms. No, Toni doesn't want to make love. She's very tired. Love locked out! Tomorrow's headlines could read,

English lieutenant found murdered on Capri!

So to bed, heavily steamed up with condensation on the Swonnicles. I take time out now to address the reader. You will be aware of the paucity of any lovey-dovey talk between us. Occasionally, I would tell her I loved her and she would call me her *'tesoro'*, that is all. It seemed we did not need an effusion of romantic communication. We loved each other and that was it. It felt strong and perfect. We never had a row or a cross word, there was no need for romantic out-pourings – that all came out in our being. It was a beautiful, invisible bond stronger than words. Meantime, back on Capri steaming Milligan is trying to sleep off his red-hot, revolving Swonnicles and desire.

Morning number four – three to go! Hurry, Milligan, don't waste the golden hour lolling in the pit scratching your cobblers. I had brought my watercolours with me and decided today I would do some outdoor painting. Toni could join me if she wished, or she could take some of my fortune and go shopping in the piazza. Yes, she would like to be rid of me for a day. After breakfast we ascend on the funicular; at the piazza, we split. I take a path wandering off the square. After a quarter of a walk through the paradise garden, I come to a small corner with a huge garden pot sprouting little white and red flowers – an ideal subject, and simple. I set up my easel and the result you see overleaf. Alas, poverty-stricken Penguin can only afford black and white.

233

Watercolour I did on Capri

As I sketch, small bees are buzzing and taking their share of the nectar of life. The colours before me blaze out; there is no subtlety on Capri, each colour stands out in the all-pervading light. I get lost in the brush strokes – disaster! I kick over my bottle of water. Just up the path is a villa. I knock on the door and a pretty young girl answers. She eyes me suspiciously. I ask, can I have 'Una po de aqua.' Let's face it, you don't often have people knocking on doors for water. She takes the bottle and I hear someone ask her what it is. She shouts that a man wants water; the mother is inquisitive, and comes to stare at me. I explain I am 'Una artista aquarello'. She nods her head understandingly. The daughter appears with the full bottle and I thank them both and return to the easel.

It's a hot day with a breeze, so the colours dry quickly. I finish one painting, then move along the path and find the ruins of a Roman tomb. Super. I set up the easel and soon get lost. I get the background of the sea and sky just right, with the creamy stones of the tomb in the foreground. It's my best effort. I stand back a little to admire it, at which moment the wind catches it and I watch it float away down the cliffs and land on the sea. Bloody luck, did Van Gogh have this trouble? Shall I chop an ear off? So, with one solitary painting I make my way back to the piazza.

No signs of Toni, no sign with an arrow saying 'Toni 3 chilometri'. I sit me down at a café, making sure people see my painting equipment. Today I want people to know I am a great artist. Tomorrow I'd be Bing Crosby again and, who knows, the day after Jimmy Cagney. For a few moments I'm Billy Bunter and order an ice-cream, then back to Van Gogh again. I'm taking my first spoonful when a pair of small, cool hands from behind me clasp over my eyes. It's Toni, she is smiling effusively. Ah, Toni, love of my life, see this masterpiece! She looks at my painting. 'Very pretty,' she says and I reward her with an ice-cream. What has she bought? She delves into her shopping bag and shows me two silk scarves, 'One for my mother, one for Lily and this,' she takes out a little velvet heart-shaped pincushion, 'this for Gioia.' Nothing for me? Not even a silk headscarf?

'You only do one painting?' she says.

'No, I've done two.'

Oh, can she see it? Yes, if she dives off the three-hundred-foot cliffs.

After the ice-cream, neither of us feels like lunch. Shall we take out customary swim and I'll show her once again my aquatic trick? She'll love my standing-on-head-legs-out-of-water bit. Crossing the piazza, we meet the Fosters. They've been to the Blue Grotto.

235

'It was a jolly nice trip,' says Mrs Foster.

'And so cheap,' he added.

Yes, I agreed; things were cheaper here than on the mainland, but a man of my wealth wouldn't notice that.

We bid them adieu and after collecting our costumes, we swim from our little beach. It's deserted again. Toni has bought a small bottle of olive oil. God, I wanted to top up my suntan. I rub it all over and smell like a mixed salad. Toni wants some rubbed on her back. Nowhere else? I fall asleep in the sun, wondering what the poor people are doing. My poor father is possibly at work and my poor mother doing laundry, that's what the poor were doing. Toni is talking: can I see if there are any jellyfish around? Can I go in and see if they are stinging? I swim under water and announce from the sea that it is free of jellyfish but, ah ha, there's me in it now – watch out for the groper fish, dear. I display my speed at the crawl and I'm Johnny Weismuller for a while. Remember the drill: three foot kicks with every one arm stroke. Little does the world know that I represented Chislehurst Laundry, Lewisham in the All-Laundry Swimming Championships of 1936, and won! And back I was again on the Monday, washing all the shitty sheets from Lewisham Hospital.

Toni gives a shriek and in a froth of water swims for the shore. Something touched her, she looks a bit touched. She thinks it was a jellyfish. I do more underwater scouting – all I can see are bits of seaweed. No, she won't go in again. We dry off, make for the hotel and an afternoon siesta. It's very warm now. I doze with nothing on save a sheet over me. Reflected in the mirror, I look like a corpse. Was there *nothing* in the world that would fill me out? I'd tried Horlicks and Sanatogen, Phosperine, cod liver oil and malt, queen bee jelly, arrowroot, Virol, Dr Collins' Enervate Mixture – with the list becoming endless, I fall into a ziz.

When I awake, it's dark. I've missed tea. I rush around, shower, dress and contact Miss Fontana. 'I come your room at tea-time, but you sleep so I no wake you,' she says. Has *she* had tea? Yes, it was very nice, thank you. She had it with

Lieutenant Foster and his wife who had told her things were cheaper on Capri than the mainland.

'Where shall we have dinner tonight?' I ask her.

She smiles and shrugs her shoulders. I wonder where she means.

'Where *you* like to go,' she says.

I shrug my shoulders and that doesn't get either of us anywhere. Shrugging shoulders rarely does. After a few minutes of mutual shrugging we decide to eat in our hotel. Again the dining-room is empty, the poor waiters standing like gloomy sentinels. At our appearance, they breathe a sigh of relief. With a fixed-menu smile, Mario takes our orders. Yes, tonight's speciality is spaghetti Neapolitan. *My* night's speciality will be Toni Fontana. She can eat spaghetti so neatly, while I have great strings of it hanging out of my mouth that need cutting with scissors. In come the 'Jolly Decent' Fosters who, no doubt, are eating here tonight as it's cheaper than Naples. They have been on a boat trip to Sorrento and it was, as he said, 'absolutely spiffing'. What had we been doing? I said we'd been for a 'jolly good' swim. It's remarkably quiet, the only sound is the clanking of our forks and spoons touching the plates. This is amplified when the Fosters start to eat. I start to laugh at how strange it sounds, like Siamese music. Toni wants to know why I am laughing. How can I answer? We hear the chef shouting in the kitchen, the food must be deaf.

After dinner Lieutenant Foster and his wife want us to have a drink with them. What a 'jolly good' idea. We join them at their table. Why not go outside on the terrace? Yes, it's a warm night. The Fosters are very 'nice' people. You can tell by his demeanour that he banks at Cox & Kings, she shops at Fortnum & Mason's and he rides to hounds. He's definitely on the defensive when I say I think foxhunting is cruel.

'Well, someone's got to keep them down, old boy.'

'Are you a farmer?'

'No, I was a stockbroker.'

'I'm baffled as to how stockbrokers are worried by foxes.'

237

'No, no, it's the farmers. That's why they let us hunt on their land.'

'But you personally aren't bothered by them?'

'No.'

'Why doesn't the farmer do the hunting?'

'Because we do.'

'Supposing you weren't there?'

'Oh, well, we are.'

'But supposing you weren't?'

'But we are, ha ha ha.'

Yes, we are, ha ha ha – no bloody use appealing to his conscience.

'They eat an awful lot of chickens,' she says.

'So do we,' I say.

But they can't be moved. One can only pray they fall off their horses and break their bloody necks. Toni and I bid our goodnight, leaving a slightly strained atmosphere and a feeling that I was now a *persona non grata*. The question at this romantic hour is am I *persona grata* with Toni? With an unspoken yes, we get into bed and go back to the beginning of time . . . In the small hours a very small Milligan crawls out of Toni's bed, clutching its clothes wearing nothing save its underpants. I make sure the corridor's clear, I tippy-toe to my door. I've locked myself out and haven't got the key. I have to dress and wake the porter for the passkey. I shake him gently in his chair. 'Chesosava,' he splutters; then I notice his teeth are in a glass on a table. He turns his back and clicky-clacks them back into place. He opens my door and soon I'm in bed and rapidly asleep. I'm not asleep very long when I wake with the runs and that continues through the night. It gets so bad I realize it's silly to go back to bed, better to sleep on the loo.

It's ten o'clock in the morning when I hear Toni tapping on the door. *'Entrare,'* I say, when I should say 'Enteritis.' I don't tell her I've got the shits; someone who sings like Bing Crosby shouldn't have them. I tell her I don't feel well. Would I like her to sit with me? God, no, I want her out of the room before the next series of explosions starts. Can she order me something to eat? Tea and toast? She leaves just before I have an attack of postern blasts. I keep the bed-clothes tucked tightly round. Mario arrives with a tray and my food. I'm ill? He's sorry. He will be if he stays here.

All through the day shattering explosions shake the room. Please, God, nobody come in except the deaf and those with anosmia. My God, I'm shaking the windows – all this wind power going to waste. Connected up, I could run a windmill. Between the shits, I doze fitfully but have to be on the alert to avoid skidmarks on the sheets. What has caused it? They say Capri water is not that safe, perhaps that's it. By late evening it's eased off and I'm about half a stone lighter. Toni comes in. How am I? Feeling a bit better; where has she been? She went to buy some more postcards and had a swim. No, I'm not getting up – I don't want to clear the hotel. Yes, I'll have some more tea and toast. I can keep it down but can't keep it in. This time the waitress brings in my order. She's a young Capri girl, beautifully simple, dark and vivacious. She smiles.

'*Lascia qui*,' I say, tapping my bedside table.

She smiles again, nods her head. '*Ecco*,' she says.

My God, has she heard the echoes? It must have escaped under the door! I eat my frugal fare (frugals are good for you!). It's been an exhausting day, I've done about ten miles of running and feel hollow. The toilet seat has never been allowed to grow cold. I fall asleep and I don't wake till the sun is shining. I move cautiously in my bed – am I better? I get up and bath without any alarms; so far, so good. I cough without any disasters. Yes, I think I can sally forth and mix with safety. Before I do, Toni arrives. She looks lovely in a simple cotton dress with thin red horizontal stripes – she is *so* brown.

'Come,' she says and takes my hand. She leads me to a table on the terrace. 'This is our last day.'

I thought that yesterday. It had gone so quick, like I was going all yesterday.

After breakfast we get to the piazza and take a landau for a ride to Anacapri again, this time in the white gasping

239

sunshine. As we drive to the hypnotic, lazy clip-clop of the horse, the view is all-revealing. We can see the sea on each side of the island; to our left rises Mount Salaro, topped by a ruined *castello* and pinpricked with white cottages. The flowers are in riot – blue, white, red, yellow, purple. It's a painter's paradise. How terrible to be struck blind on an island like this. 'Eet is too, too beautiful,' says Miss Fontana, shaking her little head in disbelief. So far, except for the shits and not seeing Gracie Fields, the holiday has been perfect.

I tell the driver not to hurry. '*Piano, piano,*' I say, which has all the effect of rapping with a damp sponge on a window. I stand up and tap him on the shoulder. '*Piano, piano, per favore,*' I say.

He tells me, '*Non posso.*'

It's a fixed-speed horse; if he lets it go slower, it will a) stop b) die.

The road veers towards the right of the island and then turns inward. Strewn before us on the plain is Anacapri and its gleaming houses of white, pink and sky blue. Toni says they look like '*Case di bambole!*'. The road descends and we finally reach the end of it as it terminates in the square. The horse looks as though he's going to terminate as well. We buy some apples from a stall and feed them to him. The driver looks at them longingly, so we feed the driver as well.

Adjacent to us is a small café with several official guides with armbands sitting at tables, drinking rough wine and playing rough dominoes. As I have no idea which direction to take for a walk, I go over to them and ask for a guide. They all stand up, then start to argue about whose turn it is. Toni and I stand like idiots for five minutes while the argument rages. One by one they drop out and finally one comes forward. He's short, about fifty, wearing a peaked cap with a badge that looks like a clenched fist. He has a face like a clenched fist with a large clenched nose. He has a silver-grey stubble, a shave away from being a beard and ears that are really supports for his hat. When he stands up to his full height, you can see he hasn't any. He has a huge head whose weight must account for his bow legs. Yes, he'll show us a walk but can we wait while he finishes his dominoes. While we wait, Toni and I have a *caffelatte* and magnificent gooey pastry, full of cream and sweet as nectar.

His dominoes finished, our guide, Alfredo, leads us on our walk. '*Un'ora,*' he holds up one finger. We pass several villas of the classic type, whose immaculate gardens burgeon with floral life. Now and then, when he gets shagged out, Alfredo stops and gives us snippets of information. Tiberius built twelve villas on the island, one for each of the Roman gods. Apparently, none of them showed up.

We are slowly climbing up the path and after an hour reach the peak of Mount Solaro. The view is indescribable, but I'll describe it. To our right, I can see Salerno and even the invasion beach where I landed that day in September 1943 – even further away, I can see the Doric temples at Paestum. '*Fantastico, si?*' says Alfredo, seated on a wall. Yes, fantastic. To our left, we see as far as the Gulf of Gaeta and the Abuzzese Mountains. It was like being in a plane coming into land at Naples. Toni and I stood with an arm around each other, silenced by what we could see. This was marvellous, better even than two eggs, sausage and chips! It was almost better than Bing Crosby in 'We're Not Dressing'.

With the view etched in our minds for ever, we return to the square in Anacapri and two chilled glasses of lemonade. Afredo returns to his cronies and plunges into the hectic world of dominoes. 'What do we do now, Terr-ee?' says Toni. I personally would like to die. It's very hot now and we decide to have our last swim on the last day. By horse-drawn, then, back to the piazza which we find full of Americans who are all a bit pissed, sitting around at tables. They've got to the shouting-remarks-at-passing-ladies stage. We edge off to the funicular, which is coming up loaded with more noisy G Is. When they see Toni, they whistle and give shouts of 'Hello, Baby, get rid of him', etc. It made me feel invisible. Fools! It's a good job they didn't know I boxed for the London South-East Polytechnic, Lewisham. It was an even better job they didn't know I'd had the shit beaten out of me.

Toni wants to know 'Why American and British soldier always shout at woman'. I tell her the Americans can afford to shout because they have lots of money and the British *have* to shout because they haven't. '*Molto ignorante,*' she says. 'When German soldier in Rome they never shout.' No, they just gassed you.

The sun is scorching down when we splash into the cool waters of the bay, which appears to be free from jellyfish. I just sit up to my waist, occasionally splashing myself to stop sunburn. Toni swims up and sits next to me. She holds my hand under water – kinky, eh?

'What you think, Terr-ee?' she says.

'I think it's time for this,' I say, and give her a salty kiss and gave one a quick squeeze.

'Ooo, Terr-ee,' she gushed, 'everybody see.'

Grabbing her ankles, I pull her under water – impetuous, playful fool, Milligan! Toni surfaces laughing and tries to splash me. I swim out of reach and pull funny faces. I'm such a bundle of fun, it wouldn't take much for me to do my handstands. Ah, look who's here – it's the Fosters.

'What's the water like?' he says.

'It's jolly good,' I say.

He wears a black full-length costume that was out of date in 1929, and a body to match. He enters the water, does a clumsy bellyflop then strikes out with a strange overarm stroke.

'It's beautiful, darling,' he shouts to his wife.

I thought it looked very clumsy. She is wearing a 'sensible' one-piece, red costume; her arms and legs from the knees down are reddy-brown, the rest of her body ghastly white. She minces into the sea until the water reaches her fanny, at which she breathes an ecstatic 'Oh'.

I had wondered why our patch of beach was alway so deserted, today I find out why. To my horror, I notice 'Richard the Thirds' floating in the water. We are only swimming at a sewage outflow – no wonder I'd had the shits. When we return to the hotel, the manager confirms it. '*Si,*' he says, '*molto sporco, molto, acque di scolo.*' Fancy, I'd been

up to my neck in *acque di scolos*! Apparently, the far side of
the island is the shit-free swimming – too late, now. I take a
hot shower and scrub my body with a nailbrush. Fancy,
after all the paper I had put on the loo seats to avoid catching
anything, there I'd been swimming in it! When I tap on
Toni's door, she is just out of the shower. She is wearing a
dressing gown – not for long. We both end up in bed,
steaming, with the Swonnicles fibrillating.

After we have consumed each other, we fall asleep and are
awakened by the maid wanting to come in and turn the bed
down. Toni tells her not to bother. It's twilight, the sky is
going from purple to blue-black, with crystalline stars
hanging like clusters of diamond grapes. Tonight we will
dine where Toni says she'd like to eat in the piazza. I must
put my Robert Taylor kit on: dark blue corduroy jacket,
blue trousers, white silk shirt and satin tie. I comb my hair
well back to show my 'widow's peak'. The mirror says I'm
a Robert Taylor lookalike. I take my silver cigarette case,
because I want to be seen tapping my cigarette on it after
dinner.

Arriving in the piazza, we find it busy with nightlife. It's
a Saturday, and the piazza is fuller than normal. I give my
bankroll a quick feel to give myself confidence. In the corner
of the piazza is the Vienna Café – very smart, outdoor tables
with snow-white starched napery and bowls of flowers. The
waiters, too, looked starched and crackle when they move.
This is an Austrian-run café: all the staff are blond and
blue-eyed. All of them look like Nazis on the run; their smiles
seem a mite pinched and insincere. However, the menu is
Italian.

'Oh, this restaurant very chic, Terr-ee,' says Toni.

'Very nice,' I say, as I made heavy with tapping a cigarette
on my case, a little too heavy – the end of the cigarette splits.
Unlike Robert Taylor, I nip the end off and light up the
remainder. Even though I'm Robert Taylor, there's no need
to be uneconomical. The waiter brings us two ridiculous
menus about two foot long by one and a half foot wide.
Mine obscures the view of Capri, Toni and the rest of Italy.

From behind this cardboard shield, I can at least hear her talking.

'Wot you have, Terr-ee?'

Terree will have Mozzarella and tomatoes, then scampi. Are you still there, Toni?

'Yes,' she giggles.

The waiter asks, any particular wine? I say, yes, *any* particular wine. Ah good, the piazza musicians have started up: they fill the night with melody – the vocalist, with halitosis, which he breathes over me when the band arrives at our table. He sings with a permanently outstretched arm, holding an inverted hat. Putting the menu on one side, I take out my roll of money so that the entire square can see it. Slowly, oh, so slow, I peel off a thousand lire bill and drop it into his hat from a great height. The amount is large enough to bring a sob into his voice, and mine. He inserts the word *'grazie'* into the song.

'You give lot of money,' says Toni.

'I know,' I say, 'everyone in the piazza is talking about me.'

The waiter brings us a bottle of 'any special wine', a white, fruity Capri. We clink glasses and clink eyes; after a long, lingering, loving, lasting look with just a touch of the lascivious, we drink.

'This time we stay here most happy in my life,' she says.

'Anche me,' I reply. She inclines her head to one side – this would make me appear to be sitting at an angle.

'I very sorry when tonight finish.'

Amen.

'When I first meet you I girl, now I woman.'

Gad, two for the price of one!

The crackling waiter arrives with out first course. *'Signori,'* he says and sets it down. *'Buon appetito,'* he says with a grin, a Germanic half-bow and a click of his heels. Why doesn't he just piss off?

Quick, my false beard and dark glasses and my Quasimodo hump! Gracie Fields has entered the piazza with three other people! One blessing, she's not singing. Thank God, she's sitting at the far end of the square. Her penetrating voice rises above the music. '*Buona* sers ee bai gum,' she is saying. People are turning and staring, she is big in England and known on Capri as *Nostra* Gracie. The question is, will she sing?

There is no scampi like Italian scampi and this scampi is *not* like Italian scampi. I call over a waiter who looks like Hermann Goering. 'Vot is ronk vid it?' I tell him it's scampi à la hard as bloody bullets. He sweeps it away and returns with scampi à la still as hard as bloody bullets. Would I like something else? Toni tells me her sole is very nice. OK, I'll have that. Meantime, I'll have another little tipple of wine. It's happened! The musicians have reached Gracie Fields's table and soon she is warbling 'Vedo Mare, Quanto Bello' in the sitting position. She has a strong penetrating voice; it can penetrate walls, battlements and eardrums. When she finishes, the whole square gives her generous applause. Is it with appreciation or relief?

The Dover sole is just as I like it, dead. The more I drink, the more I tell Toni I love her and sometimes I tell her I love the wine, I tell her I love the white-coated waiter, that horse across the square. I also love that square across the horse and the waiter's white coat; I love the white square with the waiter across the horse's coat and another bottle please. What's the time? Midnight, we'd better be getting back to the hotel or my mother will be wondering where I am. As I accompany Toni to the funicular, I hear Gracie Fields singing again: it's 'Ave Maria'. The noise of the funicular drowns her out as we descend for the last time – goodbye, little piazza.

I desperately want to sleep with Toni and Toni is desperate not to. 'No no no no, Terr-ee, no no no no, you go sleep. Stop that, no no no no no, please stop that,' she finally breaks my stranglehold on her and pushes me in the direction of away. All right, Toni, there's always Lily Dunford of Brockley, Bette from Bexhill and Norwood Beryl!!! One last bedtime cigarette: I lie on my back under the covers with a slight steam on, enjoying the process of getting lung cancer,

245

then fall into a delicious sleep. Arggghhhhhhhhhhh! I awake as the cigarette has burnt down to my fingers, bloody fool! I blow furiously on the burn and get light-headed. I run my finger under the tap – bloody fool, it's somebody's fault. To sleep for the second time, then. What a waste of time: eight hours laid out like a corpse. The trouble with sleep is that nothing happens.

NAPLES AGAIN

NAPLES AGAIN

I awake to the sound of various church bells, wassatime? Nine o'clock. We have to catch the eleven o'clock ferry. I leap from my bed and hastily pack my suitcase, then collect Toni for breakfast. Is she packed? No, but her clothes are, ha ha ha. Mario knows we are leaving today – most important to him is how much. I settle the bill with Mr Brinati.

'I hope you enjoy Capri,' he says.

'Apart from the shit-strewn sea, we have.'

It's cost us ten thousand lire.

As we leave the hotel, Mr Brinati stands at the door and waves us goodbye.

Lugging Toni's suitcase and mine, I lead down the little path to the Marina Grande. We can see that the ferry has docked. From where we are the ship looks like a toy. As we get nearer, it gets bigger. Not many people boarding. At the top of the gangplank, I present our return tickets to a scruffy-looking sailor with all the animation of a wooden leg. He is to sea travel what Charles Manson was to vegetarianism.

We go into the saloon and sit on the bench seat like lost children. At the bar, the barman is polishing glasses. 'I hope I no sick this time,' says Toni. It would certainly be a messy end to the holiday. She sits in anticipation, I give her hand a squeeze, she smiles back. A few more passengers are hurrying up the gangplank – an Italian family with two young children. They enter the saloon, the woman whoops out one of her boobs and starts to feed the baby. You don't get that on the 74a tram going to Forest Hill.

The engines throb into life and there are shouts from the bridge as the tie-off hawsers are freed from the bollards. Slowly, the ferry appears to turn on its axis and the vessel heads out to sea. Thank God, it's totally calm and by the time we are halfway across, Toni is still all right. We have made our way to the deck above and stand at the rails in the ship's slipstream. It's a hot day but the sea air is delightfully cool, like real cool, man. Behind us Capri is getting smaller; we stay the same size. We must have got off just in time. Napoli and its giant Mount Vesuvius are appearing through a morning haze. Naples is getting bigger – by the time we arrive, it's the right size to accommodate us. I realize that all through the trip, neither of us had said a word. As we are docking, Toni looks at me: 'All finish,' she says with a note of sadness. 'Never mind,' says Merry Milligan, tomorrow we journey to the Eternal City and stay with 'Momma' where our sex life will come to a grinding halt. Still, there are other things – ice-cream, spaghetti, rug-weaving and light groping.

After Capri, Naples is like a madhouse – the noise! And a variety of smells, from stale fish to guardsmen's socks.

'*Che massa*,' says Toni, as we thread our way through the dockside crowds.

'*Scusi, scusi*,' I repeat *ad nauseam*.

The taxi we catch is a scream: at the back, it's down on its springs; the front points up so the driver has to permanently elongate his neck to see the road. We at the back are in the semi-prone position. All my life I'd been prone to semis (Eh?). Toni and I discuss tomorrow's arrangements. We have to catch the 10.30 train to Rome in the morning; I'll call for her at etc., etc., etc. I drop her at the Albergo Rabicino; a goodbye kiss, and I'm off to mine.

When I arrive I go straight to Bill Hall's bedroom – my God, he's still in bed! Has he been up since I left him? "Ow you get on with your bird in Capri?' he says, searching for his fags. 'Shagged out, are you?' What has he been doing? 'I done some local gigs with Bornheim and Mulgrew. We got one tomorrer night at the Officers' Club. You want to sit on guitar?'

'No, Bill, I'm off to Rome with Toni. Any news about the boat passage?'

'No, it's being arranged through Major Philip Ridgeway

at CSE. 'Ee thinks it will be on the *Dominion Monarch*. 'Ee said 'ee thinks it will be sailing on 15 September.'

'He *thinks*? Doesn't he know?'

'Don't ask me, mate. That's wot 'ee told me.'

15 September – that would give me a good clear week of rug-making and light groping in Roma, and a few days to spare in Naples.

When I get to my room, there is a load of mail on my bed. My father has sent me a roll of newspapers, a real treat. I spend the afternoon finding how the rest of the world is faring. How good to see English newspapers again!

BREAD RATION; NO CHANGE YET

Ah, here's a good one:

Gerry Merry, father of twenty-two children, fined for stealing from chemist's shop

– he must have been after condoms.

Heath for Trial on Chine Murder Charge

– so someone's been murdering Chines. Are they small Chinamen? I loved seeing the ads again. 'Biscuits Keep You Going'. Did this mean the runs? Then, 'Repair War-Damaged Hair with Silvikrin!' 'For Inner Health, Take Bile Beans'.

Evening. Hall wants to know if I want to come down to a club on the Via Roma.

'It's a nightclub. Lot of 'Mericans down there, plenty of Eyetie birds – got a good Eyetie band. They let me sit in.'

I'm at a loose end and it's frayed, so O K. Yes, Bill, let's go in there and beat up a storm – yeah, wow, beat me, Daddy, eight to the bar. I'll bring my guitar along.

We duly enter the door of a place called The Den. We descend stairs to a basement, where a band is trying to be heard above the noise of the customers. It's a postage-stamp-sized room, the smoke so thick the band on the far side are hardly visible. Everyone is on the floor jiving. Around the perimeter are chairs and tables; we manage to get a couple in the corner by the band. The leader, one Franco Pattoni, plays tenor sax. He sees Bill and waxes lyrical.

'Ah, Beel, *vieni, vieni,*' and beckons him to come up.

'We drink first,' says Bill, miming the action.

''Ello, big boy.' I look up at an overmade-up but very pretty Italian girl of statuesque proportions, smiling down at me. 'You buy drink, I dance weese you,' she says.

I'm looking up at her directly under her prominent boobs that give a promise of pneumatic bliss. No, I won't dance but she can sit and have a drink. She pulls up a chair and crosses her legs, a good safety move.

'You American?' she asks.

'No, I'm not.'

Straight away, I lose marks. Can she have a cigarette? Yes. Can she have a light? Yes, anything else? Is there any laundry she wants doing? Yes, she'd like a brandy and coke. She also wants to know if I'm married. No, I'm single and have to depend on Swedish massage. Her name is Bianca Bianci, mine is Spike Milligan.

Bill Hall leans over with a gleam in his eye. 'If you play your cards right, you could catch it off her,' he says.

After a drink, we both get on the stand and join in the jazz. It's a very good combo, playing music of a professional standard. Bianca sits and watches – I hope she also listens. She recrosses her legs; it must be hell in there. She is whisked away by a drunken G I and waves me goodbye over his shoulder. Another woman in my life gone! How they pile up.

By midnight no one has asked us to play 'Lay That Pistol Down, Babe' – it must be some kind of record. I've had enough. As I put my guitar away, I'm confronted by both of Bianca Bianci's.

'You want good time?' she says.

No, thank you, I've just had one but don't let me stop you having one. She really likes me, lays a hand on my lapel.

'Oh, why you say no,' she says, pouting.

'Pouting is such sweet sorrow,' I say.

I leave – it had been a near thing for Toni. By taxi, back to the hotel where I ask the night porter could he get me some food. 'No, *signore*.' I hold up a hundred lire note and 'Yes, *signore*.' He raids the kitchen and comes into my room with – Arghhhhhhhhhhhh, no, it's Cold Collation! It's better than nothing, but only just! I eat it by closing my eyes and thinking of England. I next indulge in a hard night's sleeping in the kneeling load position. (What am I talking about? Helppppp.)

ROME YET AGAIN

ROME YET AGAIN

Monday morning finds me packing my best clothes for the Rome trip. I pack my Bing Crosbys, my Robert Taylors and my Leslie Howards. At breakfast Bill Hall, who in the morning looks like a mummy with bandages off, wants to know do I want a gig tonight. No, I'm going to Rome with Toni. ''Aven't you had enough rumpo?' he says. How can he be so crude about my love affair? It's not rumpo I'll be after in Rome, it will be ice-cream, spaghetti, rug-weaving and light groping in between mother-in-laws. Will he still be in Naples when I get back?

'I suppose so. 'Oo wants to go back to bloody England in the winter?'

'Oh, don't you want to see the old folks at home?'

'No.'

'Why not?'

'Because they don't want to bloody well see me. They only written to me once – that was to tell me they'd let my room.'

I take my leave, scoot upstairs three at a time, trip and fall down four at a time. I've hurt myself, elbows, shins and all parts south of the meridian. Clutching my injuries I go to me room and get the porter to order me a taxi. Limping, I lug my heavier-than-me suitcase to the waiting vehicle. 'Albergo Rabicino' I tell the unshaved, bleary-eyed taxi driver. He's one of those slow-witted drivers that lose control at speeds over twenty miles an hour. Painfully slow, he chugs down the streets of the Vomero. He's very good at shouting, ex- cellent. He shouts at all and sundry, for what reason is beyond me, but then he *is* beyond reason.

Toni is waiting at the front door of the hotel. I collect her and her two suitcases and we are on our way to the Central Station. The crowds there are frightening. I book two first-class tickets, '*Piattaforma numero due*,' says the ticket office man. Through a nightmare of people with a high garlic content, we struggle to the platform where the train is now standing. We find two seats in a *non-fumare* carriage. Thank God, we're early. Soon the train fills up with what appear to be peasant families and their furniture fleeing the wrath of Saracen invaders. Fathers shout, mothers scream, children howl. Obvious third-class passengers crowd into our carriage and the corridors. I look at Toni, who seems quite cool and undisturbed.

'Is it always like this?'

'No,' she says, 'this is a good day.'

I'd never seen congealed people before.

To shouts, whistles and flag waving, the train pulls out. Everybody seems to be in a rage. The nicest part is I'm squashed up next to Toni. On my left is a huge, heavy-breathing, fat woman with a huge basket on her lap. From it protrudes bread and the neck of a wine bottle. The thought of trying to get to the toilet fills me with dread. I pray God that my bladder will hold out for the trip. After half an hour Toni wants just that. She disappears into the crowded corridor. I don't see her again for nearly half an hour. When she comes back, she tells me there's a queue a mile long for the loo. I say, I know, I'm on the end of it. It takes me half an hour to get there. The loo is in an appalling state; no one appears to have holed in one. Back to Toni. The journey will last two hours – the question is, will we?

It is with a gasp of relief that we steam into Rome Central and fall out of the carriage. We throw ourselves in a taxi and thank God it's all over. On on on to Via Appennini! Signora Fontana is waiting at the door with sister Lily and maid Gioia. There's endless embracing and kisses on each cheek. '*Benvenuto*, Terr-ee,' they all say as the kissing roundelay continues.

'Come, Terr-ee, I show you your room.'

Toni leads me to a neat, small bedroom at the back of the apartment. I dump my bags.

Mangiare mezzogiorno has been laid on. Fussing like a

mother hen, Signora Fontana shows us our seat placings. 'Terr-ee, *qui*,' she gestures.

'How did the show go in Naples?' asks sister Lily, who will have to be killed.

'Oh, the show in Naples? Very well. Oh, yes, my word, the show in Naples, ha ha, it was splendid.'

Signora Fontana tells us there has been a one-day strike of tram drivers. Oh, really? How interesting. Does Signora Fontana know that the price of butter has gone up in Poland, and there are no dry-cleaners in Peru, and a Negro vicar has crossed Scotland on one leg, medicine is now free in England and so is illness? Soon I'm left out of the conversation as they all talk in Italian at a speed too fast for me by far. I just sit and when they all laugh I join in like an idiot. When the meal ends, Toni remembers me again. 'My mother have bought ticket for opera tomorrow night. You like see?' Yes, I'd like see. The meal ends with zabaglione. 'Gioia make for you, she know you like,' says Toni. Delicious! Now it's announced that all the ladies are going to afternoon mass. Do I want to come, too? No, I've got this bad leg.

I spent a relaxing afternoon listening to the Allied Forces Network which played unending programmes of big band music. This afternoon, I remember, it was Artie Shaw. I didn't know at the time that the days of the big band were numbered (I think this was number six). Swing music was the 'in' thing and I was part of the scene, man. When the ladies returned from mass, they found me stretched out on the sofa, asleep, with the radio on. It had been a boring service with an old priest who couldn't enunciate well and dribbled. Now some tea: Gioia disappears into the kitchen. The Signora wants to give me a present, a book, *Italia Paese dell'Arte* – was this Artie Shaw?

We sit round drinking tea and drumming up conversation. What will I be doing when I get back to England? As I step off the boat, I will immediately become famous – that's what. The Bill Hall Trio will be up there in lights, London will be at our feet, shins and groins! Toni tells her mother how successful we are. Oh yes, her mother knows, had she

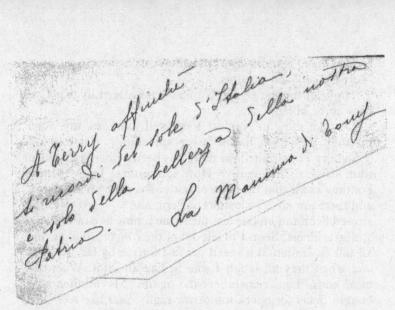

A Terry affinché
si ricordi del sole d'Italia,
e sole della bellezza della nostra
Patria.
La Mamma di Tony

Dedication by Toni's mother in the book

not seen us triumph at the Argentine Theatre, even if she herself was a bit baffled by the act? I remember her mother had no idea of jazz and couldn't understand why we all wore rags, and *why* were people laughing at us? It wasn't fair. How is my mother? My mother is very well. And my father? He's well, too. What about my brother? Would you believe he's well as well. The phone goes, Lily rushes to it. It's her beau. Immediately her body turns to jelly and she speaks *sotto voce*, blushing and giggling, running her finger up and down the wall. Toni smiles, 'This new boyfriend.' Lily is now rocking backwards and forwards and her finger is going up and down the wall faster. What *is* he saying to her?

Toni unwraps the presents she bought on Capri. They are all delighted. Gioia is delighted with her pincushion and hugs it to her; Signora Fontana tries on her headscarf. Lily is weaving from side to side and trying to drill a hole in the table with her index finger. She is nodding her head – how can he hear that on the phone? She seems to be going into a trance. Who is she speaking to, Svengali? I have another cup of tea. They want to know have I any plans for the evening?

Yes, but I left them in my other jacket pocket – I remember, though. I thought Toni and I might go to the pictures. 'Oh, yes,' says Toni enthusiastically. Splendid, her mother is expecting an old schoolfriend and will no doubt spend the evening going over the old school exams. 'Do you remember $2 \times 2 = 4$?' 'As if it were yesterday.'

The drag of going to an ENSA cinema is that I have to wear my CSE uniform to be allowed in free. When we arrive, we see they are showing *Fantasia*. I'v seen it before but it's good enough to see again, if only for the hippo and crocodile ballerinas in the 'Dance of the Hours'. In the dark, we sit holding hands and sucking boiled sweets. It's a very enjoyable, relaxing evening until three soldiers sit in front of us. The one in front of me has a head the size of a Dickens's Christmas pudding with ears that look like another two heads looking over his shoulders. He totally obscures the screen and Italy. I have to watch with my head inclined at sixty degrees.

Film over, we usher forth. It's now dark and Rome is at its best – people in their Sunday clothes, the streets thronged with those just out walking or sitting at street cafés. 'Come,' says Toni, 'I show you nice place.' Back home, at this time of night, I could have shown Toni Reg's Café opposite Brockley Cemetery where you could get eggs, sausage and chips with bread and butter for half a crown. I daren't tell, I didn't want to make her jealous. Three streets up she shows me a little trattoria where we settle. Would she like dinner here? No, 'Just glass wine.' She tells me, with a note of sadness in her voice, that when her father was alive he sometimes used to bring the family here for dinner. Did my father ever take me to dinner?

'Yes.'

'Where?'

'50 Riseldene Road, Brockley.'

'That is restaurant?'

'No, that's my home.'

Toni laughs, a plus mark. We sip our wine watching life's circus pass by.

'People in Rome very chic, Terr-ee, yes?'

Those who are perambulating do so at a pace that is not far short of standing still. The ladies throw their weight on to alternate feet to give their bottoms a slow rotating wobble. All Italian women have it. Rome must be a voyeur's paradise. Toni and I point out people that interest. For instance, what is the old bald man with watery eyes doing with a sixteen-year-old temptress? What tablets is he on? Toni releases titbits of scandals.

'All men in Rome like young girl,' she says with a knowing look. 'When I in Rome ballet, many old men come to stage door and give me flowers, many.'

We finish our wine and taxi back home. She shushes me as the rest of the family are in bed. She rustles us up some sandwiches. We sit and eat, listening to the AF Network turned low.

'I lak jizz but I no understand.'

'If you like it, that's all that matters. It's like wine – you like it or you don't.'

In retrospect, I realize how simple our conversations were, almost mundane.

After a quick canoodle on the couch and a lot of lascivious whispers from me and a clothesline of no, no, noes from Toni, I go to my bedroom. I lie in bed, my mind wandering lonely as a cloud that drifts on high. I couldn't wait to get to England and start the act on its road to fame . . .

What a treat: I'm awakened by Toni, all bathed and perfumed, with my breakfast on a tray. Her mother has gone to work, sister Lily to college, only Gioia in the flat – she'll have to be killed. 'How you sleep?' she says. I tell her I slept on my left side with my knees drawn up under my chin. 'Theeese bed OK for you?' Yes it's OK for me, but too narrow to be OK for us. 'You naughty.'

When I've bathed and dressed, she tells me we are going visiting to see Luciana Campila, her ballet friend from the tour. '*Via XXI di Aprile*,' she tells the taxi. Why is the street called 21 April? She doesn't know. It might be after some special occasion, then again it might be named after 21 April.

You can never tell with a local council – in Brockley, we had a Fred Street and an Enid Terrace.

The Campilas are a bustling middle-class Italian family with two daughters. When we arrive, the middle-aged plump Signora Campila is in the kitchen massaging a huge lump of dough to make pasta, with the aid of her daughters. They all break into animated conversation but, after a brief introduction, *I* might as well be tied up in the garden. As they continue, I wish I was. There are bursts of conversations, then shrieks of laughter – every now and then one of them giving me a sympathetic look as though I *should* be tied up in the garden. Luciana has become engaged to Dennis Evans, a military pianist at CSE Naples. They are to be married and live in Cwmllynfell, which he can't even spell. He's a miner; they will live with his mother and father in one room and live happily ever after, until she flees back to Rome two months later, covered in coal dust and pregnant – but that's all in the future. My future will start the moment this cabal of females breaks up. 'Terr-ee, you lak cup of coffee?' says Toni.

How nice, she still remembers me! I sip my coffee like I've just come back from the dead. From what I can make out of the conversation, it's all scandal. When they get excited, the Campilas attack the dough with greater ferocity. It looks like three women beating up a malleable midget.

After a couple of hours in Coventry, Toni says we are leaving. I'd left hours ago. We go back home where Gioia has prepared us a salad lunch.

'The opera this evening, tell me about it!'

'Ah, you lak very much – Aida in the Terme di Caracalla.'

Did I hear right? We're going to watch an opera being held in Caracalla's bath?

'Yes, Terr-ee, in the, how you say, *rovina.*'

Ah the *ruins* of the Baths of Caracalla, how hygienic! Do we have to take soap and towel?

It was an evening I'd never forget. The first bonus was we had a giant full moon, a cool evening. We arrive to crowds already entering the seating area in front of the stage, which is built into a giant arch in the ruins. I even thought I heard nightingales . I'd never seen this opera before. It was such a spectacle! And a giant cast. I was pretty stunned when, in the Grand March, it seemed every film extra in Rome was on stage, including two elephants! There was a wonderful vibrant orchestra of about sixty. The principals were Maria Caniglla and Giuzzo Neri; it was *bel canto* singing, soaring in the Roman night with ecstatic applause after each favourite aria. I was completely entranced. This was better than Harry James, better than two eggs, sausage and chips at Reg's Café. At the end I sat there stunned, what a production! Time and again I was moved to tears by the music, was it really written by a man called Joe Green? Amazing.

After the opera I had promised to take Toni and her family to dinner at an hotel they had recommended – Albergo Tenente, wow! As Secombe would say, 'There's posh for you.' It's modern but wonderfully tasteful; everywhere, it's white marble and gilt. The dining-rooms are on the sixth floor overlooking the Tiber, the ruined Roman Ponte Sublicio and the Tiberine Island. A fawning manager greets us and a fawning waiter attends our table, how I love it. The Fontanas aren't a well-to-do family – the mother has to work – so this is a treat for them, I can tell it by the delighted expression on Signora Fontana's face. Mind you, the expression on my face when I saw the bill was something else. I mean there's a limit to everything, even 72,000 lire!

The head waiter renders us a list of this evening's specialities; he delivers it all with flamboyant gestures, rather like an excerpt from Shakespeare. It's all a waste of time, as none of us want any. He deflates visibly like an actor who's been booed. He hands us to a second waiter who takes our order with a slightly crimped mouth that looks like a chicken's bum under pressure. The ladies are all agog with the munificence of the surroundings.

'*Un bel posto,* Terr-ee,' says Signora Fontana, whose head is all but revolving.

264

'Did you know, Terr-ee, Mussolini come here to eat?' says Toni.

'So have I,' I said.

'Mussolini,' says Miss Fontana, 'is not bad man, he stupid.'

He must have been to pay these prices.

We talk about the opera. I lament the fact we don't have such a plethora of wonderful voices back home.

'But you hev Gracie Fields,' says Toni.

'Yes,' I say, 'we have Gracie Fields', and leave it at that.

The meal passes with me trying to interject into the conversation. I knew a few Italian words that would suffice: '*Avero*' (is that true), '*la penna del mia zia è nel giardino*' (the pen of my aunt is in the garden) or '*Mio cane ha mangato il gatto*' (my dog has eaten the cat) and '*nostra cameriere ha profumati ginnochii*' (our waiter has perfumed knees) – all said much to the bafflement of Signora Fontana, but it has Toni laughing.

'My mother think you mad,' she says.

'I see, then I must tell you that *il papa non suona la fisarmonica bene*' (the Pope cannot play the accordion well).

At this Signora Fontana laughs out loud, then stops herself with a hand over her mouth.

The chicken's-bum waiter brings the bill, face downwards on a silver tray (not him, the bill). I turn it over and fake a heart attack. 'Call a doctor,' I say. 'No no no, on second thoughts, call a financier.' After this clowning, I make big of paying the bill. How I loved those huge Italian bank notes. As they are carried away, I fake tears and sobbing.

We are all fairly merry with wine as we taxi back home. Lily, who has heard that I can croon, wants me to sing '*una canzone come la jizz*'. I'm well lubricated enough to go straight into 'Boo boo boo the thrill is gone, the thrill is gone, I can see it in your eyes'. I couldn't fail, I had three captive females and *I'd* paid for the dinner. Lily claps. 'Bravo, Terr-ee,' she says. Good, a lone clap is better than a single herpe.

Arriving back home, Signora Fontana looks at her watch: 'Mama mia', look at the time, she has to get up early for work. So, with a chorus of *buona nottes* we retire for the night.

Alas, we collide a little later when we all try to use the loo. Flushes and blushes. I lie in bed going over the evening – how nice this all was, I would certainly miss it.

What was this new terraced house my parents had moved into in delightful Deptford like? Did it have a coke boiler and baths every Friday night? Did my father still wear long underwear in one piece that he shed like a butterfly emerging? Could his socks still stand up on their own? With these fond memories, I fell asleep.

A new dawn, a new day, the same old me. I awake to catch Toni emerging from the bath, wrapped in a towel. Temptation at this time of the morning: she looks glowing. I grab her and kiss her – holding her up so her feet leave the ground, only to drop her at the approach of Gioia who will *have* to be killed.

Toni has arranged for us to have our photo taken by 'Very good photograph man, best in Rome'. Go on, say it, and the most expensive!! I remember the great days when my roll of money was 72,000 lire – now it's down to 30,000, just a ghost of itself! The photographer's trade name is Luxardo; his real name is Il Conto Julio Di Sacco. He is of noble blood and six foot tall – so good-looking, it hurts. He speaks flawless English, has been to Caius College, Cambridge, wears a dazzling white shirt and trousers and a black silk neckerchief and is as queer as a coot.

'Good morning,' he says. 'Let's see, it's,' he looks up his leather appointments book, 'Mr and Mrs Fontana.' Wrong. Mr Milligan and Miss Fontana. 'Oh, I'm so sorry.'

From his posh front office, we enter his studio: very large, a mass of equipment and lights and a young boy. 'This is Francesco, my assistant.' And queer as a coot. Would we like to sit on this couch? He stands behind a large wooden box camera, talks rapidly in Italian to the lad who is putting a plate in. The Count comes forward and arranges us with our heads together. He's different, he *doesn't* want us to say cheese, he doesn't take pictures of those unending grinning idiots that plague the world of photography. 'I want you both to look serious.' He pauses for a look through the lens. 'Are you both in love?' Yes, I'm both in love. 'Good, then you think that when I say ready.' He takes a giant stride 'twixt us and the camera, very much like Jacques Tati. Finally, he settles. 'Ready? In love, hold it.' Hold what? A light flashes. 'Very good,' he says to himself. 'Now I'm going to take you individually. Miss Fontana, then.' He giantstrides towards her and places her hand under her chin. 'Like that, very good.' He giantstrides back, lights a cigarette, tosses his head back to eject the smoke and aims through the lens.

'Think nice things,' he says. The flash of light, then it's my turn. Please, God, can he make me look like Robert Taylor. 'No, don't look at the camera, Mr Milligan, just to the right. Think nice things.' I think of my nice things – a flash and it's all over. 'They'll be ready day after tomorrow.' With great courtesy, he bows us out.

Toni and I decide to walk for a while. We are on the Via Tritoni, right in the heart of the city – well, actually, more in the kidneys. Toni eulogizes about how handsome the Count was. 'He very good-looking man.' Not quite, Toni, a very good-looking *it*. Am I sure? Positive. No! Yes!! We have a nice, long, lazy walk and eventually end up at the Fonte di Trevi, its gushing waters giving a scene of cool relief in the hot atmosphere of the city. 'We must throw in money and make wish,' says Miss Fontana. I peel off a thousand lira note as though to throw in. 'No, no,' she takes some small change from her handbag and gives me a coin. 'We throw together.' She smiles. We watch our coins slither to the bottom. 'Make wish now,' she says. What I wished for, I can't remember. I wonder what, in those distant days, it was ... I wonder, too, what Toni wished for and did it come true? ...

It's time for a coffee, etc. We find a small café, etc. and sit outside. It's a delightful day; it seems that Rome has endless sunny days that pass by almost unnoticed, etc.

Here my diary suddenly stops. All it says is 'Measured for a suit!' I remember this was done at the prompting of Toni, who knows a 'good, cheap tailor!'. He has a shop on the ground floor of the Teatro Marcello. Inside it's small and dark, *he* is small and dark. He smiles, he has small dark teeth. All the time he nods his head as if the neck is loose. Oh, yes, he can have the suit ready in three days *if* we pay a small service charge. I choose a cloth but Toni doesn't like it. Has she something against purple and yellow check? I'll be the talk of Deptford. 'There he goes,' they'd say, or 'Here he comes,' depending on which direction I was going. No, no, no! She chooses a dark cloth, with a faint stripe. 'Theese more elegant, Terr-ee,' says the little devil. Of course, I say yes. If she asked me to wear a transparent loin cloth, gumboots and a revolving hat, I'd have agreed. Standing on a chair, he measures me. Inside leg, which side does the *signore* dress? Near the window, I told him. He takes my chest measurement twice. He doesn't believe it the first time. Do I like padding? Oh, yes. Where? Everywhere. Do I like wide bottoms? On some women, yes, Boom Boom.

So, dear reader, we come to my two blank days. However, on 23 September my diary continues. 'Lazy day, went to Parco Botanico. Lunch in park. Carriage drive back home. Madam Butterfly in evening, awful singing. Toni tells me organized by black marketeers, claque in evidence.'

Yes, *Madam Butterfly* was at the Rome Royal Opera House. Toni has two free tickets that her mother had given to her by a customer at the CIT travel agency. What a treat to look forward to! But it was a night of suppressed hysterical laughter. The whole opera was financed and cast by black marketeers. I couldn't believe it. When first I saw Madam Butterfly, she was *huge,* with a heaving bosom. I thought, out of this frame will come a most powerful voice. When she opened her mouth to sing, you could hardly hear anything. To accentuate the shortcoming, she overacted, throwing her arms in the air, clasping her hands together, falling on her knees with a groan, running across the stage with loud, thudding feet – all to thunderous applause from an obvious claque. Then we wait for Lieutenant Pinkerton: my God, he's half her size! He can't be more than five foot five inches and so thin that when he stood behind her, he vanished. He has a piercing tenor voice, high up in the nose, with a tremendous wobbly *vibrato* that fluctuates above and below the real note. He is obviously wearing lifts in his shoes that make him bend forward from the ankles as though walking in the teeth of a gale. If that isn't all bad enough, he is wearing what must be the worst toupee I've seen. It appears to be nailed down, the front coming too far forward on the forehead with a slight curl all round where it joins his hair.

Trying to laugh silently, I'm almost doubled up in pain. All around me are Mafia-like creatures – one wrong move and I'll be knifed. So be it, no comedy could exceed this. We notice that when Pinkerton tries for a high note, he shoots up on his toes, putting him at an even more alarming angle. When he and she embrace, she envelopes him completely, his little red face appearing above her massive arms as though he's been decapitated. I'm carried on the tide of enthusiasm. When the claque jump up applauding, so do I. *'Bravo, encore,'* I shout. It was a night I can never forget.

At the little restaurant after the show, I keep breaking into fits of laughter as I recall it all. Toni is split down the middle, both halves being equal to the whole. She's ashamed that something so bad should go on at the Royal Opera House. *'Disgrazia,'* she says, but continues to laugh through it.

I remember that, as we sat outside eating, for no reason it started to rain. We retreat inside while a waiter rescues our food. The waiter is amusing; he apologizes for the rain and says even though some has settled on the food, there'll be no extra charge.

Seated inside, Toni suddenly says to me, 'You know, in two day you leave me.'

My mood changed, was it that soon? I was so impervious to days that each one came as a shock. Why wasn't time timeless?

'Toni,' I said, 'I'll come back as soon as I can and I'll write as much as I can.'

That's followed by us just looking at each other in silence.

'I miss you very much, Terr-ee.'

She looks so small and helpless; I *feel* so small and helpless.

'I tell you what, we have some champagne, yes?'

She pauses reflectively. 'OK,' she says.

The restaurant hasn't any champagne. '*Tedeschi hanno bevuto tutto*,' says the waiter. Would we like Asti Spumante? Yes, when in Rome.

When midnight strikes in some campanile, we toast each other. We'd done it so often before, but this time it's a little more meaningful – our sand is running out. In the taxi back, I sit with my arm around her, her head on my shoulder (sounds like a transplant). I hum her favourite tune, 'La Valzer di Candele' . . . We tiptoe into the apartment and I instinctively wait for my mother's voice, 'Where have you been at this time of night.' No, it's Signora Fontana asking is that Toni. Yes, so goodnight.

The day is suit-fitting day. When we arrive at the tailor's, a man is leaving wearing a terrible suit that appears to have been made by a blind man. No, no, no, says the little tailor, he didn't make that. It's only his father-in-law visiting to collect the alimony. My suit is all ready on a hanger. Will I step into the cubicle and change? The suit is a great success; I can't wait to get outside for a photograph.

Oh, yes, this is a Robert Taylor suit. Quick! I must be seen walking about the town. What's the best street? Ah, yes, driver, the Via Veneto and step on it. When we arrive it's midday and the morning promenade is coming to an end. Nevertheless Toni and I and the suit walk up and down, then down and up. Toni and I and the suit sit at a restaurant and Toni and I and my suit have an ice-cream. All Rome must be talking about me. My suit is now smoking a cigarette. Toni is totally bemused: is this a man or a little boy she's going out with, or is it a suit? If only they could see me in Brockley now, standing outside the Rialto Cinema waiting for Lily Dunford. My picture would be in the *Kent Messenger*.

By mid-afternoon I think Rome has seen enough of the suit, so we return to the apartment. Gioia opens the door to my suit, *she doesn't seem to notice it*!!!! She'll *have* to be killed. I have a good reason to take my suit off: Gioia has to go out shopping. It's the last chance of Toni and I being alone. I draw Miss Toni's attention to this by making her take her clothes off and getting into bed, where we foreclose on the world. There *is* a Father Christmas. He was early this year. However, though it was divine making love to her, it lost a bit by Toni breathlessly telling me all the time to 'hurry up' as Gioia was due back. I did my best, finishing in under twenty-three minutes – beating Gioia by five and my own record by ten. With Gioia fiddling at the door with the keys, I rush madly back to my room, just slamming the door on my bare bum in time. Worn out by pressurized love-making, I have a siesta. It's a warm afternoon but nice and cool in the room. I can hear Gioia clinking and clanking in the kitchen . . .

I awake in the evening to the sounds of Signora Fontana and Lily talking. As this is my last evening here, they want me to have dinner 'a casa'. They know my love of pasta and have prepared spaghetti Neapolitan. Toni wants her mother to see 'the suit', so I put it on and do an 'entrance' into the sitting-room. Oh, yes, her mother thinks it's very smart. But should the flies be undone? Oh, dear. Today is Signora Fontana's wedding anniversary. She shows me a photo album: that's her as a young woman on holiday with her mother and father in Savona. Did I know her mother was French? No? Well, I did now. I see grinning photos, from her mother-in-law grinning in Ravenna to her husband grinning outside his soap factory in Abyssinia in 1936. It was possibly one of the best records of grinning I had seen.

We dine to a mixed conversation about the world: things aren't getting any better. I agree, I know my thing isn't getting any better. Shoes are very expensive, '*Troppo caro*,' says Signora Fontana. Has she thought of bare feet? They must be economical. The Communist leader Togliatti is a very dangerous man. 'He want revolution in Italy,' says Toni. So a ragbag of conversation. Gradually, I'm left out of it altogether as they all jabber heatedly in Italian. As the conversation swung from Toni at one end and her mother at the other, I must have looked like a spectator at a tennis match. I call out the score: 'Fifteen, love . . . thirty, fifteen . . .' They ignore me, but it's fun.

Dinner over, they listen to the news in Italian on the radio as I sip a glass of white wine. After the news comes Italy's premier dance band led by Angelini. Lily wants to know if I can 'jitter bugger'. Try me. We move back the chairs a little and Lily and I 'cut a rug'. She's very good, I am not. Toni and Mother watch on with amusement. Gioia looks on in amazement. The phone rings, Lily hurls herself at it: it's *him*! She is running her finger up and down the wall. The evening ends with us playing snap. How delightfully simple it was, the simplest of all was me . . .

Comes the morning of my final departure. I put on my CSE uniform for the journey, then comes amnesia, folks. I remember that I made the return journey by military lorry, a three-tonner returning empty to a depot in Salerno – but as to why and how I managed to get a lift on it, I can't remember. I've racked my brains, I've even racked my body and legs, but to no avail. Anyhow. There I was, saying goodbye to the Fontanas: they all cry, even Gioia, the maid. So with one suitcase and a much-reduced bankroll, I depart.

I depart to amnesia because where I picked up the lorry is lost for ever. However, I remember the journey back. The driver was a north-countryman, he hardly said a bloody word all through the journey. I sat there in silence with Rome falling farther and farther behind. It was a hot, dusty day and I dozed frequently in the cab. When we reach the Garigliano plain, I can see Colle Dimiano where I was wounded. It all seemed so unreal now, but I think I left part of myself up there for ever; after the incident, I was never the same.

Suddenly, as we near Naples, the creep driver seems to speak. 'Do you know what time is?'

'Yes,' I say. Period. I'd make the bugger suffer.

He pauses and repeats, 'Do you know what time is?'

'Yes.'

'Oh, what is it then?'

Finally, I tell him. He nods his head in acknowledgement, his vocabulary expended. He drops me at the bottom of the Via Roma. I delighted in saying goodbye. 'Tatar, you little bundle of fun,' I said.

I'm in the welter of the Neapolitan rush hour and garlic. I manage to get a taxi back to the hotel. The old fragile porter grabs my bag; he'll take it to my room. He strains and staggers to the lift. I have to wait for him, I have to help him into the lift where he stands gasping for breath. He must be training for a coronary. On my floor, he staggers behind me. I offer to carry it. '*No, no signore, tutto a posto*', he'll just have a little rest in the corridor. I go ahead and wait in my room – poor old bugger, he's doing it in anticipation of a tip or death, whichever comes first. I give him two hundred lire – it's a good tip. '*Mille grats, signor*,' he says in Neapolitan dialect and shuffles out the room. I put through a phone call to Toni. After a delay it comes through.

'Hello, Toni.'

'Terr-ee,' she gasps, 'my Terr-ee, you go all right Napoli?'

'Yes, I go all right in Napoli.'

''Ow lovlee 'ear your voice, *mio tesoro*. I miss you much already. Why you go away?'

'What are you doing?'

'Just now we have dinner. Tell me you love me.'

'I love you.'

A little more of that type of chat and we finish. Yes, I promise I'll phone tomorrow. No, I won't go out getting drunk with Mulgrew. No, I won't go near other girls. Now, where is that man Hall. I buzz his room.

''Oos that?'

'Me, Spike. Are there any gigs going? I'm at a loose end till the boat sails.'

No, no gigs tonight. There's one tomorrow. Do I mind playing in a sergeants' mess? Well as long as it isn't too big a mess.

'Wot you doing tonight?'

273

'I'm not doing anything tonight.'

'Well, good luck with it,' he says.

I met him in the dining-hall for dinner. Has he seen Mulgrew or Bornheim lately? Yes, he's done a couple of gigs with them. What about the *Dominion Monarch* and the sailing date? That's all fixed, I have to collect my ticket from Major Ridgeway. So the end is in sight: it's goodbye Italy and hello Deptford.

The remaining days were very very boring. So I won't bore the reader. I do a couple of band gigs on guitar with Hall, Bornheim and Mulgrew at military establishments. I collect my boat ticket and passport and I buy a few trinkets for my mother and father. Most days I spend in my room reading books from the hotel library. The very last one was the story of San Michele by Axel Munthe, a most moving story about Capri.

The night before I sail, Jimmy Molloy checks into the hotel. He's booked on the same ship as me. He wants to have a night out; he knows a good officers' nightclub on the seafront. OK, I'll come with him and wear the suit. It's the Club Marina, 'Officers Only'. We show our C S E passes. Down a corridor to a large room with a central dance floor, where a good Italian band are playing the music of our time. There are hostesses at the bar: no, Jimmy, I'm not interested. Well, he is. He goes over and chats to one and brings her back to our table. Ah, good, wait till she sees my suit. She is pretty stunning, small, petite, saturnine-dark with a pair of giant olive eyes.

'This is Francesca,' says Molloy.

'*Piacera,*' I say.

She throws me a dazzling white-toothed smile. More than that, as the evening progresses I realize that she fancies me and my suit. 'I fink I've picked a loser here,' chuckled Molloy. Do I want to take her over? No no no, Jimmy, I am promised to another. He gives me a disbelieving look. 'Come on, a bit on the side won't hurt.' I told him I had no bits on my side, all my bits were at the front, so I'd be the wrong fit for her. However it's nice flirting with her.

274

The lights go down: a spotlight on the stage illuminates an Italian M C in a white jacket. 'Laddies and Gintilmin, nower oura starer of thee cabareter, Gina Escoldi.' He points left, the band strikes up and a ballerina on points pirouettes on the the floor and sings 'a hubba hubba hubba' with red-hot accompaniment. She has a coarse croaky voice, loaded with sex – all the while standing on points. It was a head-on collision between jazz and ballet, but very successful. She goes down big with what is in the majority, an American officer audience.

At the end of the evening Molloy says, 'You takin' this bird or not.' I decline, cursing the fact that I have a conscience. 'One day,' he laughs, 'you'll regret this decision!' What did he mean 'one day', I was regretting it *now*. While he offs with her, I off to the hotel and bed. While I lay there, my mind was going through the long years away from home. Had I really been in action in North Africa? Had I really taken part in the Tunis Victory Parade? Did I land at Salerno? It all seemed unreal, like a distant dream ending up in the most distant dream of all – Toni and me on Capri. Would the sun ever shine like that again?

On departure morning I awake and, first thing, put in a call to Toni. We say our final goodbyes – tears on the phone from Rome. At breakfast, I meet Jimmy Molloy. 'That bird last night, what a con. When we get to 'er place, she just kisses me goodnight then pisses off. I think it was all your bloody fault, Milligan.' Smugly, I say, yes, it undoubtedly was.

Our ship sails at midday. We have to start boarding at 10.30. We take a taxi to the quay where the *Dominion Monarch* awaits. We both have first-class passages – I'm nominated a cabin on the port side. A young English steward carries my bag and calls me sir. It's a fine, single-berth cabin with a porthole for looking out – or, if you hang on the outside, for looking in. 'If there's anything you want, sir, just ring the service button.' I locate the Purser's Office where a grim-faced staff change my lire into sterling, which looks much

On board SS Dominion Monarch from Naples to the UK

less. Up on the promenade deck I find Molloy and I get him to take my photo.

The ship is alive with bustle, with sailors shouting yo ho ho and pouring hot tar down the hatches. At midday the gangplank is removed, the ship gives a long mournful blast on the hooter and a tug starts to manoeuvre us out to sea. Molloy and I stand at the rail. Slowly, the great ship puts on speed, the Italian mainland recedes into the distance, finally lost in a haze. It's over: it's goodbye Italy, goodbye Toni and goodbye soldier.

SPIKE MILLIGAN

ADOLF HITLER: MY PART IN HIS DOWNFALL
VOLUME ONE OF THE CLASSIC WAR MEMOIRS

'The most irreverent, hilarious book about the war that I have ever read' *Sunday Express*

'At Victoria station the R.T.O. gave me a travel warrant, a white feather and a picture of Hitler marked "This is your enemy". I searched every compartment, but he wasn't on the train . . .'

In this, the first of Spike Milligan's uproarious recollections of life in the army, our hero takes us from the outbreak of war in 1939 ('it must have been something we said'), through his attempts to avoid enlistment ('time for my appendicitus, I thought') and his gunner training in Bexhill ('There was one drawback. No ammunition') to the landing at Algiers in 1943 ('I closed my eyes and faced the sun. I fell down a hatchway').

Filled with bathos, pathos and gales of ribald laughter, this is a barely sane helping of military goonery and superlative Milliganese.

'Our first comic philosopher' Eddie Izzard